D1491717

COUNTY
CHAMPIONS

The Publishers will be donating part of the proceeds of this book to the Lord's Taverners, whose charitable objectives are:

*To enable youngsters to keep physically fit and mentally alert through the playing of team games, principally cricket.

*To build and run Adventure Playgrounds for under-privileged children through the auspices of the National Playing Fields Association.

*To provide minibuses for handicapped children to enable them to get away from the confines of Homes or Hospital.

COUNTY CHAMPIONS

Heinemann·Quixote

Heinemann/Quixote Press
10 Upper Grosvenor Street, London W1X 9PA

LONDON   MELBOURNE   TORONTO   JOHANNESBURG   AUCKLAND

The chapters are copyright respectively:
© *Richard Gordon Ltd 1982* © *Bill Tidy 1982*
© *Leslie Thomas 1982* © *Donald Trelford 1982*
© *Duncan Kyle 1982* © *Colin Cowdrey 1982*
© *Alan Melville 1982* © *Barry Norman 1982*
© *Trevor Bailey 1982* © *Frank Tyson 1982*
© *Michael Jayston 1982* © *Hugh Pickles 1982*
© *John Arlott 1982* © *Alan Gibson 1982*
© *Ted Moult 1982* © *Charles Palmer 1982*
© *Tim Heald 1982*

The Publishers gratefully acknowledge permission to quote
extracts from *Ted Dexter Declares* (Stanley Paul/Hutchinson Publishing Group)
and from Alan Ross's poem 'Watching Benaud Bowl' (Alan Ross).

SBN 434 98024 2

Phototypeset by Tradespools Limited, Frome, Somerset
Printed and bound in Great Britain by Butler and Tanner, Limited, Frome, Somerset

Contents

And see where busy Counties strive for Fame,
Each great and potent at this mighty Game!

James Love

Cricket, an heroic poem in three books, 1765

There is no talk, none so witty and brilliant, that is
so good as cricket talk, when memory sharpens memory,
and the dead live again—the regretted, the unforgotten—
and the old happy days of burned out Junes revive.

Andrew Lang

Surrey

Richard Gordon: Qualified as a doctor and became the celebrated author of such medical classics as *Doctor in the House*, *Doctor on the Job* and *Doctor in the Nest*, among others.

The South Bank Show
Richard Gordon

Venice never recovered from the introduction of the *vaporetto*, nor the Oval from the disappearance of the trams. They grated round the low wall past mid-wicket, ungainly as mobile conservatories, driver's foot-bell clanging a knell like the Abbot of Aberbrothok's on Inchcape Rock.

These ringing grooves of change were inaugurated on Wednesday, July 10, 1901, and silenced on the Saturday night of July 5, 1952. London's last tram entered the eternal peace of the New Cross Depot with frenzied crowds bending pennies in the lines like medals blessed by the Pope, demonstrating the fatal English passion for the obsolete. Lacking a Test seat in the 1930s, you bought a shilling all-day ticket and scrambled to the top deck between the Vauxhall and pavilion ends, aboard a scarlet-and-cream, double-bogie, fully-upholstered E/1 type, equipped for both conduit and overhead-line current collection, the No 40 which ran from Victoria to Kennington decorated with advertisements for Force, Virol, Wincarnis Tonic Wine and Sunlight Soap.

The gas holders endure. In my youth—I was born shortly after the fifth Test against Australia there in 1921, when Percy Fender got a duck and no wickets—the Oval had a "gasworks end" opposite the pavilion. The encroaching purity of cricketing prose abolished this, when writers discovered the gas to be made in Vauxhall, only stored at the Oval to cook the Sunday dinners of Lewisham and light the lamps of the Old Kent Road.

Five gasometers were built in 1869, one demolished 110 years later. They are as readily identifiable in photographs of Jack Hobbs or Bill Lockwood as Windsor Castle behind any English monarch. When they stopped making gas from coal in the 1950s, the Oval was connected to the bottom of the North Sea via Shorne on the Kent marshes, and looped by the Gas Board with another sporting centre at Ascot.

The Oval gasometers are a public relations spectacle as important for British Gas as Concorde for British Airways. The Board keeps them clean

1

and freshly painted, instructing its site foreman during Test matches to hoist Union Jack and tourists' flag atop the vast one, which squats awesomely above the scoreboard with the massive benignity of the Great Buddha at Kamakura in Japan.

Middle-aged Englishmen idealise their cricket grounds like their old schools. What heart is hard enough to resist engravement with the picture of the beautiful ground at New Road, Worcester? Where the touring side were once directed for their opening match in April, the west face of the magnificent cathedral mirrored in the swirling floodwaters of the River Severn, the trees bending and creaking in a north wind sheering round the Welsh mountains. (It is inarguable that we have done worse in the Tests since the fixture was postponed to midsummer.)

The Oval's nearest cathedral is Westminster Abbey, two and a quarter miles away. You could see it, like Hackney Marshes in the music-hall song, if it wasn't for the houses in between. The River Thames, up Harleyford Road, sweats its oil and tar between massive embankments, as unsweet as the M1 at Watford. Around lie 1933 LCC flats, scruffy shops in Brixton Road and stuccoed Victorian terraces now becoming fashionable, like the artisan's dwellings of Chelsea which in the 1950s acquired duck-egg blue front doors, window boxes and a few noughts on the prices. Everyday life is separated from the spectators by an encircling brick wall, as abruptly as from other Londoners judicially deprived of its enjoyment for longer.

The Oval *was* a prison, a distinction among county grounds. During World War II, the turf was pierced with stakes and criss-crossed with barbed wire for a prisoner-of-war camp, the Colditz of Kennington. Five such transit camps were scattered round London, Cockfosters becoming a familiar name in the Luftwaffe. The Oval held no wartime prisoners, but in 1945 a bunch of SS officers ended their careers beyond even Nazi imagination, in a Nissen hut in the covers.

The view from the back row of the pavilion roof is magnificent, like watching cricket from an alp. The beflagged Victoria Tower of Parliament, which dominated the skyline until Millbank sprouted its concrete beanstalk, is insignificant against half a dozen later higher-rising blocks. A Centre Point was to be raised on the Vauxhall end in the 1960s, the idea collapsed with the property boom, but the model in the Long Room fascinated the members all season. From nearby factories, the smell of pickles wafts fitfully across the ground according to climatic conditions, like the famous sea-fret at Hove, but does not swing the ball so noticeably.

Apart from the double-fronted, red-brick, lead-roofed 1884 pavilion, the Oval has six stands—the free terracing, the Peter May Enclosure with pastel-coloured tip-up plastic seats, opened on May 5, 1981, the stand with a bar and the stand without a bar, the Vauxhall Stand and Archbishop Tenison's Grammar School.

The school across the road, where clanking trams are replaced by the sirens of fire-engines from Kennington station, was founded by Thomas Tenison (1636–1715), a Cambridge man like Peter May, who opened London's first public library and preached Nell Gwyn's funeral sermon. Its seemly 550 boys from the dioceses of London and Southwark, are taught by masters who sensibly see the advantages of employment allowing a deck-chair on the roof during all Test matches.

The Oval contrasts to the conventionally romanticized county ground as Thomas Hardy's sheep-dappled downs to the municipal abattoir. This is its singularity and charm. Its green face, beautifully shaved, shines from the surrounding jumble of brick-work like—as a former Dulwich College right-arm fast bowler put it, about a lovely girl at a dull party—a diamond in a pile of coke.

The Oval in the 1980s is a £1m-a-year entertainment business, with departments for administration, finance, marketing and advertising, a Prince of Wales room for private parties, boxes and rows of reserved seats for companies—what customer can refuse an invitation to a cricket match, especially with free booze? For the Club's latest annual report to start, "Things get better", marks the Secretary as a unique man in Britain.

The Oval in the summer of 1844 was a market garden, separated by a hedge of laurel and box from a dozen sycamore-shaded white villas and Doric-columned St Mark's, one of the Commissioners new "Waterloo Churches". A tall-windowed, two-storey building with its stables anticipated the Hobbs Gate and the Surrey Banqueting Suite. Ringed by its dusty, rutted, dung-spattered road, the Oval showed on the map as plainly as a full stop on a page. London lived north of the River—business in the City, fashion in the West End. Only two railways ran south of the Thames, the London and Croydon from London Bridge and the Bricklayers Arms, the London and South Western from Waterloo and Nine Elms. To the south opened the green slopes of Peckham Rye and Herne Hill, and the village of Lewisham on the River Ravensbourne, which flowed into Greenwich Reach opposite the Isle of Dogs.

The Oval lay in a wedge of south London from Camberwell to the Thames belonging to the Duchy of Cornwall—the Duke was aged two. The Montpelier Cricket Club, under a mile away near the Elephant and Castle in Walworth, had seen their ground sold from under the toes of their bats. They decided to defy disaster and play elsewhere, as the Dodgers 100-odd years later shifted nonchalantly from Brooklyn to Los Angeles, electronic scoreboard, Dodger Dogs, Dodger cheer of "Charge!" and all.

The unfailingly industrious and amiable Gordon Ross, Surrey's

3

historian, discovered that a Montpelier member called William Baker suggested a deal with the Duke's man of business, and got a 31-year lease of the Oval for £120 annually. The Dukes changed, the lease remains. At some £2000 a year until 1983, the Oval is the best property bargain in London after Lord Knollys' Seething Lane garden, which goes for a yearly red rose to the Lord Mayor.

The peas and carrots had to be dug up, the turf laid. With our sophisticated town-planning schemes, our computerized contractors' estimates, this might now be achieved within two or three years. In cumbersome Victorian days, the Oval was grassed in good time for the following season, by Mr Turtle of Clapham, who in March 1845 started transplanting 10,000 turves from Tooting Common, four miles away, for £300.

On Friday, August 22, 1845, the Montpelier Club dined at the Horns Tavern, a vast red-brick pub which endured into the 20th century long enough for me to drink a respectful pint there. The port circulated, the kettles steamed for the gin-and-water, spirits glowed like the cigars, the mood made everything seem possible and the impossible only to take a little longer.

After the second grace—*Non nobis*, sung—the toastmaster bellowed for silence, the Queen was toasted, the Prince, Sir Robert Peel and Her Majesty's ministers, and General Gough, who had gone to defeat the Sikhs. A hundred members of clubs playing cricket all over Surrey were admitted to the dining-room. The Chair proposed "That a Surrey Club be now formed", to mobilise the cricketing skill of the county from remote villages beyond the rivers Wey and Arun and over the Hog's Back. The motion was passed amid cheering, shouts of "Bravo!", hammering with knife-handles on the table, gentlemen embracing each other like bears and slapping each other's backs as though slamming carriage doors. It was a fertile age for the birth of clubs, and how Mr Pickwick would have twinkled behind his pebble glasses.

The first match at the Oval was already in its second day, the Gentlemen v Players of Surrey. When the County Championship was codified 28 years later—no one could play for two counties at once, how refreshingly artless was all legislation then—Surrey were among the eight first-class sides. Their maiden Championship match started on Thursday, June 5, 1873, against Sussex, in freezing fog which delayed play until lunch. The notion that enviable Victorians lolled overdressed in unbroken summer sunshine arises from their incapacity for taking photographs without it. Constable painted plenty of clouds, Turner lashings of rain, gales and snowstorms.

Surrey lost by 29. Fourteen years later, they won the Championship nine years running, except for Yorkshire putting the clog in during 1893.

Surrey played as champions the first year of the new century, when their landlord won the Derby and was shortly to ascend the throne. They won it again during the battle of Mons. By 1918, they had to wait longer to make a come-back than did Hitler.

Under the Metropolitan Management Act (1855), Surrey disappeared from the Oval in the direction of Croydon. In 1965 it receded further, to suit the GLC. Middlesex vanished completely, and the side should rightly have changed their name to I Zingari. In the lovely prose of Victorian sports writers, from which you can almost smell the beer, Middlesex were "The Metropolitans" and Surrey "The Transpontines", but the only use London has now for either county is providing edges to the Boat Race course.

Lord's is the cathedral of cricket, the Oval low-church. Its pavilion is homely with curtains, plain and clean like a well-kept pub, the walls with framed scorecards of famous victories, its basement hiding magnificent marble urinals. Its bars sell plain cottage pie and sprouts, pigeons strut and coo on the girders as self-assuredly as in Trafalgar Square, to the despair of the Lambeth pest control officer (the Oval can offer pigeon shooting now and then).

The atmosphere is unbuttoned—though not wholly so, *Please Note That Shirts Must Be Worn At All Times*, demands a notice in the pavilion. It is the Cockney's cricket ground, ever since the supporter who observed in *Punch* it was funny arf the bloomin team started with 'H'—Itch, Obbs, Ayward and Habel. Its Cockneys in recent times are equally likely to be born within the sound of Bow Bells as those of St Michael's Cathedral, Bridgetown. Cricket cannot weld races and classes, but it can solder. "If the French aristocrats had played cricket with their peasants," said the historian Trevelyan, "their châteaux would not have been burnt."

I became a Surrey member in 1952, when the audience never ran across the pitch, even with all their clothes on. When no one yet scoffed at players wearing protection for their brains, though considering it perfectly normal to wear it for their testicles. When cricket balls never lost their shape—Stuart Surridge, who makes bats and balls, blames poor modern leather, but thought my notion of a sacred herd bred for cricketing purposes impractical.

My membership was as unthinkingly shrewd as any angel that same year taking a share in *The Mousetrap*. The Surrey show ran seven years, a succession of County Championships unmatched—and probably now unmatchable, with the season a scramble of motley matches and the counties stuffed with mercenaries.

Surrey shared with Rommel's Panzers and Napoleon's Grande Armée the reputation for invincibility which is half the battle. Their opponents arrived at the Oval with defeat in their bags. "All cricket is in the mind,"

Peter May told me perceptively, if modestly. (Cricketers are as neurotic, and as prone to such obsessions as always putting on one boot before the other, as any other overtaxed public performers.)

Surrey had Peter May to make the runs, Stuart Surridge to mastermind the captaincy. They had Micky Stewart and then John Edrich. They had Ken Barrington, who later—sadly, not much later—had to walk bravely through life knowing that his heart ticked like a time-bomb in his chest. They had Laker and Lock. To scotch suspicions of conspiracy with the other Lock (Bert, the groundsman), these took more wickets away from the Oval. They had the two Bedsers. Or the four Bedsers. Or the Bedser. The hypothesis is interesting.

Most people assume there are two Bedsers, Alec and Eric. The twins dress exactly alike, down to their cufflinks, and doubtless underpants. Alec is entitled to an England tie, Eric is not, so Alec never wears it. Communication across London on the wardrobe of the day is unnecessary. They do it by extrasensory perception, saving enormously on their phone bills. As Swansea will not allow their cars identical registration numbers, they have successive ones. Anyone floundering to discover which Bedser he is addressing is cunningly confused by their never referring to Alec or Eric but invariably to "my brother".

Such duplicity and duplication is clearly impossible between men always in public view. There are two other Bedsers, Cedric and Ringo. The quadruplets are equally good at cricket, and took it in turns to be bowler or batsman and to play for England. Three of them were always hiding in the dressing-room lockers, to bowl with devastating freshness after lunch and tea. Alec Bedser is credited with 1,924 wickets, but 481 of them belong to Ringo. Alternatively, there is a single A.E. Bedser, and the other is a well-fostered mass hallucination, like the Loch Ness Monster.

Nobody goes to a cricket ground just to watch cricket. With the gap between overs and between balls, there isn't that much to watch. Members go because Englishmen are as addicted to clubs as Australians to Foster's. A companionable bond is reassuring in a world where everyone is a stranger, some stranger than others. Many of the Surrey members are senior citizens, even senile citizens. Each new season they observe with *Schadenfreude* winter's ravages on each other's frame, their comfort at having missed viewing cricket in the Elysian Fields tempered by recalling the stands there are of unlimited capacity.

Many go to meet people. I encountered more distinguished doctors at the Oval than at the Royal Society of Medicine. Mr Arthur Dickson Wright, for whom I once gave an anaesthetic (his trousers fell down during the operation, there was a dreadful fuss), kept me up-to-date on the boundary—"The duodenum was ulcerated right through, y'know, came apart in two pieces in my hands." He was a surgeon of infinite skill, wry wit, unflawed wisdom and adroit anecdote. I wish I had invented him.

In the sixties I met the Monster. Boris Karloff was pushing 80, and had just finished a distinguished career with the Hollywood Cricket Club. He played with such world-famous cricketers as E. Flynn, N. Bruce and D. Niven, under C. Aubrey Smith of Cambridge and Sussex, one of the few cricket captains to be knighted. Lady spectators were encouraged in the pavilion, as during the last five years at the Oval, Sunday afternoons often gathering the Misses de Havilland, Garson, Cooper, Oberon and Laye. I eyed its pitch, opened at Griffith Park in 1936, with the feelings of a rural dean encountering some particularly successful missionary chapel among the benighted. Now it is to become the Hickstead of Hollywood.

Boris Karloff was really Bill Pratt, his brother was Sir John Pratt of the Foreign Office, who always bicycled to Whitehall. I once enquired idly during a Test match which dramatic academy Boris had attended. He stared with greater horror than he had ever aroused in his audiences. "*Dramatic academy?* Dear boy, I was employed laying railroad track, and the line happened to finish at Hollywood." It was a boring Test, but we came every day. "See you on the cross again tomorrow," he would bid farewell, in the spirit of *The King of Kings*.

The stage sees the importance of being earnest about cricket. When Sir Terence Rattigan excused himself from two actors during the dreary half-hour before lunch, for an essential phone call from New York, he left a shocked silence. "You know," remarked one to the other sorrowfully, "I don't think Rattigan's taking the game *seriously* any more."

Actors always leave at the tea interval, lest anyone imagine they weren't working. They clap gratifyingly, generally with hands above head. I once enticed Ben (*Rookery Nook*) Travers from Lord's to the Oval. Sitting him in the pavilion with a proprietorial air, I asked, "Do you come much to this ground?" "No, I haven't been here since I came to watch W.G. Grace play," he replied matter-of-factly.

Stephen Potter, the master of Gamesmanship, amazingly took little interest in cricket, though he had recorded 8,400 instances of it in Sussex v Derbyshire at Hove, a match reduced by rain to one and a half days. I proposed him for the Oval, where a seat in the pavilion quickly completed his education.

I attend cricket to dabble in doctoring. When the loud-speaker enquires anxiously, "Is there a doctor in the ground?" I move quicker than a slip-fielder to a catch. At my first Oval consultation, I hurried with pounding heart, wondering if I should be asked to reduce Tony Lock's dislocated spinning-finger. Alec Bedser was the captain, who greeted me

7

jovially: "Would you take a look at Peter Loader's throat, doc? We want to know if it's worth while paying his fare to Nottingham tomorrow."

Other consultations were less formal. "You're a doctor, aren't you?" Herbert Strudwick asked on the players' balcony. "Could you give me some advice about my eyes? I don't seem to see as well as I used to, in my weekly game of golf at Brighton with Jack Hobbs." He was 81. I advised masterly inactivity. "I fancy I've broken every bone in my hands, one time or another." He clasped them reflectively. "The gloves I started with were like the kid gloves you'd wear to go out. For a better grip, I'd wet them in that fountain over there." He indicated a corner by the scoreboard which had no fountain in any other living memory.

I work in cricket grounds. During a midweek county game in dull weather, alone in the stand, unbothered by telephone or family, with just enough activity in the middle to keep me awake, I have written several novels. I have a technique for writing while watching the Tests on TV with the sound off. The only necessity is an accurate knowledge of the run-up time for all international bowlers. The author writes, say, "To be, or not to be: that is the quest ..." looks up, sees the delivery and continues, "... ion: whether 'tis nobler in the mind to suffer the slings ..." and watches the next ball. When fielders jump all over the screen, sound is restored for the instant replay. This is my one contribution to English Literature. The quickies compose elegant sentences, but the spinners read like Hemingway.

The Oval has its literary associations. Yorkshireman Albert Craig was "The Surrey Poet", touring the ground with his works at a penny a time until he died in 1909 in befitting poetic poverty, though the Prince of Wales sent him a get-well telegram. In 1960, four years after taking his 19 Australian wickets in a Test, Jim Laker published *Over to Me*. It enjoyed, as we authors say, a *succès de scandale*, too bloody much. Jim hit the Surrey side all round the wicket (he was a fair lower-order bat), making himself as popular in the committee room as Alexander Solzhenitsyn in the Kremlin.

Perhaps he suffered from the author's pathetic vanity that what he writes remains as unconnected to his real, lovable self as his lines to an actor. The world is depressingly empty of people who would agree, *Je n'approuve pas ce que vous dites, mais je combattrais jusqu'à mon dernier souffle pour votre droit de le dire.* (Voltaire of course knew nothing about cricket.) Jim Laker later became the game's equivalent of Dixon of Dock Green, time's heavy roller smoothed the memories, but an apposite remark at the Oval can still take a nasty spin.

My greatest moment in cricket came at the Oval on the Saturday afternoon of August 15, 1964. In the Test against Bobby Simpson's Australians, Fred Trueman had N.J.N. Hawke caught at first slip by

Colin Cowdrey for 14, and became the first to take 300 Test wickets.

This was achieved in one of those squalls of excitement which blow across the placid cricketing sky. Incandescent Fred was 33, who knew how much longer he might blaze for England? He had been taken off, the weather was dodgy, a second innings might not (and did not) materialise. Would he get another spell? I can reveal the true story. While Ted Dexter, the captain, was deliberating between overs who to bowl next, he observed Fred hurtling like a comet from the pavilion end. He had put himself on. Most sensibly too. Fred ended the match with 4 for 87, and his career in the glow of seven wickets over the record.

Since then, tobacco has moved into the Oval and everywhere else. "The cricket administrators," wrote *World Medicine* in 1979, "say that without cigarette sponsorship their sport would die. In short, they accept that 50,000 unnecessary UK deaths every year is an acceptable price to pay for keeping cricket alive. They could, however, reduce the carnage and raise the same amount of money by mounting a monthly spectacle at Lord's at which they could publicly execute some lowly persons, maybe by throwing them to the lions. They could expect a full house no matter how much they raised the price of admission and even if they allowed themselves a generous ten deaths per session they would still reduce the cost in human lives to a small fraction of 1 per cent of what it is now."

I couldn't—so sadly—agree more.

Glamorgan

Leslie Thomas: Bestselling author of *The Virgin Soldiers, Tropic of Ruislip, Dangerous Davies: The Last Detective*, and many others.

Daffodil Summer
Leslie Thomas

In the fading August of 1948, on a day by the southern seaside, J.C. Clay, the gentleman of Glamorgan, bowled a measured off-break which struck Charlie Knott, of Hampshire, on the pad. The story has it that Dai Davies, the umpire, a brown, beaming man, raised a dramatic finger and, unable to contain himself, bellowed at Knott: "You're *OUT*—and *WE'VE* won!"

Glamorgan had indeed won. Not only a remarkable match, but the County Championship, and for the first time. On that dun afternoon in Bournemouth the pavilion trembled with Welsh singing, voices that floated over the English regular roses, causing raised eyebrows among the gardens and where the band was playing by the sea.

For Johnnie Clay, the lean, grey man, wise as a heron, the triumph had come in his fiftieth year and after seasons of failure, disappointment, even ridicule, for his beloved county. I remember that day, trotting on my trivial rounds as a junior reporter on a local newspaper in Essex, hearing the wonderful news on the radio while I was cross-examining a lady about the thrills and spills of the Women's Institute flower arranging contest. "Why," she asked briskly, "are you grinning like that? Flower arranging is *no* laughing matter." "I'm sorry," I remember saying, knowing she would never understand. "I'm doing it because I'm happy."

Happy indeed I was, along with a throng of others. Of the four hundred telegrams sent to Arms Park, Cardiff, the next day was one from an exile in Paris. The news, he said, had made him decide to return home to Wales. What, after all, had Paris to offer?

For me the love affair was new. It is a confession I hesitate to make, even after these years, but, brought up in wartime Newport, I hardly knew of the *existence* of cricket, until I was gone twelve years. Then, after the war—after I had heard about it and was growing in love for it—one day in 1947, I went for the first time to Lord's and had scarcely had time to place my spam sandwiches and myself on one of the free seats (as they were loftily called) below the heads of the trees at the Nursery End, when I witnessed the most exquisite sight of my youthful life. Willie Jones, small as a button, batting against Middlesex, leaned back, folded his body like a spring, and square cut to the boundary. The ball hit the boards with an echo I can hear now. It was as though he had waited for my arrival, after all those unknowing years. From that moment—and although I had left the Land of my Father's and my birth—I had Glamorgan written on my heart.

*   *   *

The trials of the early days of Glamorgan County Cricket Club are nowhere better contained than in a tale told by Jack Mercer, eighty-odd now. He was a Glamorgan player when almost anyone who owned a bat could get a game. "We had six captains and five wicket-keepers in one season," he recalled. "The oddest people used to turn up and get in the side. A great big fellow was in the team one day and Johnnie Clay, being a gentleman, didn't like to ask him whether he was a batsman or a bowler. So John asked me and I didn't know either. 'Well,' said Johnnie, 'we'll put him in the slips. Even if he can't catch, he's a big chap—something might hit him'."

J.C. Clay, the dear man, the quiet cricketer, in the phrase of Wilfred Wooller, was a member of the side which first played in the County Championship in 1921. The application for first-class status had been grudgingly approved. Cricket authority sniffed and intoned: "If you can get eight other clubs to play you, then you are accepted." Glamorgan got six and Lancashire and Yorkshire agreed at the last moment to join the list. Certainly the Roses Counties never overrated the urchin Welsh team. "Yorkshire only ever booked a hotel for two nights when they came to Cardiff or Swansea," sighed Wilfred Wooller.

The team amazed itself and everyone else by winning the opening match against thoroughbred Sussex. From then on it lost. *Wisden's* comment that Glamorgan's entry into first-class cricket "was not justified by results", was honestly echoed by the county's annual report which related sadly: ". . . Glamorgan were like no other side; some say it was not a side at all." The main bowlers were Harry Creber, who was forty-seven and Jack Nash who was forty-eight. In that first season Nash only just missed his hundred wickets.

The sickly infant years were slow to go. After two seasons in county cricket Glamorgan not only had a solitary specialist slip fielder, they were also £6,212 in the red at the bank. But John Clay believed and others

12

joined him in his faith. Cricket had never been considered to be a "Welsh game" but now, from the valleys and the sandy seaside towns of the south, men who could play took tentative steps towards Cardiff. Dai Davies, the man who, as umpire, played his part in the fateful day many years later, Emrys Davies, a staunch opener, Arnold Dyson, a poetic batsman, and, momentously, a man called Maurice Turnbull.

Turnbull, as captain and secretary, pulled Glamorgan up by the laces of its cricket boots. He organised both the bowling and the finances, he made centuries and friends, he was as articulate in the chair as he was in the field. He was the first Glamorgan cricketer to play for England and then—outrageously—he was killed in the war before all his selfless work came to splendid justification.

In the final seasons before the war the county finished in positions of untold respectability—midway up the table. At that time Wilfred Wooller first walked out to bat, the rugby hero come to the summer game. A big man, combative, unyielding, some said, and still do, too forthright, but a leader born to lead. He was to be Glamorgan's man of destiny. But first he had to wait six years and a war.

* * *

They say that when Wilfred Wooller played his first match after his repatriation from a Japanese prison camp and went out to the wicket, tears were running down the cheeks of grown men.

"Like a big skeleton, he was," an uncle of mine told me. "And yellow."

But it would have taken more than the Japanese to daunt Wooller. "We played a game at Changi prison camp in Singapore on Christmas Day," he remembers. "Somehow we found a ball and a bat and we made some stumps. We had an England versus Australia Test match right there in front of the Japanese guards. They looked puzzled."

Forty years on Wooller is still a big man, tall, unstooping, broad-shouldered, broad faced. He prowls rather than walks. A man like a large leopard. His was the sad but familiar story of a return from years of captivity and privation only to find that life had changed behind his back. His pre-war marriage was quickly over. "I remember getting in my car and driving from London up the Great North Road—anywhere," he said. "I had no idea where I was going." The road, oddly, led to Africa and a frightening adventure in a crash-landing airplane which made him, abruptly, realise that life was still precious. He decided to do something with his—and returned to Wales to become captain of a Glamorgan team that was to make history.

"At the beginning there was really only half a team," he recalled. "The remnants of what we had before the war. But there was a new generation of young cricketers wanting to play, boys like Phil Clift, Gilbert Parkhouse and Alun Watkins, all gifted, all eager. Then we took on some chaps from outside, players that their own counties had decided they did not want." Three of those cricketers, Len Muncer, Norman Hever and a lad called Eaglestone, were from the richly-endowed Middlesex team. With the rag-tag-and-bobtail already assembled in Cardiff they became, under the steely leadership of Wooller, a side of supermen.

It was Johnnie Clay that Wooller patently admired and still remembers with affection. "He was the most wonderful of men. Quiet, a true gentleman. He loved cricket and lived for it. All the winter he bowled on a practice wicket in his garden. But he was never so serious that his sense of humour would not come bubbling out. One day we were playing against Somerset and C.C.C. Case—'Box' as they used to call him—was batting. He was always a difficult man to get out, he would block ball after ball and never take risks, and on this day Johnnie Clay became so exasperated with the stone walling that he substituted a rubber ball for the cricket ball and bowled that. You should have seen Box's face when the thing took off vertically right in front of his nose."

Alun Watkins, a Plymouth Argyle footballer, a man built like an armchair, but not in the least static, came into the side. He was a pugnacious batsman (I once saw him hit a ball for four to leg—after it had passed the wicket-keeper), a good medium pace left-arm bowler. He was also a fine close-to-the-wicket fielder, one of the clutch which Wooller recruited, taught, inspired, and to whom he gave faith. Wooller says: "In the season we won the Championship there were plenty of county sides who had far better batting than us, and quite a number with better bowling. But not one had a more brilliant fielding side."

The county which, only a generation before, had only one man brave enough to call himself a slip fielder, and which had found it necessary to "hide" four old men in the field, now had a roost of men who were capable of the most miraculous catching feats. Wooller remembered how Ernie Toshack, the Australian, had bowled to a leg-side close field and he employed that in his Glamorgan team. Around the corner the Glamorgan fielders loitered like shop-lifters. "Our secret weapon," smiled Wooller. "In our championship season Watkins, Phil Clift and I took about 120 catches."

Emrys Davies and Arnold Dyson opened the batting, until the veteran Dyson went to take a coaching appointment at Oundle School, reappearing to play a notable part in the finale to the Championship. Both players from Glamorgan's days of struggle, acquainted with grief, they gave their sober experience to the younger players of the side. Emrys coached the elegant Gilbert Parkhouse and the dapper Phil Clift who became his opening partner. He would stare down the wicket at Clift like a minister in chapel. "Emrys was a good man, a sober, dedicated fellow, a great father-figure to the team," said Wooller. Arnold Dyson studied the game every moment, winter and summer. They used to say that he was such a perfectionist that if he touched a catch to slip he always walked even if it were dropped. Morally he was out.

Willie Jones, the bean-sized batsman, topped the county batting averages that summer of 1948, amazingly hitting *two* double centuries but no single centuries. Welsh-speaking Willie had to be encouraged, bolstered. After scoring two thousand runs in a season he was worried in case his contract was not renewed. He never went to the wicket without trembling, scarcely believing that he was capable of doing the things he did. Jones played his favoured square cut like a man prodding a bear. At Gravesend, against Kent, in June he scored 207. "When he came in after batting," remembers his captain, "his hand was shaking so much he could hardly hold a glass of orange squash. 'I'll never be able to do that again, skipper,' he mumbled." A week later he *did* it again—212 not out against Essex, with Emrys Davies getting 215 in a total of 586 for five declared.

They used to call Haydn Davies, the wicket-keeper, The Panda. He was large and dark of head and eye and adopted the stance of that curious, benign and powerful creature. For all his heaviness, both in body and aspect, he was the lively one, the joker, the charmer, the boy for a night out, even when the stern Wooller disapproved. "He telephoned me one day and said, 'Skipper, I've got a broken finger'," said Wooller. "I asked him what he intended to do about it and he said, 'I'll go on playing. I'll try to keep it out of the way'."

There were others who came in and out of the side as the summer progressed, George Lavis, Jim Pleas, and an absorbing spin bowler from Swansea eponymously named Stan Trick. "He worked in his father-in-law's garage and he couldn't always get away to play," smiled Wooller slowly shaking his head. "But the Swansea wicket was made for him. There he was just about unplayable." In his first match at the St Helen's ground against Somerset, he took six wickets for 77 in the first innings and six for 29 in the second. But only at Swansea could he do it. They said his sort of bowling didn't travel well.

Of the three imported players, all from Middlesex, the most significant was Len Muncer, a beaming, oval-faced spin bowler, approaching his final seasons. He got through twice as many overs as anyone else, apart from Wooller, and took 156 wickets in the season at an average of 17.12. He was also only just short of a thousand runs. Young Eaglestone batted soundly when he was needed and Norman Hever, the fast bowler, topped the first-class averages for some weeks. At Lord's against Middlesex, the county which had rejected him, he took five wickets for 34. With relish.

*   *   *

But Glamorgan were never players of mere matches. They had the fun and charm and good companionship of a touring repertory company. J.B.G. Thomas, the legendary sports editor of the *Western Mail*, travelled around with them that Daffodil Summer. "They had an old mangle, the sort your mam used to have at home, and this was transported on the back of a little lorry, together with a pile of tattered, suspicious-looking blankets," he remembers. "If Glamorgan arrived at a ground and there had been overnight rain then everybody would set-to spreading the blankets and putting them through the mangle to get the pitch fit for play."

"They were a lovely bunch of boys. I don't think they quite knew what was happening to them when they won the Championship that summer." Bryn Thomas would travel by train with the team, sometimes taking his infant son along also. "We used to be crowded into the compartment, talking cricket, laughing, a whole bunch of us, and little Craig would be up in the luggage rack, staring over the top, taking it all in." Such an exotic childhood, travelling suspended above those gods, no doubt gave Craig Thomas the seed he needed to become the successful novelist he is today.

The first match of the 1948 season told nothing of the amazements that were to follow over the sunny early weeks. Glamorgan played a friendly game against Thomas Owen's XI, an occasion which, however, was not without its oddities. The year was scarcely out of winter and the conditions were chill, indeed so inclement that Maurice Leyland "retired hurt" in the visitors' first innings. He had cramp. Emrys Davies, grey as the weather, assembled a painstaking 31 before being dismissed by Len Hutton, a thoughtful bowler in those days, who took two further wickets in the Glamorgan innings at a cost of 22 runs. Sporting declarations in the weather-washed game resulted in Thomas Owen's team being required to score 85 in 45 minutes to win. They were four runs short at the end. One of the umpires was Douglas Jardine. I wish I had seen him. And Hutton bowling.

Another friendly, against Somerset, was played at Newport where once, it was gossiped, the wicket was prepared with more than a touch of witchcraft. Certainly, before the war, the Glamorgan groundsman, was rumoured to have prepared a strip of mystic components including silt from the River Taff, coal dust from the River Ebbw and mud from the River Usk "all boiled up in a Welsh cauldron". It was forecast that the potion would help the Glamorgan spinners against Gloucester in the summer of 1938. Gloucester made 581 of which Hammond got 302. He liked batting on coal dust.

The 1948 match against Somerset at Newport went better for the Welshmen. Somerset crumpled to the diminutive spin of Willie Jones (who also got 93) and lost by 98 runs.

Essex next were defeated at Cardiff (where the cricket ground was behind the Arms Park rugby stand) by five wickets; then Somerset again at Swansea with Stan Trick from the garage, taking his famous twelve wickets. At Derby, at the end of May, against a strong bowling side, came defeat by the not inconsiderable margin of 301 runs. But there followed three successive triumphs—against Kent at Gravesend (Willie Jones's nervous double hundred) and versus Hampshire at Cardiff, where Hampshire scored a hundred in an hour, going for victory, and were then summarily dismissed in the next hour, mostly by the flighted left-arm bowling of, once again, Willie Jones. "He made the ball 'ang in the air, aye like a grape," my old uncle said.

Kent were humbled at Swansea in June, Stan Trick, having more time off from the grease pit, taking ten wickets and Len Muncer eight. More than 30,000 people watched this match over the three days, the multitude that were to follow Glamorgan throughout the season. Wooller, the rugby man, the winter hero, was bringing Welshmen out of the valleys to see a different game, but one which they embraced with hardly less heart and, naturally, with as much singing. It was the first time choral works had been heard at first-class matches.

The uplift was needed, not only in Wales but throughout a Britain bled grey by a war that had finished three years before. Clothes and food were still rationed, there were shortages of almost everything. But the pundits were unimpressed. "It was not a vintage year," decided a cricket aristocrat. He was one of many who refused to believe that this unfashionable, even *foreign*, county could actually win. Victory after victory was discounted even when the Welshmen led the table in June, and the setback period which followed in July was acknowledged by those who knew, or thought they did, as only right and to be expected. Lesser counties simply did not ascend like larks. At the end there was a multitude who were not so much surprised as shocked. It was as though the prize had been taken by stealth.

That same season up and down England, in the Test matches and through the counties, went the conquering Australians on their first post-war tour. They scored seven hundred runs *in one day* against Essex at Southend.

At the Oval, England were briskly dealt with: all out for 52. Don Bradman walked out for his farewell innings. He was cheered and applauded all the way to the middle, only to return minutes later in the silence of disbelief—bowled by Hollies for no score. I was there in that throng. I had never seen him bat and now I never would.

On that day Alun Watkins played his first match for England, and received such a battering from Lindwall, that he was too bruised to play in the historic game at Bournemouth which took the Championship.

*   *   *

Meanwhile Glamorgan appeared to have lost their way. They fell to Middlesex and to Leicestershire and there came a faltering series of drawn games, partly through the summer weather turning sour. The game with the Australians never came to any flourish, although with lumpy rain clouds hanging on the Bristol Channel and not an inch of room in the ground, Keith Miller made 84 in the only innings, which came to a stop in a downpour with the tourists at 215 for three. In another July game Gunner G.A.R. Lock, playing for Combined Services, the only squaddie in the parade of Lieutenant Colonels, Squadron Leaders and Commanders, took six wickets for 43, a taste of the great days that were to come for him with Surrey and with England.

A victory against Warwickshire, at Neath, kept Glamorgan's nose near the top of the table and then came, in mid-August, with the Welsh weather mending, a wonderful and crucial victory against Surrey at Cardiff. Wilfred Wooller's brave batting, driving and hammering square cuts, ensured a Glamorgan total of 239. Wooller scored 89, his best of the season. Then Johnnie Clay, coming into the team in the absence of Watkins, and having reached the age of fifty, bowled out one of the strongest counties in England for fifty runs. Clay took five wickets and when Surrey followed on took another five. The long, frail, silver man was almost bowled over himself as the Arms Park Welshmen charged across the pitch at the end to acclaim him and the Glamorgan team. The smell of success was in the Cardiff air and very sweet it was.

And so to the final match against Hampshire, at Bournemouth—not the *last* match of the season but the one that had to be won. "It needed to be then," remembered Wilfred Wooller laconically. "Because the last game was at Leicester." Jack Walsh, the Australian-born spin bowler, played for Leicester and Wooller's team knew they would be pressed to scrape even a draw on the home side's wicket. (So it proved for, having secured the Championship, Glamorgan went to Leicester and were soundly beaten by an innings—the second time that the Midlands county had defeated them that season.)

The habitual champions, Yorkshire, who might have finally overtaken Glamorgan, were engaged against Somerset at Taunton, on the other side of Dorset, and Glamorgan began their innings at Bournemouth with conspiratorial clouds on the sea. Arnold Dyson, on holiday from his school coaching, was asked to play because Phil Clift was injured. Johnnie Clay came into the side instead of the Test-match-bruised Alun Watkins. Both replacements played crucial roles in the events of the next two days.

Emrys Davies and Dyson went forth to bat. Emrys's wife went off to walk around the town. As she shopped she listened for sounds from the ground.

Only ten minutes after the innings had begun dull summer raindrops sent the players to the pavilion and there they remained for the rest of the day, staring out at that most glum of views, the English seaside in the wet.

Sunday was spent wondering. On Monday the skies appeared kinder and once more Emrys and Arnold went to the middle. There now remained eleven and a half hours to win the match. The pair batted steadily as the clock turned, but knowing that the time would come for acceleration. Dyson was out for 51, trying to force the tempo, and at lunch Glamorgan were 99 for one wicket. Willie Jones emerged (tentatively) and, locking up his dashing shots, stared low and anxiously down the wicket at the fiercely advancing Shackleton, one of England's finest pace bowlers.

In mid-afternoon Emrys stroked (yes, *stroked*) a six, an extravagance greeted with almost chapel-like pursed lips from the Welshmen present. Emrys smiled apologetically. Willie sidled his way past his fifty, and when Emrys was eventually out for the most important 74 he had ever accumulated, the unassuming little man from the valleys assumed the mantle, stitched his way patiently through the whole innings while Wooller and Len Muncer and Norman Hever, at the tail, threw their bats. The side were all out for 315, Jones returning, smiling unsurely, with 78 not out.

It was still only early evening and the Hampshire openers, Arnold and Rogers, went out with over an hour left for play. Wooller and Hever bowled. In the captain's second over Rogers played a true leg glance and Gilbert Parkhouse, who had failed with the bat, swooped like a local gull to catch the ball an inch from the ground and no more than three yards from the bat. It was the catch that made Glamorgan really *believe* they could do it. Before the end of play on that brief evening six Hampshire batsmen were back in the pavilion. Glamorgan went to bed looking forward to the morning.

There seemed hardly room or time to breathe on that ground the next day. Not long ago I played in a match there and I sat after the game, in the lemon sun of the evening, years later, trying to imagine how it had been. Wooller, seriously, sent a telegram to Somerset playing Yorkshire at Taunton. The two counties, having for so long been treated lightly, disdainfully, had a mutual bond, and the message "Hold on to Yorkshire. We're beating Hants" was received and understood. "Don't worry," came the reply. "We're beating Yorkshire."

With that assurance Glamorgan set about the Hampshire second innings. Every so often a whisper would go from the pavilion around the crowd that Somerset were keeping their word.

John Clay had been out early to sniff the salty air. He pressed his finger tips into the wicket and knew everything would be all right. The information he kept private. He and the oval-faced Len Muncer finished Hampshire for 84. There were now four hours during which to get them out a second time.

Arnold and Rogers batted without any crisis for twenty minutes and four hours began to look a short time indeed. Then young Hever got one under Rogers' bat, pitched right up and moving a shade. Clean bowled. Hope rekindled.

Desmond Eagar, a fine player, charged the Glamorgan bowlers, hitting Willie Jones for a six that came near to disturbing people on the beach. But Muncer and Clay came back and that was enough. Muncer curled one around Eagar's feet to bowl him. The next man Bailey was promptly run out and the two spinners, so disparate in physique and style, whittled their way through the tail. Muncer had claimed five wickets in the first Hampshire innings and Clay three. Now it was the tall Johnnie's turn. The man who had played in Glamorgan's first county match in 1921, bowled as he had never bowled before. By the time he had Knott lbw, and had received the historical affirmative from Dai Davies (Knott swears to this day that the umpire appealed as well!), he had taken six for 48. It was still only mid-afternoon.

So there it was. The miracle at last. They still talk about it in Wales and wherever one Welshman meets another. It was wonderful that time long ago. That Daffodil Summer.

Yorkshire

Duncan Kyle: A contented traveller and writer of adventure stories, who suspects he would have been happier still as a cricket correspondent: preferably for the Bradford *Telegraph & Argus*!

Bradford and Bradman, and Times Gone By . . .
Duncan Kyle

It was a long time ago, that first sight of Yorkshire cricket, remembered now only as a brief and inevitably distorted film-clip to be projected occasionally and at will on some mental screen: Bowes at mid-off, none-too-mobile, but very sure when the hardest shot was within reach; but then bowling remarkably freely and from enormous height. And Verity, graceful as some white cat, flicking the ball to hand with his toe, then turning—and turning the ball, too, all bounce and bite and sportsmanship. He went to war as a Green Howard, to die of wounds in Italy in 1943, and my neighbour here in Suffolk, a farmer and no cricketer, was with Captain Verity in that battle and will not forget a fine quiet gentleman, much mourned as war ground bloodily on.

A year after fighting ended, Yorkshire, with Lancashire's typically generous co-operation, held a memorial match for him, proceeds to go to Verity's young family. A newly-demobilised flight sergeant, one Washbrook, made 97, Eddie Paynter 47 n.o., Wilf Barber 88—and the *tax collector* £1,100. Thirty thousand people had attended to pay their tribute and give the odd shilling and they were, not to put too fine a point on it, bloody cross. They sat stoically in the rain, the players went ahead like ducks in a downpour, and that damned tax man sat in the dry and counted his take with greedy fingers.

But Yorkshire won the Championship again that season, the right and natural thing, it seemed, and it muted the fury a bit. By then we had been starved for years. I was a badly deprived child, swindled by Hitler out of seasons 1940–45 inclusive. Never even saw Sutcliffe play.

Only once during the war was any cricket which might reasonably be described as first-class played in my home city of Bradford, and for me it was finer far than six extra rations of sweets. Army played R.A.F. and there were several sights for longing eyes: Flight lieutenant Hammond, for instance, firing sixes off tiptoes into the football stand, and Lieutenant Leyland banging the ball left-handed, off the back foot, past cover's right hand.

After that I was living suddenly in a new world. For five years we had had only the Bradford League (though I'm far from sure that "only" is the aptest of words!). Local sides were speckled then with great players, but they were odd-looking teams all the same, composed of fortyish men and boys still too young for war. We saw Constantine, Achong, C.B. Clarke, Paynter; Copson bowling for, I think, Windhill; and George Duckworth, standing in those days on the wrong side of the Pennines, red-faced and rotund and screaming his *How's that?* very loudly, as if to remind them in Manchester that he was still about. Young names, too, were creeping higher on the scorecards. An Aireborough Grammar School boy named Close was performing prodigies at fourteen, lifting Test match bowlers over the boundary. ("Bit big 'eaded, so they say." "Aye, an' if 'e is, t'lad's summat to be big 'eaded abaht!") And at Farsley, in the second team, a lad named Illingworth. A pair of schoolboys, then, both to be very good captains of England, though neither could then have guessed it, and wouldn't have believed it, anyway, because amateurs skippered England and each already had a foot on the professional road.

They'd get there, though, along a path trodden first by Hutton. (Time you mentioned *him*, do I hear? Thought I'd forgotten, did you? *Forgotten!*) In 1945 his magic was feared to be in abeyance, the subject of much earnest prayer from lads my age—and older people, too. Sergeant PTI Len Hutton had tumbled in an army gym and smashed that high left elbow. Stitches, operations, even grafts had followed: now it was whispered there was a crater in the forearm that would nicely contain your fist. Yet on Bradford League wickets not always of the truest Hutton was pushing that ruined elbow straight down the line, for his nursery club, Pudsey St Lawrence, against some quite bouncy quick bowlers; and busily finding out whether he could still bat a bit with one arm inches shorter than the other. By July, for Yorkshire now, against an Australian Services side (which included an ex-fighter pilot named Keith Ross Miller) he scored 82 out of a total of 122, and eighteen months later, facing that same Miller (by now in dangerous tandem with one Lindwall), he was still pushing that fragile elbow structure immaculately down the line with the ball flying off a length on a ruined pitch at Brisbane. A very brave player. And yes, he *could* still bat a bit.

The Championship season of 1946, A.B. Sellers leading 'em out once more, that sailor's gait of his, and the great names following him down the steps at Park Avenue. Brian Sellers grinning and hurling the ball jokily at Arthur Wood from a range of about five feet, and Wood, with his trencherman's shape and his fox-terrier reflexes, taking it sweetly and

24

flicking it back, and the crowd delighted and relieved to see that these were still the same men—laikin' yes, but laikin' very hard. No Verity, of course: instead somebody named Booth, left-arm-slow from the League, getting on a bit and denied a chance for years because Verity had been unchallengeable. Arthur Booth took his chance *that* season. Top of the first-class averages, no less, a hundred-plus wickets for eleven apiece, and all Yorkshire was reassured, because the bag of talent seemed bottomless still.

A year or so later, Big Bill Bowes had retired, the Viking body slowed by years in a prison camp. He went into the Press box, to report cricket for the *Yorkshire Evening News*. (They headlined one of his reports from Australia: "Brisbane pitch flooded—by Bill Bowes"!) And I was in the Press box too, learning, running copy for the encyclopaedic Dick Williamson of the Bradford *Telegraph and Argus*, who seemed then, and seems still, to have had the best head for cricket facts and figures of anybody I ever met. A day was to come, not many years later, when Hutton, in a Test match, was given out "obstructing the field". *Sensation!* From the office I telephoned Dick Williamson. He was reporting a football match that day, twenty thousand voices yelling around him and no reference books to hand, but he reeled off the three previous times it had happened, the teams involved, even the dates.

He was a hard man, too. Hard and generous. I can still see his face the first (and last) time I applauded in the Press box. Heads turned, heavy with disapproval. The patrician J.M. Kilburn looking down a longish nose; busy John Bapty glancing in irritation at a copy boy who knew nowt. And Dick, with blue eyes like a pair of cannon, jerking his brown-trilbied head. I approached, trembling. "Not here, son. Never in here."

I was there very much on sufferance. Few things and no persons came lower than a copy boy hoping to become a junior reporter. Other aspirants were back in the office, fetching tea and racing along corridors with sheets of paper, but *I* was at a Yorkshire match! One word from Dick Williamson would have ended that for ever.

After a time he even began to trust me with small things. He'd been out of the box, telephoning, when a catch was taken, and asked *me* about it! I carried on as his copy boy long after the junior reporter hurdle had been crossed. It was indulgence by the news editor, and by Dick, and I'm grateful still because I was present at some of the Marvels of the Age. I met *Gods* . . .

Last summer, in one of the many rain-breaks in the Tests, I listened as Arlott, Johnston, Trueman, Bailey and Co talked about great Test matches. Headingley, 1948, was on everybody's list. Well, *I* was there, first ball to last. A great uncle, very old then, and believing, wrongly, that he wouldn't be alive on my twenty-first birthday, offered an advance present: tickets for the London Olympics. It was the hardest choice I ever faced, weighed thus: *Bradman was playing at Leeds*. There would be more Olympics, but no more Bradmans.

So I saw the little man in the big green cap. Saw him get fifty-odd, bowled by a persevering Pollard, in the first innings; saw him dropped at slip by Jack Crapp, saw Godfrey Evans improbably juggling with the ball and failing to stump him—*and* saw him make 173 with Morris (182) and win the match. What an ovation as he came off the field! The great Don was to say later that the finest compliment ever paid him came that day: as he walked into the crowd, an old Yorkshireman slapped him quite hard on the shoulder and said, "Aaaah, you *bugger!*"

It was during that match that Mr Ernest Holdsworth was elected either a life—or an honorary—member of MCC, I forget which. Ernest who? No need to ask if you knew your Yorkshire cricket. He was chairman of the Cricket Committee of the County Club (chairman, also, of some giant company in the wool dyeing trade, too, as if *that* mattered). He was, simply, The Boss. So there he stood at Headingley: a proud and powerful old gentleman, crimson-and-gold silk new-knotted at his neck, before the pavilion at lunch-time, accepting congratulations. A spotty youth stopped before him. A grimy hand pointed accusingly at the tie. "'Ey," the youth demanded, "When did t'a play for Brig'us Rangers?"

There, too, as Bradman flogged an England attack consisting at times of the wrist spin of Compton and Hutton, Dick Williamson told me of Bradman's only appearance on "our" ground—Park Avenue. The year was 1930, his first tour. Australia played Yorkshire twice that season, the first time at Sheffield. At the Bramall Lane nets, the young marvel was keenly observed by a fiery Yorkshire bowler named Macaulay. The examination was lengthy. At last Macaulay turned away. "I'll do you so-and-so catched and bowled." (Bowled, thus spoken, rhymes with howled.) And he did: for 78. "Aye, well, wait till I 'ave 'im at Bradford." But at Bradford the chance never came. Emmott Robinson had first snap: Bradman lbw Robinson 1. Bradman, on succeeding tours, stood down at Bradford . . . Nerves? I don't know, but check the reference books, if you will. A sharp and humorous character though, Macaulay, and wonderful in the field. He stood one day at third slip. A young player, name unknown, playing his first match in the County side, stood at second. Off Bowes an edge came, fast and low, a red flash at the ankles. The young man, unaccustomed to such speed, but well taught, was busily getting his heels together to prevent the ball going through, when a white blur passed before him, scooped up the ball, rolled over three times, then fixed him with an angry eye. "In this team, lad," snarled George Macaulay, "we cop *them!*"

But all that happened before my time, and there is richness enough in

26

the few years I watched Yorkshire to make digression unnecessary. Giants walked the land in those days: giants of old, present giants, giants-to-be. I lived in Toller Lane. A hundred and fifty yards away in Jesmond Avenue I used to see Emmott Robinson walking his terrier, and touch my school cap; one of my friends was the grandson of Schofield Haigh. (For that matter, John Boynton Priestley, that Yorkshireman of Yorkshiremen, was brought up one hundred yards due north, and it is one of the continuing mysteries that he, somehow, apparently never fell deeply in love with cricket. Football, yes. Incomprehensible!)

But back to the giants—perhaps to *the* Giant. I met him only once, but unforgettably. It was on the 6th of September, 1951, and I was sent by that indulgent news editor to interview him for an eightieth birthday piece next day. Morning bus to Huddersfield, a knock at the door of a very modest house. It was opened by the great man's sister, in a pinafore, wiping her hands.

"Is Mr Hirst in?"

"No," she said, "he's not."

"Are you expecting him back?"

"Aye, love, he'll be in for his dinner."

"You don't happen to know where he is?" (The news editor was, as I say, indulgent, but it was not his intention that I spend all day on one article.)

"Aye, love. He's up in the park, top of the road."

"Thank you." I was turning away.

"With Wilfred," she said.

I *ran* up that road. *With Wilfred!*

Boys were playing cricket—two rather old boys among them. The wicket was a pile of assorted jackets, and those nine- and ten-year-old Huddersfield lads were playing with the two greatest all-rounders who had ever lived: Wilfred Rhodes and George Herbert Hirst. (Sobers came later.) The boys knew who they were, of course, but didn't seem awed, or conscious of any great privilege. It was just a game of cricket, for them— and, truly I think, for Hirst and Rhodes, too. No point in listing the achievements; you need only open *Wisden*. But I'll remind you of two things: Rhodes played against both Grace and Bradman, and in a Test match at fifty. And Hirst? Well, there *was* the season of 1906. If you open *Wisden*, and look in the Cricket Records section headed The Double, you will find his name right at the top, entirely alone. The little old man I saw, playing that day in the park, once scored 2,385 runs *and* took 208 wickets in a single season. When, at the end of it, he was asked if he thought anyone else would match those totals, he said gently, "Nay, I don't know. If they do, they'll be tired." You have heard that observation before? It was repeated, more than half a century later, embellished a little, by Frederick Sewards Trueman, when *his* total of Test wickets passed three hundred. I always thought that a pity—Trueman had no need at all of other men's flowers.

Rhodes, then, was already losing his sight; he was quite blind soon afterwards, but still to be seen on the scattered county grounds, asking young players to hand him their bats, feeling at the blade's edge to check if a youngster middled the ball.

But what about Hutton? Never fear, all roads lead back to Hutton, eventually. When he was a boy, fourteen or so (no teenagers then) and already performing prodigies (it is said the ten-year-old Hutton went in to bat in the schoolyard at Pudsey the day after the Easter holiday and was still there, not out, when they broke up for summer), he went to the Yorkshire nets, to be watched by Hirst. Bill Bowes later asked Hirst about the lad.

"Nay, ah can tell him nowt," said Hirst.

"Is he deaf?" asked Bowes. "Or won't he listen?"

"Nay, neither. The lad's a player."

A player. He was an' all! I have countless memories of Hutton. There was a time when I watched him with such emotional concentration that I could sometimes sense what he would do. He emitted little signs. Something in the way he prodded the wicket and touched his cap told of his form. Once, in something like agony, I actually *knew* he would be out next ball, and he was—bowled. Hutton was bowled an awful lot for a player of his matchless quality.

Interviewing him, once, I asked about it, and he said, "Yes, I know." Fatuously, I pressed the point. "Can you do anything about it?" He gave a weary little smile. "I've been trying all my life. I try to get a few runs between times."

Didn't he, though? And what runs they were!

Just occasionally, when he was free of responsibility—and that was rarely, whether he was playing for Yorkshire or England—just occasionally, when he was feeling at the very top of his form, he used to take his cap off in mid-innings. And then . . . oh, and *then*! I saw him take seventy between ten-to-one and half-past off the Derbyshire attack. Forty minutes for seventy off Gladwin and Jackson, then the most dangerous pace attack in the land. He pushed the field back with stinging drives, then drew them in with short-run singles, then skimmed drives over their heads. And at the other end "Posser" Lowson, a slimmer look-alike for Hutton, and a fine player himself, was doing much the same. *He* made forty more that day before lunch; hardly surprisingly, considering the onslaught, a few extras came along, and Yorkshire went in for their tea and salad at 120 for no wicket. In forty minutes. Was Hutton L. wearing his cap? He was not.

28

But he wore it the day I watched what I still believe is the finest innings I ever saw. It was played, and rightly, against Lancashire—at Bramall Lane in the early fifties. A brute of a pitch, damp, with a hot sun on it, and Bob Berry turning the ball and fizzing it and making it sit up and beg. (Recently my publishers produced a beautiful cricket book, full of interest, information and fine writing. It says of Hutton that he had an unfortunate effect on other young players, because he played too much from the crease. They should have seen him that day!) Berry was skilful, the pitch was made for him, and he was a flighter of the ball. Hutton danced. Right forward and right back. Feet like lightning, full stretch to the ball, or curled over it. At the other end there was a procession. At Hutton's end timing, elegance, grace, watchful defence, supremely punishing attack. I've never understood how so slow a swing of the bat could move a ball so fast. Specifically I remember two strokes. The first was—what else?—that peerless cover drive, fielded near to me in the crowd by a man a long way from the wicket, who threw it back and then stood there wringing his stinging hands. The second, on that brute of a wicket, was a late cut, very late, the sort of thing you might associate with a Keith Miller feeling cheeky. It passed between wicket-keeper and first slip.

He became Sir Leonard, of course, but Len Hutton he was, for us. There were those who said Compton was the better player, but they read E. W. Swanton in the *Daily Telegraph*, and everybody knew *he* was weighted on the Southern side. (Compton, about this time, fielding at Sheffield and in his pomp, encountered one of those stray dogs which sneak into cricket grounds without tickets and run like streakers all over the field. It seemed drawn to Compton, attracted, a few suggested, by the scent of his hair cream. "Bite 'im!" yelled the crowd delightedly. "Bite the . . . !" Whether it did or not, I've never been sure, but he had a deal of trouble fending it off. A Tyke of Tykes, that one. Laughter rang round the ground. To be fair, there is no doubt the Yorkshire crowds treated Denis Compton abominably. He was a splendid and chivalrous batsman, and a brave one; furthermore, he is the only great player I can recall who was so treated: the Yorkshire crowds were, with that exception, unfailingly generous. But once, at Leeds, when his celebrated knee was acting up, Compton made a couple of misfields and was hooted for the rest of the day whenever the ball came near him. I'm ashamed of it, but I know the reason. It was felt in Yorkshire that Hutton got the kicks and Compton the ha'pence, and the fault lay with the Southern cricket writers who, it seemed in Yorkshire then, couldn't wait to have a dig at Hutton while they were praising Compton to the skies.)

To this day some of that feeling persists in Yorkshire. It may be an inferiority complex manifesting itself, but I'm inclined to think it is a hatred of things unfair. Boycott has been England's most successful batsman of the last two decades, but the Yorkshire spectator feels that what praise he's given is grudging, that the Southern critics are ever ready with big sticks.

And by Jove! didn't *they*—the cricket writers—hose him down with bile and venom when he returned from India just before Christmas last year! Boycott, having scored more runs by then than anyone else in Test history, couldn't have had a worse Press had he been the Yorkshire Ripper. I have little doubt he's a difficult chap to live alongside. The dedicated always are, especially if one is not quite so dedicated, or so successful, oneself. I also seem to recall that Bradman, according to the late, wonderful Jack Fingleton, was not especially adored in the Australian dressing room.

As a digression—I'm even tempted to make it a competition with a bottle of Tetley's and a parkin pig as prizes—try to imagine what *The Times* and the *Telegraph*, daily and Sunday, might have said had Boycott, rather than Fletcher, skippered England to defeat by India in a stupefyingly dull series and with an over rate of about three a fortnight. As guidance, remember that Close, admired *and successful* as England captain, was sacked in mid-series for slow play.

As someone once said darkly to me at Scarborough: "There's a commandment, lad, about charity, but it only applies if you're born south and east of Marlow. It's the axe and the block for Yorkshire players if they're not fully paid-up saints!"

Still, that's a sour note, and I must damp it. Though Yorkshire cricket seems to have had its sourness, too, in the dressing room in those days, it wasn't to be seen on the field. What was in evidence was class, some of it sadly fleeting; like Appleyard's Season. Big Bob from Bradford, whanging down medium-paced off-breaks that spat up around the hip pocket: 200 wickets in his first full season. A bowler of something near genius, so dogged by illness and injury that his career was woefully short. Gerry Smithson, left-handed and suspect of technique ("picks 'is bat up toward second slip," said Maurice Leyland, "they'll york 'im all ower t'place.") And they did. But against Lancashire, of all people, he hit ninety-nine before lunch, all eye and timing and punch.

There were stayers, too: Coxon, running in like an angry whippet, teeth bared, a batsman-hater who'd bowl all day up the cellar steps, as the saying went; and the superb Willie Watson. Was there ever a cricketer as graceful? In my mind's eye I can see him now, chasing in the field, running fast and upright, fair as some Nordic god—he had a kind of easy-easy sprint, if such a thing is possible, and played as straight as anyone I ever saw. A hundred in his first Test match against Australia, but far more than that: with Trevor Bailey he saved both match and series that day.

Don Brennan and Jim Binks, beautiful wicket-keepers both, the one ever-immaculate, the other ever-present. Binks came into the Yorkshire side and never left it until he retired. No absences through injury, no broken or split fingers—you can't say more for a wicket-keeper than that.

And then there was John Wardle. You need only look at the figures: 1,842 wickets at an average of 18.95 between 1946 and 1958, and a buzz-buzz of excitement whenever he came in to hit.

He won a lot of matches, spinning skilfully and exuberantly, with that long swing of the arm from behind his back. But he lost one, too—a very fine bowler, bowling really rather badly at a moment when it counted, in the most exciting game of cricket I ever saw.

The year was 1948. Bradman's magnificent Australians playing Yorkshire at Bradford. (The Don elsewhere, naturally.) Hassett in charge and one of those Bradford wickets that set your teeth chattering. Really it could have happened on no other ground. For those who don't know Park Avenue, a short description: at one end the football stand; at the other the pavilion, high on a bank behind row upon row of seating; and a short boundary in front of the wicket both ends; but long wide expanses to square leg and point; a ground for six-hitters and strong drivers, with a wicket which, true enough in good weather, was a pig and a half when rain and sun touched it up.

Yorkshire batted and were shot out. Johnston and Miller hunted as a pair—but not quite as you might imagine. Miller abandoned pace and bowled off-breaks. Furthermore he bowled them brutally well. Six for 42. In went Australia, and Frank Smailes, who could turn his hand to most things, tore through Hassett, Morris, and Co like a quart of Epsom Salts, also bowling off-breaks. He had six for 51. (Miller strode out with his cap on and banged Smailes' first ball directly back over the bowler's head for six. He made 34, brave and almost contemptuous. But he couldn't last; no one could.) When Yorkshire batted, wickets again fell fast, so that in the fourth innings, the 1948 Australians, undoubtedly among the strongest sides ever to play the game, needed sixty to win.

That's all. Just sixty. But the wickets tumbled. Smailes had Hassett, Brown, and Morris for next to nothing. A few runs came—not many. Australia six down for 31, and Loxton hurt and unable to bat. The suspense was indescribable. Thirty to get, four wickets to go, and at the wicket a small, dark eighteen-year-old, by name Neil Harvey, whose experience of muck-heaps like this one must have begun that day. The ball turned and reared as it had done all through the match, and Harvey faced John Wardle, latest in the long and aristocratic line of left-arm spinners that went back through Booth and Verity to Rhodes himself. Harvey had already been dropped—doom's bell was tolling. Long hop outside the leg stump. Four. Long hop outside the leg stump. Four more.

31

Strong men all around turning their faces away. "'E's giving 'em t'bloody thing," someone groaned beside me. "All 'e 'as to do is keep it straight. T'pitch'll do t'rest." But he didn't. Harvey straight drove for six to win. Yorkshire lost by four wickets. Nobody else came near to beating the Australians that season. But my heroes gave them the fright of a lifetime.

They gave the West Indians a nasty time, too, a couple of years later, in the season Ramadhin and Valentine put everybody through the mincer, and the 'Three Ws'—Walcott, Weekes and Worrell—cut England to ribbons. Beautiful cricket was being played. After the Bradford match against Yorkshire I interviewed Hutton on the subject of Ramadhin, encountered for the first time that day. He'd been studied closely, and finally "read". Everybody on the ground saw it happen: Hutton feeling his way for a while then suddenly blossoming: the delicate dance forward, the slow swing of the bat, and something small and red accelerating past cover. I've forgotten how many he scored—it must have been seventy or eighty.

Ramadhin, dark hand partly obscured by flapping shirt cuff, turned the ball either way with finger spin, providing a mystery that seemed insoluble. Had Hutton solved it?

"I don't know," he said slowly, "but it seems to me he flights the leg break just a bit higher."

"How much is a bit?" I asked.

"Six inches or so. Maybe a bit more."

I wondered then, and wonder still, how it is that such judgment can exist in a human being. Nothing to go on but flight. Hutton had two eyes, like the rest of us, and a bat in his hand. How on earth . . .? But then, his judgment was uncanny altogether. One day Yorkshire took the field and play began. The bowlers didn't notice anything. The batsmen were unaware. The umpires happy. But Hutton said, "There's something wrong." The pitch was measured, it was twenty-three yards long.

I have said I saw Wonders, and I did. Laker in that 1950 Test match trial—at Bradford again. Eight wickets for two runs for England v. The Rest. Laker was much approved; after all he was born just down the road, in Shipley. He picked the petals off the fine flower of university batsmen that day: Doggart, May, Carr and Sheppard, and he was spinning the ball so wickedly they couldn't get their bats within inches, and sometimes not within feet.

And then, when England batted, Hutton at his dazzling best (said *Wisden*)—until he was bowled neck and crop, with 85 on the board, by a violent, young, fast bowler with miner's hips and shoulders and a mane of black hair flapping. I was behind the bowler's arm and that delivery pitched leg and middle and nipped the top of the off stump. I doubt if God could have played it! Thousands of spectators didn't know whether to laugh or weep. They'd been done out of a Hutton hundred, *but*—the new young Yorkshire quickie had done it, Trueman by name. And if he could bowl Our Len like that, he could bowl anybody. Saddened, the crowd yet gloated over a beautiful future.

And of course, it materialised. If I criticised Trueman a little earlier—and I didn't really, merely cavilled a bit at a single observation he once made—it is necessary to make amends. F.S.—great bowler, wonderful fieldsman, and a considerable batsman on his day (nearly ten thousands runs in first-class cricket). He generated excitement and enthusiasm for cricket across the world. Above all, he tried, and then tried some more, and never, never, never gave up. I for one never saw Fearless Fred have a lazy day. He might, on occasion, bowl less than well, but it was never less than the best he could give. And that best could be extraordinary. I saw him decimate the poor Indians at Headingley in a Test match, so controlled and hostile, so accurate, so lethal, with the ball lifting off a length, that poor Polly Umrigar was trying to play him from a guard somewhere near the square leg umpire. At one point the Indians were 5 for four.

It was at that moment I said to Mr William Eric Bowes, tapping at his typewriter in the seat next to mine, "What do you think they'll get?" There were visions in my mind of a record low Test score.

He gave me that enigmatic beam of his. "Between five and six hundred," says he, very promptly.

"*What!*"

"You heard."

"But they can't!"

"Want to back your judgment?"

I offered half a crown. The Viking head was shaken. Ten bob, then. "All right, ten bob," said Mr Bowes. "You might as well pay me now."

"But they're only five down!"

"Think about the bet. Between five and six hundred, I said. Well, didn't I? So they've got seven now, and they certainly aren't going to get six hundred. Pay up, lad."

Much grinning around me. A lesson learned: watch out for the sucker bet. I paid up, and resolved I'd find another innocent and recoup. Over the years it *has* worked a time or two.

Perhaps one is simply older; perhaps the one-day game has taken something out of cricket; but it doesn't seem like that any more. One sees the fine young players, the Atheys and Sharps, having to slog cross-batted for urgent runs on Sunday afternoons, polish and quality clearly apparent, and this the wrong way to develop it. Brian Close departed from Yorkshire, so one understood, over the matter of one-day matches. He didn't like them, and neither do I. Can you imagine Hutton or Compton,

May or Dexter, doing all that desperate scampering? Nor do the covered wickets help. That marvellous exhibition of skill by Hutton and Berry couldn't have taken place in recent seasons; nor could the Australians find themselves on a snorter against a county side, though I see the rule's now been changed. People say: oh, but the fielding has improved wonderfully, and indeed it has; but good fielding should complement the best of bowling and batsmanship, not replace it as a spectacle.

That's why I'm so glad I was born *where* I was born and grew up *when* I grew up. I'm sorry I never saw Sutcliffe, or Leyland at his thumping best, and only glimpsed Verity. But that period after the war was full of good things, imprinted in the memory—things I haven't even mentioned, and must mention now. Snapshots, no more:

The telescopic arm of Brian Sellers at short point, flicking out like a lizard's tongue, picking up Washbrook's square drive.

Norman Yardley's wife making a car dash to Yorkshire from the South so that her child could be born in the county, and therefore qualify to play.

The ever-chivalrous Yardley again, making a blinding catch and calling the departing batsman back because he, and only he, knew the catch wasn't a fair one.

Trueman being straight driven for six by Richie Benaud at Scarborough and the pair of them grinning at each other, each knowing all about the ball to come.

Brian Close standing doggedly still and taking the bruises against Wes Hall.

The uniquely sweet sound of Jack Hampshire's bat.

The sight of Richard Hutton, in a brand new county cap, following in father's footsteps (and following in them well enough to be there in the record books: "Record Partnership for the 7th wicket v India: 103 with Alan Knott").

Above all, there is a photograph taken on the Headingley ground, during the Test match against Australia in 1977. In that match Geoffrey Boycott scored his hundredth century and in the photograph, he stands on the left, in whites. Next to him, in a wheelchair, a well-groomed figure still, sits Herbert Sutcliffe, scorer of 149 centuries. And making up the little group is Sir Leonard Hutton. He made 129.

It happens to be a picture of the batsmen; but I saw bowlers to match.

Sussex

Alan Melville: Author of many successful West End plays and revues; actor, broadcaster and television personality.

A Fair Ground by the Sea
Alan Melville

"The season for resuming this athletic and manly exercise being now returned, we shall review the promise of sport which the season holds out; and it is with pleasure that in doing so we have to congratulate the admirers of this noble game upon the position in which this justly celebrated county stands."

It has to be admitted that these uplifting sentiments appeared in the *Brighton Gazette* a hundred and forty years ago; they could well have been written today, except that no doubt they would be more crisply phrased. "Barclay's Banking On Jackpot" would be how the *Brighton and Hove Argus* would put it. After all, it was only by the most damnable combination of bad luck, bad weather, bad wickets (elsewhere, of course; never at Hove), dubious mathematics and downright chicanery on the part of lesser breeds without the law that last season Sussex finished runners-up instead of in their rightful place as the physical embodiment of this book's title. (It is still inadvisable to mention the decimal system anywhere near the County Ground at Hove; even though it was not in a Championship match and had no bearing on the final pipping at the post, members turn puce, or pucer, when reminded that—after appeals, counter-appeals, and a serious threat to take the matter to the House of Lords—it was decreed by the other Lord's that we had "lost" a vital match by .17 of a run.)

As a matter of fact, Sussex—the first County Club to be formed in the country—has *never* won the Championship. It seems incredible, especially to Sussex supporters who are well known for their lack of bias, strict impartiality, and generous appreciation of the talents of other counties, even Nottinghamshire, but there it is—a mystery comparable to the disappearance of the *Marie Celeste* or the working of OPEC's Law, whereby every time the price of oil comes down the price of petrol goes up. (Though there is a letter in the Sussex C.C.C.'s excellent library, written by the great Doctor W.G. himself, maintaining that we *did* win the Championship, or at any rate should have won it, somewhere way back in the 1890s. Another argument over a tied match, it seems; chicanery again, of course; we were playing Nottinghamshire, and obviously they were up to their usual tricks.)

In Sussex, we take these blows of Fate in our stride; last season, when it was realised that yet again we had been denied our rightful due, the stride-taking consisted of the team streaking round the Hove ground starkers before or after, or probably both, getting at the Moet and Chandon. It is pleasing to observe that the media reported that "no objections were raised by any of the ratepayers occupying premises overlooking the County ground." I should think not, either, considering the amount of free entertainment they had during the season. Where else could you lean on your balcony and watch characters with good old Chestertonian Sussex names like Imran Khan or Garth le Roux at the top of their form without paying a penny piece for the privilege? If one may paraphrase Mr Kipling—the poet, not the cake man . . .

> *God gives all counties runs to make*
> *And wickets that may fall;*
> *And some may get the lucky break*
> *And some no breaks at all.*
> *But one's unique . . . who else would streak,*
> *Four points from victory?*
> *No umpire's call rings out "No ball!"*
> *In Sussex-by-the-Sea.*

(Incidentally—and we ask this in all innocence, never having won the thing in a hundred and forty-three years—do you *get* anything, apart from the glory, a bit of lolly, a word in edgeways with Frank Bough on "Sportsview" and with luck a perk or two from the sponsors—for becoming County Champions? I mean a cup or a shield or a medal or anything of that sort. No one at the Hove ground seems to know, not even Ossy Osborne the County's encyclopaedic librarian. We're only asking in a plaintive sort of way: what, if anything, is parked at this moment on Nottinghamshire's mantelpiece or sideboard? Temporarily, of course.)

Sussex first padded up as a County Club in 1839, the opening fixture being The Gentlemen of Sussex with Two Given Men v. The Players of the County. With due respect to Lord Dexter and the Nawab of Pataudi, the whole thing was rather more aristocratic than today. The 2nd Duke of Richmond was the pioneering spirit, and Prinny—though understandably none too nimble in dealing with bouncers or bodyline stuff—was a keen supporter. One is inclined to wonder how the Two Given Men felt in such company.

But cricket had flourished in Sussex—and, let's face it, in less salubrious counties like Surrey and Hampshire—long before this. There's a report of some court proceedings in January, 1598, involving a parcel of land somewhere near the Sussex-Surrey frontier; the coroner, one John Derick, let it be known that he "had known the land in question for the last fifty years and he and diverse others did runne and playe there at crickett and other plaies". One of the original rules of the Henfield C.C.—Henfield, a few miles inland from Brighton, still has its attractive and well-kept cricket ground on the common—would be promptly annulled at most of today's Club A.G.M.'s . . .

> **Rule 13** that any Member degrading himself by
> getting in Liquor before the match
> is played out, he is under Forfeit of Two
> Shillings and Sixpence.

And those of us who enjoy Sunday cricket, either semi-recumbent in a deck-chair at Hove or totally so goggling at the box, might feel a pang for the goings-on in 1622 in another Sussex village, Boxgrove. There the Vicar, the Reverend Daniel Earle, took a hefty swipe from the pulpit at the flannelled fools in his flock who played the game on the Sabbath, and the fact that the village team included two of his own churchwardens didn't help much. He preached a long and vehement sermon accusing the players of three mortal sins:

> 1st., that it is contrary to the 7th Article,
>
> 2nd., that they breake the Church windows with
> their Ball,
>
> and 3rd., for that a little childe had like to
> have her braynes beaten out with a
> cricket Batt.

Just how the third offence happened isn't clear; but apparently in those days the batsman was allowed a second strike at the ball if he could re-establish contact with it before it touched the greensward, and no doubt the stupid infant got in the way. One feels a faint reluctant sympathy for the Vicar (as well as, of course, for the childe); in the absence of a proper ground, the Boxgrove home fixtures were played in the churchyard.

Sussex, you see—both its players and spectators—has been enjoying cricket in one form or another for at least four hundred years. And every so often during that time things have happened inside the county boundaries (I mean the geographical ones, not the ones that slip so smoothly off Parker's bat when he's in the mood) which have earned a place in the history of the game, and even revolutionised it. It was the Duke of Richmond's star turn, Lillywhite (known as Nonpareil in the same complimentary way that Arnold is known as Horse), who really settled once and for all the change-over from under-arm to round-the-arm bowling. He wasn't the first to try it out on a presumably demoralised batsman; Willis at Lord's had had a go, with unhappy results. He was no-balled, and in a fit of pique vowed that he would never play again. Nor did he: according to contemporary report, he "mounted his horse and rode out of Lord's and out of cricketing history".

But Lillywhite of Sussex it was who legalised and polished, no doubt down the leg of his flannels, the ferocious new technique—and incidentally introduced for the first time among the extras the word "wide". A great guy: but for him, bouncers would be unknown except on certain pitches where they are inevitable; we'd have been spared all that Jardine body-line brouhaha, and the manufacturers of helmets, shields, guards, cages and other assault-course kit would be feeling the pinch. And fast bowlers would be an even more cantankerous-looking lot than they are; it's just possible to imagine Derek Underwood being every bit as crafty bowling under-arm as over-arm, but difficult to picture, say, John Snow ambling gently up to the crease and sending down a soft one leaving his hand around calf-level.

Another Sussex name for the records, though not a character to be emulated today, is one Thos. Pierpoint who—before the County Club came into existence—played for representative Sussex sides in the mid-1820s. Though the names are somewhat similar, he was no very swift executioner; playing against a Men of Kent XI in 1827 he took seven-and-a-half hours to score 31. Wisden himself played his first match for Sussex in 1841. At a lively supper party one night in 1845 at the Blenheim Hotel in Brighton, the I Zingari came into being. The one and only Maurice Tate is down in the annals as having taken 27 wickets for 145 runs at an average of 5.07 in a match against Glamorgan; how this was achieved, without putting Glamorgan in and presumably out three times, is not made clear.

The lowest score ever made by Sussex in its entire history totted up to 19 in the year 1873. The highest score ever made against this justly celebrated county was 726 in the year 1895. It need hardly be added that both matches were against Nottinghamshire. Nottinghamshire, in fact, are the *bête-noire* of the martlet; and as reliable ornithologists inform me that the martlet is a bird which never shows its feet (if it does, it's a swallow) the sooner we start showing them, preferably wearing bovver boots, and trample down this unseemly

Nottinghamshire domination the better.

And, bringing this patchy historical survey rather more up-to-date, in 1934 Alan Melville was elected captain of Sussex. Fortunately for the county, it was the other one. Sussex has had quite enough captain trouble (no names, no pack drill, and happily no trouble at all last season under Barclay: quite the reverse) to be lumbered with a Melville Mark II.

I've said that the county, both its players and spectators, *enjoyed* their cricket over all these many years. The word was used purposely. It must seem strange—sacrilegious, even—to the dourer Northern counties that there are times (many, many times) when Sussex seems to take the field in an extraordinarily carefree mood, suggesting that whatever happens, win or lose, they are actually hoping to enjoy themselves and have (it's an odd word to use in connection with the present three- or four-day game) *fun*. The essence, the character of Sussex cricket is hard to explain to anyone living north of, say, Leamington Spa; but then cricket—any cricket—is hard to explain to the unconverted or the heathen.

Towards the close of last season, when it seemed that only a grave miscarriage of justice (or Nottinghamshire, which amounts to the same thing) would stop us from at last becoming County Champions, I happened to have staying with me in Brighton an old friend from Provence. Well, you know what the French are like about ball games: perfectly happy to spend two-thirds of their lives playing *boule* on the most uneven surfaces they can find, gesticulating non-stop, and making up the rules as they go along. As luck would have it, on the very first night of his stay *chez moi*, one of the headlines on the back page of the *Evening Argus* was HORSE ROUTS KENT. It took some time to make it clear to my guest that the central figure in the story was not some maddened equine running berserk through the hopfields but a delightful, quite docile biped called Geoffrey Arnold.

I then switched on the TV to hear the cricket scores and learned that that excellent and (in my view) rather underestimated batsman Hampshire—who at that time was still playing for Yorkshire—had hit a brilliant innings against, as it happened, Hampshire. Try explaining that to a fanatical boule-merchant from Aix-en-Provence when your French irregular verbs are none too hot and you have trouble with the genders.

I thought the best plan was to take the visitor round to the County Ground and let him get the hang of the whole thing quietly and calmly. By the time I had translated third man into *troisième homme*, first slip into *premier faux-pas* and silly short leg into *jambe brève idiotique*, it was pretty obvious that my guest was wishing he was back playing a sane, conventional game of *boule* on some bumpy gravel under the poplars, muttering *"merde!"* at regular intervals, and sending for another Pernod. We were sitting in and among the Members, two of whom on our leg-side

41

began rumbling about the current rumpus in the Committee, a section of which was stirring up a sort of let's-get-rid-of-Maggie campaign against the Club's President. (We conduct our rumpi in a more seemly way in Sussex than they do in, say, Yorkshire, scheming quietly in corners rather than giving the media a benefit match as in the Boycott/Illingworth affair.) "When a feller's given out, dammit," said the sprightlier of the two octogenarians within earshot, "he ought to bloody well *walk*."

I had just translated this into colloquial Provençal when the two comparative youngsters sitting on our off-side brought up yet again the still burning question of that iniquitous .17 of a run. "All Ted Heath's fault," said the pinker of the pair. "If he hadn't fiddled us into the Common Market and got us all mixed up with those damn Frenchies, only a few piddling maths teachers would have even known there was such a thing as the metric system." Confused thinking, admittedly, but Monsieur had caught the words "damn Frenchies" and insisted on being given the gist of the Member's remarks. "I zink," he said, having been given it, "you are all 'ere at 'Ove per'aps a leetle crazy, yes?"

It would be going too far to suggest that a slight mental instability is a *sine qua non* for a true appreciation of Sussex cricket, but there are times when one feels that it helps. At any rate, it is a definite draw-back to watch Sussex expecting the expected, anticipating the norm, and not be prepared for surprises. Whatever else may be said about Sussex cricket, it is seldom dull—certainly not when we're batting (memo to J.R.T. ("Trout") Barclay, Esq.,: bowling rate last season slowest in the country: action, please). Perhaps the weather and the Hove wicket have something to do with this pleasurable feeling that anything might happen, and very often does.

Contrary to what has been suggested from time to time by some of our visitors, there is nothing wrong with the wicket at Hove; but the weather along the South Coast can be—as Trev the Wev, our regional TV met expert finds to his cost almost daily—fickle. At the very moment when things seem to have settled into a conventional routine and the outcome of a match almost boringly pre-determined and just a matter of time, in comes our notorious sea-fret and the whole situation changes dramatically.

The fret—it's a pleasant understatement in a single four-letter word which is the cause of so many other four-letter words—is cunningly composed so as not to be dense enough to stop play altogether, but just dense enough to make peculiar things happen to the flight of the ball. Or, more probably, make the batsman imagine that peculiar things are happening to the flight of the ball. Successive Australian sides, caught in mid-mist just when they were doing rather nicely, thank you, have used the most unprintable Antipodean oaths about our fret, even hinting that in some underhand manner it is pre-packaged some distance out at sea by Machiavellian arch-schemers like Parks or Marlar or even the present Bishop of Liverpool, and blown inshore at exactly the right moment by heavily bribed members of the ground staff. All nonsense, of course; but the fact remains that many an O.A.P. has dozed off in his deck-chair at Hove in brilliant sunshine and awakened cold, moist, surrounded only by scores of abandoned deck-chairs and in urgent need of a hot toddy and a brisk rub down.

But more than the weather as a cause of Sussex unpredictability are the players themselves. We seem to be a county which attracts characters, and every now and then some pretty extrovert characters at that. There is generally room in the side for at least one slightly larger-than-life swash-buckler; whether individualism or the swashing of buckles makes for a good team spirit and a contented, placid atmosphere in the dressing room may be open to question, but for the paying public it certainly adds up to entertaining cricket.

Lillywhite, the first big name in Sussex cricket, seems to have buckled no mean swash; Ranjitsinhji, Duleepsinhji, C.B. Fry, Maurice Tate, C. Aubrey Smith, Arthur Gilligan and in more recent times Dexter, Greig, Jim Parks, John Snow . . . none of them could be considered reticent or self-effacing characters, on-field or off. When they appeared, the onlookers sat up prepared for action instead of—as is so often the case today, except in limited-over cricket—leaning back with eyes half-closed thinking of the good old days when Arthur Gilligan went in at No. 11 and scored 101 against Cambridge University. (It was only yesterday, dammit: 1919 . . . things have gone to pot since those days.)

Many of the names mentioned were captains of Sussex: can any other county (Nottinghamshire? . . . don't be ridiculous) produce an equally star-studded list? In this century alone (omitting the war years and captains who were probably very good at the job *because* they were not quite such individualists as the others):

1900	K.S. Ranjitsinhji
1904–7	C.B. Fry
1922–30	The Gilligans
1931	K.S. Duleepsinhji
1934	Alan Melville (the clean one)
1950	James Langridge (the county's first professional captain; brother of John, the finest opening bat *never* to play for England)
1953	David Sheppard, the Rev.
1955	Robin Marlar
1960–65	Ted Dexter

1966	The Nawab of Pataudi
1967–8	Jim Parks
1973–7	Tony Greig

Characters, all of them, each in his own way: personalities, individualists, scene-stealers, stars. Fry, as well as topping the batting averages for six seasons, managed somehow to break the world record for the long jump, play in an F.A. Cup Final, and be an exceptionally brilliant classical scholar. That splendidly aquiline character actor, C. Aubrey Smith (known as "round the corner Smith" because of a somewhat devious bowling action) was still showing Hollywood how to play cricket the Sussex way at the age of eighty-three. Ranji, who captained the county from 1899 to 1903, scored two centuries against Yorkshire on the same sunny day in August, 1896; Duleep, his nephew, notched up the county's highest individual score (333 v. Northants in 1930) and in all scored over 2,500 runs in each of his three seasons before ill-health ended his career at the absurd age of twenty-seven. The Langridge brothers both scored over thirty thousand runs in first-class cricket; Tate took 2,783 wickets. And in the sixties and seventies, when swash-buckling seemed to be out of fashion and there were precious few Errol Flynn characters in first-class cricket, along came first Dexter, then Greig.

In his autobiography, Dexter is honest enough to quote from one of his school reports:

> He shows promise at cricket but he must
> remember he has still much—in fact almost
> everything—to learn and is not yet in a
> position to control and give instructions
> to his fellows, who quite rightly resent it.

No comment, except to say that the headmaster was obviously far-seeing. And Greig? I remember being introduced to him on his first evening at Hove and thinking . . . what a pleasant, well-mannered modest young man: let's hope he'll be able to stand up for himself among all these hardened old sinners. How wrong can you be? Both were brilliant cricketers; both did great things for Sussex; both were at times disturbing influences.

There has always been a sort of family feeling about Sussex cricket; the fans support the county as families rather than as individuals; among the players, clans stay loyal—the Langridges, the Parks, the Busses (mini- and maxi-) are obvious examples—unthinkable, almost, that their names should be linked with any other county. Family spirit is a great thing only when each member of the family—paterfamilias, especially—keeps thinking of the rest of the clan. There were times when one had the feeling, however brilliantly Dexter or Greig was playing, that their minds—at least in the brief waits between elegantly executed strokes or, for that matter, massive clouts into or over the pavilion—were on other things. Milord's perhaps on racing, golf, a career with the media: Tony's maybe on money. But both of them added to no mean degree to the zest of Sussex cricket, and for that we should be grateful. I think we are. I hope so.

Which brings us, by a meandering and wayward route, to last season and the seasons to come. Despite the last-minute pipping at the post by Nottinghamshire (a county I had resolved not to mention in this chapter, but which seems to have kept creeping in in its usual presumptuous fashion), 1981 was one of Sussex's most successful seasons for years; certainly one of its happiest. We—both players and spectators—*enjoyed* our cricket, and the results underlined that enjoyment. The committee may have rumbled and grumbled and mumbled, but then that is expected of committees; the people who matter are the eleven characters who take the field, and the frame of mind in which they take it is all-important. In another combative area, I've been involved in more than one production which appeared smooth and polished while turmoil and near-civil war raged backstage.

For last season's peace of mind, all credit to Barclay; he came in as captain virtually unknown to the general public, and in a single season—perhaps through *not* being a larger-than-life, swash-buckling individualist—welded the side together in a way which I don't think has happened since the days of David Sheppard. With, of course, the added bonus for the players of freedom from self-restraint due to respect for the cloth; nothing more inhibiting than having to remember to say "bother" when a vital catch is dropped. One can't do much better than quote Richard Streeton, one of *The Times'* more perceptive cricket correspondents, in his summing-up of the last match we played last season (the one which led to the streaking):

> Barclay has obviously had a splendid first
> season as captain, in spite of the final
> disappointment. He has got the best out of two
> dangerous and temperamental opening bowlers in
> Imran and le Roux and helped Ian Greig's
> all-round improvement to telling effect. There
> has also been an unselfish and generous team
> spirit in the Sussex dressing room, which has
> not always been the case in recent years.

To which one can only add a fervent *Amen*. The prospects look good;

45

the main props of last season are still with us; there is a satisfactory supply of promising youngsters waiting in the wings and at the nets; the West Pier may be crumbling and the multitudinous dog-lovers of Hove worried about the local councillor who maintains that all dogs *and* dog-owners should be chopped up and canned; but there is the sweet smell of success around the County Ground. As poetry, it may not be in the John Snow class, but if we may again maltreat Mr Kipling (the versifier, not the sponge merchant) . . .

> God gives to counties ups and downs—
> Some conquering, some defeatist.
> The parting shots may go to Notts
> But Sussex downs are sweetest.
> The treasure trove eluding Hove
> For all these years will be
> Out rightful due in '82
> In Sussex-by-the-Sea.

Essex

Trevor Bailey: Cambridge University, Essex and England. Captain of Essex 1961-6; Secretary 1955-65.

The Essex Way
Trevor Bailey

With four titles available and only seventeen first-class counties, it is obviously far easier to capture a title these days than when there was only the County Championship at stake. Nevertheless, it took Essex over a hundred years to achieve their first honour. They did this in considerable style by "doing the double" of the Schweppes Championship and the Benson and Hedges Cup in 1979. However, in terms of results over the years, outstanding world-class players, facilities, size of support and financial resources, Essex cannot be numbered among the great county clubs.

It has been said, with some justification, that Essex have always been among the records. The highest opening partnership in this country (Sutcliffe and Holmes) of 555—quintuple Nelson strikes—was made against them at Leyton. Percy Perrin amassed the county's largest individual score of 343 n.o., containing an almost indecent number of boundaries, but Derbyshire won the match. When the Australians, under the Don, were steamrollering their way through England in 1948, Essex bowled them out in a day at Southchurch Park—but then again there was the slight snag of the 721 runs the visitors scored in the process.

Although Essex are not the greatest county, I have no hesitation in claiming that they were and, praise the Lord, still are a great county to play for. I cannot think of any club where the players have gained more enjoyment from their cricket. Although they have played the game seriously and keenly, there has always been an abundance of laughter and humour. This is something to be proud of, because cricket which is not enjoyed is not worth playing; a fact which has been appreciated by the club's supporters, who are certainly among the most tolerant.

This is also one of the reasons why the club has turned out so many players who besides being good cricketers have been characters in their own right. There were the Smith cousins, Peter, the best Essex leg-spinner in an impressive list of this now almost extinct species, and Ray, one of the most hard working of all-rounders. Ray was most unlucky not to have gained recognition for England. He would regularly open the bowling and then, after some eight overs, put on his cap to bowl off breaks until the second new ball became available, when he would revert to his long run. He was also a spectacular attacking batsman and excellent cover, who would have revelled in the limited overs game.

It was by no means unusual for opening batsman Dickie Dodds to hit a six in the first over of a match and he made a perfect foil for his partner, first Sonny Avery, and later Gordon Barker. If one said "bad luck" to Sonny after he had lost his wicket, the odds were that his reply would be "lazy old shot"; while Gordon not only remembered every stroke he played in every innings, but if anyone had an hour to spare he would be only too happy to elaborate in elegant detail.

The debonair Barry Knight was a frequent match-winning all-rounder for both Essex and England; and Ray East, in addition to being one of the funniest men in cricket, is a very good left-arm spinner, possibly the finest Essex have ever had. Keith Boyce, whom I signed in Barbados before he was in the island side, brought with him all the excitement of the Caribbean. He was essentially an entertainer whether bowling, batting or fielding. Today, Graham Gooch, an excellent imitator of other people's bowling actions, is one of the most devastating opening batsmen in the game.

The list is enormous . . . the fielding of Michael Bear; wicket-keeper Paul Gibb's remarkable appetite; Roy Ralph, the keenest of all "nightwatchmen" . . . but space alas does not permit.

One result of the way Essex approach the game can be seen in their happy relationship with the other counties. They have avoided those petty wrangles, sometimes lasting for years. In my early days I was surprised when the skipper of one opposing side said, "We never have a good game with Glamorgan"—and he was not alone at the time—as we invariably had good contests with the Welshmen. And this applied equally to the rest of the clubs.

A major reason why Essex cricket was so much fun was having eight different centres. It was rather like being on tour. By moving from ground to ground we were constantly meeting new faces, not to mention different pitches. Life in those circumstances was never dull. There was also a genuine festival atmosphere, with deck-chairs, marquees and improvised facilities, which all helped to provide gaiety and charm.

There were occasional snags: Alec Bedser once asked me where the shower was at Brentwood, the most attractive of our many grounds, and I was delighted to show him a minute basin, cold water only, which just about accommodated one of his big hands.

Before the recent upsurge of sports sponsorship, without which there could be no first-class cricket on the present scale, Essex had always, despite careful management, lived a hand-to-mouth existence. Back at the turn of the century the county had to rely on the patronage of the President, who frequently made up the losses out of his own pocket. Later, when unable to pay the mortgage on the Leyton ground, the Committee again had to seek assistance. After Percy Perrin, the current skipper, who was wealthy but cautious, had refused to help, the father of J.W.H.T. Douglas agreed to take over the debt, providing his son was appointed captain. It was a somewhat unusual start to his eventually becoming, until Keith Fletcher, the only Essex player to lead England.

Despite the never ending battle to make ends meet, Essex have, since the thirties, had one great advantage over many counties: a committee which was controlled by men who had actually played first-class cricket, and understood the game. They have indeed been lucky to have avoided the fate of those clubs that have been cursed by powerful committeemen who not only knew nothing about county cricket but, far worse, thought that they did.

In my twenty years as Assistant Secretary, and Secretary, of the club, I can think of only three occasions when I was overruled. The first, and most vital, was in the early fifties when, having learned how the Worcestershire Football Pool operated, I recommended that we should start an Essex Supporters' Association and Pool. It was turned down because the Committee—Doug Insole was almost the only exception—felt that the game should not have to depend on gambling. Years later, and years too late, they changed their minds.

The importance of a sensible, stable committee, which not only has an appreciation of the needs of the game but also of the spirit in which it should be contested, is enormous. It has given the club a continuity which few can match, and has meant that since the war there have been only five regular captains. The first was Tom Pearce, who took over the captaincy in the thirties; so if one includes the war years, it means there have been only five in nearly fifty years. This is a remarkable record when one thinks that Derbyshire, for example, have managed to go through five in five years, and helps to explain how the club's basic approach to the game, which might be summed up as hard, fair and yet always fun—the Essex way—has been maintained.

The post-war captains of Essex have been Tom Pearce, Doug Insole, Trevor Bailey, Brian Taylor and Keith Fletcher. All have been fortunate in that they were granted far more freedom of action than most county skippers. The Committee, having chosen somebody in whom they have confidence, leave the cricket problems entirely in his hands. Although a selection committee is appointed annually, as a safeguard for the captain in times of difficulty, it never met in the twenty years I was with the club.

51

The final decision on who is included in the XI and the way the cricket is played was, and still is, left entirely to the skipper, which is exactly as it should be.

The five Essex captains have possessed four important attributes. First, they could more than justify their place as cricketers. This was especially important when the team was not too strong. Although it is feasible to "carry a captain", if the side is very powerful, it simply makes the job more difficult when it is not.

Second, all had gained considerable experience before taking over. Although this did not apply to Tom Pearce in the thirties, he was certainly the ideal person to mould together the pre- and post-war players on resumption after hostilities.

Third, they were all natural ball players proficient at another team game. Their association with soccer, rugby or hockey helped to provide them with a much broader outlook than if cricket had been their only sporting interest.

Finally, although the five had different outlooks, temperaments and backgrounds, all had a keen sense of humour and a deep feeling for the game.

Tom, or "Burly T" as he was known, was one of the most unflappable of captains. It was almost impossible to ruffle his composure whatever the situation, and he scarcely ever lost his temper. One of the rare occasions when Tom's perpetually beaming face reddened slightly occurred during an almost unbelievable spate of dropped catches. Every member of the side, with the exception of Tom, but including the twelfth man, had managed to put one down; then, inevitably, Tom himself became a victim of "droppers" disease, and the entire team collapsed with laughter.

Tom was not only very popular with his own side, but also with the opposition. Indeed it was hard to imagine anybody disliking him. He made sure that cricket never became too serious, believing that it was a game not a war.

On the third day of a game against Leicestershire, we seemed destined for an easy win, providing we could remove quickly their one real threat, Maurice Tomkin. When he mishooked my long hop, to give mid-off the easiest of chances, we looked to be home. Unfortunately the fielder managed to trip over his own feet and drop the ball, and I had some fairly pungent things to say. At the end of the over I remarked to Tom that he could have caught it in his teeth, to which Tom replied, "Yes, Trevor, the trouble was that he tried to use his hands." Again Tom's instructions to his batsmen when chasing a target were masterly: "Play your shots, but don't get out."

Tom was a determined, cheerful, front foot batsman who played straight, and whose philosophy might be summed up as "when in doubt, push out". If a spinner, like Leicestershire's Australian Jack Walsh, beat his forward push because of his failure to pick the googly, Tom would simply smile down the pitch and suggest that he should bowl at the wicket.

Doug Insole, who succeeded the benign Tom Pearce as captain, had a very different attitude and temperament. He brought to the job a burning enthusiasm, though it took him a few years to realise that leading a university eleven was not the same as leading a professional side of varying ages and outlook. There was nothing that Doug could do about the handicap of having an unbalanced attack, which was top heavy with seam and contained no match-winning finger spinner; this meant that his side was painfully vulnerable on any turning pitch. But he did drastically improve the fielding by daily practice, and so increased the effectiveness of his bowlers.

There have been few skippers who have taken to heart more the ups and downs of their team. Doug felt personally every collapse; he would ceaselessly pace up and down the dressing room throughout a recovery, and was fearful to move from a certain spot when things were going smoothly. His fingernails were non-existent long before the end of the first home week, and he carried his superstitions to intriguing extremes. When his shirt was very dirty it was a sure indication that he was in the middle of a good patch with the bat, and it would not be changed until this eventually came to an end. Lucky trousers, lucky shirts, lucky gloves and even, distinctly unhygienic, lucky socks—Doug had them all at one time or another.

One of the many duties of an Essex captain was to pay out expenses and "win money" at the end of each match. On one occasion against Glamorgan at Westcliff, Doug, in order to save time, did this while we were knocking off the sixty-odd runs required. Suddenly wickets started to tumble and he realised that he had angered fate by assuming victory; so he immediately started to collect back all the money he had distributed. By the time this had been done, we had just scraped home by one wicket, and he had to start again.

In the talking stakes Doug had no serious rival. He seldom stopped chatting, both on and off the field, which is one of the many reasons I enjoyed batting with him so much. It did on one occasion provoke the Sussex captain, Robin Marlar, to make one of his less sensible statements when he said, "From now on this game will be played in silence." Doug's reply was fast and blunt. Knowing his quick wit and succinct repartee, few were prepared to engage him in a verbal duel.

Doug believed, quite rightly, in the unimportance of cricket records which did not occur naturally in the context of a game. He showed this as skipper of Cambridge University against Essex in 1949. At the close of the first day the University were 441 for one, as a result of an unbroken stand of 429 by John Dewes and Hubert Doggart. If he had allowed them to continue batting on the second day they might well have broken the world record second-wicket partnership, but he declared, much to the annoyance of the large crowd and the cameramen who turned up on the Monday to see if the pair would succeed.

As a captain he was shrewd and imaginative, always prepared to set or chase a reasonable target, while opponents knew that he would never go back on a deal. This could produce problems, as happened in one match against Glamorgan at Colchester. The game which had been ruined by rain was drifting to a seemingly inevitable draw, and Doug declared our second innings closed in order that Wilf Wooller and his team could pack up their gear in comfort and be ready for an early departure on their long journey back to Wales. All would have been well but for a sudden, short, sharp shower which livened up the pitch to such an extent that, though we had not bothered to take the new ball and they had opened with two tailenders, wickets started to fall rapidly. The outcome was that we walked off the field as had been agreed without claiming the extra half hour, to the boos of the Essex members.

In addition to his own enthusiasm and drive, some of which had to rub off on his team, Doug was also the leading run-getter. At his very best when the going was hard and the wicket poor, he led by personal example. I liked batting with him enormously, once we had reached an agreement of what constituted a run. This was important, as I discovered in a Cambridge v. the Australians fixture, when we found ourselves both running hard for the same end, and I had to continue to the pavilion!

Doug was not an attractive batsman from the technical angle because he would tend to drive the half volley outside the off stump wide of mid-on, rather than through the covers. As a result, he failed to gain the recognition at international level which he deserved. In fact his treatment by the England selectors was quite incomprehensible: four Tests at home, all in different series; while on his one overseas tour he played in all five Tests and, though we had a powerful batting line-up, he headed the averages. He was certainly underrated by all but his own side, and those who had to bowl at him, and it is significant that he scored a century against every county. He was especially good against off-spin and in-swing bowling.

As well as batting skill, Doug had a very safe pair of hands, which seldom put anything down, whether in the deep or the slips. His one weakness was his firm conviction that he was never wrong—which in a captain could even be considered an asset.

I took over from Doug in 1961 with mixed feelings, because it meant that the county had lost their best run-scorer and I had lost my permanent room-mate. On the other hand, I enjoyed captaincy, and it gave me a fresh challenge at a time when I knew I had been written off as a Test cricketer (Doug was now a selector and he *never* changed his mind!).

My first problem was to find a name for the players to call me. They had known Doug as "Skipper" for so long, and anyway it was hoped that he would still be available for a few games. The team eventually settled on "Chief", in memory of the countless Westerns I had seen with Doug during away games. In those days the first and most important job of the junior professional was to look up all the cinema programmes in the area where we were playing.

From the playing angle, all went well for the first few seasons. Although we were not strong enough to win the Championship, we remained in the top half of the table and achieved several notable victories, including one over the Australians and one when we came from behind against Warwickshire, to turn a first innings deficit of some 300 runs into a remarkable win. But first-class cricket was in a sadly depressed state. There was no commercial sponsorship, apart from the Gillette Cup which was still in its infancy, and the players had to be accommodated privately to reduce costs. As a result, it became necessary to cut our staff so drastically that we lacked the necessary reserve cover and our performance suffered.

In retrospect, I believe I made two mistakes. First, I should have retired a couple of seasons earlier because my bowling had started to lose its bite. The "nip-backer" was no longer gaining an lbw, merely finding the inside edge. Second, I went on playing while "carrying" one leg, the result of a severely torn muscle, while a bad back reduced the effectiveness of my bowling still further. Against that, I did persuade the Warwickshire C.C.C. to make us an interest-free loan, which enabled the club to buy the County Ground at Chelmsford, and I bequeathed to Brian Taylor a young side of real potential which was bound to improve.

Although Brian made his first appearance for the county as a teenage wicket-keeper, he was kept out of the first eleven for a long time by Paul Gibb and forced himself into the team as an unorthodox batsman before eventually taking over behind the stumps.

Brian's ability to hit the ball very hard, combined with his unconventional methods, earned him the name of "Tonker". The "Tonker" was at his most valuable when Essex wanted runs quickly, especially against quality seam bowling. He had the rare talent of being able to pick up straight, good length balls from bowlers as tight as Les Jackson and Derek Shackleton, and hoicking them over the mid-wicket boundary with a stroke not to be found in any coaching manual. Unused to such treatment, the recipient often made the mistake of digging in one short, and this would be instinctively hooked to square or fine leg. His range of attacking shots included a fierce cut and a drive which did not always go where it was intended; he used the lap to good effect against the spinners, although he was normally happier, and more effective, against pace. It was said that he would make many more runs if he hit straight through the line rather than across it, but he was never able to do that.

Although Brian as a wicket-keeper lacked the agility of a Godfrey Evans or the style of a Bob Taylor, he did a fine job for Essex behind the stumps. And he was extremely reliable, as is shown by his record of 301 consecutive appearances for the county. In many respects he epitomised the old-style professional cricketer. He took pride in his appearance. His cricket gear was never less than immaculate. He was always neatly dressed, could be relied upon to be early for any match or function, and never gave less than his best.

I always felt Brian would have made a splendid sergeant-major as, in addition to his other virtues, he had one of those stentorian voices which made telephones unnecessary. He was at his best in a practical crisis, like a car breaking down late at night on a deserted road. There was, in fact, not a little of the sergeant-major in the way he skippered Essex. He, rightly, tightened up on the discipline and was at his most successful in limited overs matches. My regret is that his considerable efforts in the John Player League were not rewarded with the Championship, which they certainly deserved.

As one would expect, Brian's sense of humour, like his captaincy, was straightforward rather than subtle. I shall always cherish the remark he made one evening when the Essex side attended a distinctly sub-standard music hall in Leeds. The comedian, rather foolishly, decided to finish his act by singing "I may never pass this way again", which was greeted by that unmistakable foghorn of a voice saying, "Can we have that in writing, mate?"

Brian's first appearance on the golf course—assault might have been a rather more accurate description—also produced considerable laughter. Early on, a Taylor drive predictably ended in a stream. Gordon Barker told him to pick it up and drop it over his shoulder. What none of us had foreseen was that he might drop it back into the water, which left all but Brian in a state of near hysteria for the rest of the round.

Keith Fletcher was only a schoolboy when I first invited him to play in a Club and Ground game. It was immediately obvious that he possessed exceptional talent. Given good health and the right temperament, I was convinced, as I had been many years before when I first saw Barry Knight, that he would eventually play not only for Essex, but also for England.

In addition to batting ability, Keith had a keen cricket brain, illustrated by the following anecdote which the late Don Smith loved to relate. Don ran the Young Amateurs of Essex and was not too pleased when I insisted that he include Keith, who at the time was a diminutive fourteen-year-old from a village school, in his carefully chosen side containing the best youngsters in the county. Keith retained his place by the simple expedient of scoring runs, and was chosen for the big match against Middlesex. On this occasion, he found himself running out of partners and went up to Don, who was umpiring, and asked shyly, "Would it be alright if I gave it a bit of a tap now, sir?"—showing at an early age the instinctive appreciation of a situation which all captains need.

When Keith joined the Essex staff he was a small, quiet, rather diffident lad with a delightful country burr. He gained his nickname, "The Gnome", when he arrived wearing winkle-picker shoes with pointed turned-up toes. But he learned fast and showed his pedigree by establishing himself in the first eleven while still in his teens: an exciting stroke-maker with the ability to drive medium-pace bowling over extra cover off the back foot. He was, in fact, very far removed from the correct, sound accumulator of runs he was to become in later years. All captains require a mental and physical toughness and this attribute could be seen in the way Keith, before he was twenty, handled fast bowlers Wes Hall and Charlie Griffith when batting for Essex against the West Indies; it was evident, too, in his development as a specialist fieldsman in that unpleasant bat-and-pad position, where fast reflexes and courage are essential.

When Gordon Barker retired Keith Fletcher became Brian Taylor's first lieutenant, always at hand to give sound advice drawn from the knowledge he had patiently acquired over the years for both Essex and England.

Ever a thinker about the game, this, combined with his outstanding record as a batsman for both county and country (many are surprised to learn that his batting average in the fifty-odd Tests he played in before being recalled to the international scene in 1981 was over 40), made Keith the obvious person to succeed the "Tonker". Again the Essex committee had chosen wisely, as he quietly, methodically and very efficiently steered his team to the "Double" in 1979 and to the John Player title in 1981.

It would be true to say that Keith, both as a batsman and as a captain, has never received sufficient recognition; he lacks the glamour of the more extrovert players who constantly make the headlines. There is no swagger when he goes out to bat, and at times he appears almost apologetic; while his captaincy is completely without histrionics. He lets his players know exactly what he wants and expects from them without informing the crowd, television and the rest of the media at the same time.

Not surprisingly, Keith's humour is essentially gentle and restrained.

In his early days with the county, he came under our coach Frank Rist—they don't come much nicer—who used to tell the youngsters not to hang around at the wicket if they knew they were out. If they had hit the ball, they were to walk. In one unimportant Club and Ground game, Keith forgot his intructions and afterwards Frank asked him what he had been waiting for. Keith thought for a moment, his eyes twinkled and he said, "Well, Frank, the wind was blowing so hard down the pitch that I thought he might not have heard it."

Appointing Keith Fletcher captain of England for the 1981 Indian tour was both a sensible and an obvious choice. He is an astute and experienced skipper with a proven record. This was his third tour to India, so that he knew the conditions and what to expect as well, if not better, than anybody else in England. And, unlike many England captains, he was worth his place as a player: he is one of the most accomplished batsmen against spin, and there was likely to be plenty of that. Most of all perhaps, he is both liked and respected by his fellow professionals for his ability, honesty and for the way he has always played his cricket.

The Essex way.

Nottinghamshire

Michael Jayston: Leading stage and screen actor whose long list of credits includes *Equus* and *The Sound of Music* (stage), *Nicholas and Alexandra* (film) and *Tinker, Tailor, Soldier, Spy* (tv).

Trent Bridge Heroes
Michael Jayston

My grandfather was the inspiration for my love of cricket, and especially cricket played by the men of Nottingham when I was about seven years of age. Usually my grandfather seemed to be in another world and given to violent and unpredictable changes of mood (this I discovered later was due to an overfondness for drink); but he became another person when he talked of cricket. His eyes shone and his voice took on a passionate intensity. He would repeat stories over and over again until I knew them by heart. The names he mentioned—Shrewsbury, Gunn, Larwood, Voce, Hardstaff—sounded to me like a litany of saints; indeed at school I often confused them with biblical characters, much to the annoyance of the teachers. He made his stories far more interesting than school, and Brer Rabbit and Humpty Dumpty were very tame meat in comparison. My grandfather was of course speaking of heroes. Although other cricketers were mentioned, like Hobbs and Grace, he was totally biased towards Nottinghamshire players as being the best there were, and Trent Bridge as being the finest ground in the world. Considering his proclivity to drink, I was astonished to find in later years that his stories were hardly ever exaggerated.

He told me of a young man called Copley, coming from the obscurity of Notts second team, substituting for Larwood in a Test match at Trent Bridge, making a brilliant catch to dismiss McCabe, thus playing a major role in England's subsequent victory. He then returned to obscurity.

Grandfather showed me a scorecard of the match, Sussex v. Notts at Hove, 1911, where a hitter of uncertain form by the name of Ted Alletson scored 189 runs in ninety minutes. Before lunch he had scored 47 in fifty minutes; between 2.15 and 2.55 he added a further 142, and his last 89 runs were achieved in the space of a quarter of an hour! Fifty-six runs came from two overs by Killick and two from Leach produced 34. This is probably the most extraordinary exhibition of hitting in the whole history of the game.

Harold Larwood always figured in the stories. I heard of the time he smashed the pavilion clock with a prodigious hit. "The ball was still rising," my grandfather said. Larwood's claim to fame, of course, was not as a batsman, although in that department he acquitted himself well. It was as the fastest and most feared fast bowler of his time that his name appears in the roll of honour. Hammond once cut him for six over point, smashing a car window in the process. Larwood's name is still mentioned at Trent Bridge when a fast bowler arrives on the scene. "Yes, he's fast but you should have seen Larwood," the greybeards mutter. If lightning struck the pitch during a match I'm sure they would say, "Yes, pretty quick, but . . ."

Arthur Shrewsbury, Notts opener at the turn of the century, fascinated my grandfather, not on account of his prowess as a great opening batsman but because Arthur had never been seen in public without a hat on. On the pitch he wore a cap, off it a top hat. His wife claimed she was the only person to have seen his head uncovered. The reason for his head being thus hidden was the fact that Arthur was as bald as a billiard ball—or so his wife said.

Of all the players of whom my grandfather spoke, the name George Gunn occurred most frequently and was mentioned with awe and reverence. He had first played for Notts in 1903 and was the strangest figure that the game has given us. He possessed a genius for batting but his attitude and a quirk of temperament prevented him from achieving his full potential. He seemed to delight in annoying bowlers and fieldsmen. His contemporaries said he could score a century in an hour or in four hours under the same conditions, depending on his mood. Recuperating from TB in Australia in 1912, he replaced an injured batsman and scored a century on his Test debut.

There was one story about George Gunn of which I suspected my grandfather of embellishment, and it puzzled me until I was about ten years of age and first starting to attend matches at Trent Bridge. One day when rain showers had stopped play for a while I was sipping a Dandelion and Burdock in a sweet shop opposite the ground, when I saw an elderly gentleman slip on the wet kerb and fall into the road. I helped him to his feet and then across the road. He thanked me and gave me sixpence: "Here lad, buy yourself an ice cream." As he handed me the coin I realised that here in the flesh was one of the legends of whom my grandfather had enthused. I stuttered, "You're George Gunn." He laughed and then with a quizzical look said, "Now, young feller me lad, how the devil do you know that, you could never have seen me play." I recounted everything I knew of his career. He seemed modestly pleased that I knew so much about him, and after that first meeting, when I saw him from time to time, he always had a smile and a cheery wave of his stick for me.

That September, on the last day of the season, I had my cricket bag with me after a game at school. As I strolled round the ground I came to the nets, and who should be there but George Gunn. "Hello, it's the Good Samaritan," he said. "Have you got a cricket ball in your bag?" I said I had. "Come on, you can turn your arm over and we'll see how good you are . . . And you can see if I'm any good," he added. For a good half an hour I bowled to the great man. He didn't use a bat, he used his walking stick. He missed one ball during that time, whereupon he picked up a stump. "This is a bit better," he said. "My eyes aren't what they used to be." He was then over seventy years of age. He could have gone on for much longer but I was tiring, and I jokingly said, "Don't you think you ought to declare, Mr Gunn?" He looked at me oddly. "That takes me back a few years—what you just said." He then told me a story which I had only half believed when recounted by my grandfather, but which I have subsequently verified.

In 1919, a local amateur cricketer of meagre ability had the audacity to challenge George to a single-wicket competition for a £100 side wager; a considerable amount in those days. George, not being avaricious and knowing that the game would be completely one-sided, refused the invitation. The amateur persisted and badgered George for weeks. Eventually, George, out of sheer exasperation, agreed, reducing the wager to a fiver, but determined to teach the fellow a lesson. The match was played on the Trent Bridge practice ground from five until seven-thirty in the evening. George won the toss and decided to bat. At the end of the first evening he had scored exactly 300 runs. By the end of the second session he was 620 not out. At this point his opponent suggested that George might like to declare. George declined, saying he never declared in a single-wicket match, but adding that the amateur, if he so wished, could replace the stumps with a heavy roller which was six feet wide! The amateur shamefacedly agreed to this generous offer. It made not the slightest difference. George continued on his merry way and halfway through the third evening he had increased his score to 777.

He had run nine off one ball when the amateur finally cracked. Perhaps the realisation that he could be bowling to George until Doomsday eventually decided the issue in his mind. He threw the ball down, jumped on it, conceded the match and stomped off to the Trent Bridge Inn, from where he was seen emerging, many hours later, in a deplorable and maudlin condition. He never paid the wager. George did, however, top the national averages for that year and he maintained that the practice over those three days had had a lot to do with it. "I hope I didn't ruin his enjoyment of the game," he was heard to say, with a wicked twinkle in his eye. O, rare and wonderful George Gunn.

It was said many times that if Notts ever needed a fast bowler all they had to do was shout down the nearest pit shaft and, lo and behold, up would come an aspiring Larwood or Voce.

One of my favourite memories of my early years as spectator was watching a match between Sussex and Notts. Notts were badly depleted by injury and illness. The Notts coach Bill Voce, who had not played for some time, was pressed into service. He answered the call magnificently. His days of glory as Larwood's fearsome partner were long since behind him, and little could have been expected. In the event, he rolled back the years, bowled thirty-three overs and took five Sussex wickets, including those of John Langridge and David Sheppard, the two openers. This alone would have satisfied most 42-year-olds, short of match practice, but there was more to come. Notts started their innings badly, losing five wickets for a few runs. Voce came in, attacked from the start, and scored 45 hard-hit runs, including two colossal sixes over the ladies' pavilion. The ball which caused his dismissal snicked off the edge of his bat on to his nose, and was then caught by the wicket-keeper. He walked from the wicket, blood pouring down his face, like a triumphant gladiator. He was fifty yards from the pavilion when the spectators all round the ground rose as one man to applaud the warrior.

Years later, I met him when he came to work at the Bestwood Colliery Offices, and spent many happy times chatting about cricket when I should have been at my desk aspiring to be a cost accountant. Once I played against him in the Notts Amateur League. By now Bill's bowling had reverted to his original slow left-arm spin. I hit his first ball for four. The next ball was certainly not slow. It whipped through, short of a length and hit me painfully in the lower ribs. A vision came before me of Bill bowling to Ponsford and Bradman. My nerve was gone. Next ball, I was bowled neck and crop.

It was said that women put their knitting to one side, small boys rushed to the pavilion gate, and strong men emerged from the bar, when Joe Hardstaff junior went in to bat. Nature had cast him in an heroic mould. He had the looks of a film star, fair-haired, a slim yet muscular build. These attributes and the balance of a natural athlete combined to give an impression of quiet strength: a man to be reckoned with, one from whom great deeds are expected. It was against Somerset in 1947 that I first saw him in his splendour, on a deathless afternoon in the height of summer. He scored 200 not out with an ease and elegance that took my breath away. On the three further occasions I saw him that summer, he scored 127 not out, 221 not out and 45 not out. In fact, including the first two matches of the 1948 season, I saw him score 878 runs before he lost his wicket!

As a boy, I couldn't understand why Joe had not played for England more often. Many years later, I found out from a few of his contemporaries that he was never overly polite to the selectors. On the boat trip back from the 1947–8 tour of the West Indies, Joe allegedly called one of the playing selectors a "daft old clodpole"—or words to that effect! The apoplectic official is said to have claimed that he would ensure that Hardstaff never played for England again. Joe laughed and told him not to bet on it. The selector said no bet was involved—he would give Joe £100 if he ever made the England team again.

The following season arrived and with it the 1948 all-conquering Australians. In the Notts match before the first Test, Joe scored 48 in the first innings and in the second became the first batsman in the country to take a century off their mighty attack, which included Lindwall and Miller. The selectors had to pick him for the Test.

The selector, to give him his due, was true to his word and a cheque for £100 was despatched, presumably with much swallowed pride. Joe tore the cheque up and sent it back—quite a gesture when professionals in those days were paid about £20 a week.

That Test against the Aussies was the last time Joe played for England. He scored a duck in the first innings, brilliantly caught by Keith Miller (for years afterwards I bore murderous instincts against him). Joe made 43 in the second innings in a century stand with Compton, and those were his last runs at international level. In 1949 he finished top of the national averages, above Hutton, May, Washbrook, Compton, and took a century off the New Zealand touring side, but this was not enough in the eyes of the selectors.

As I grew older, my boyhood idolatry hardened to a deep, knowledgeable appreciation of Hardstaff's art. He had every stroke in the book. It was the way he played those strokes that burns in the memory. His straight- and off-driving were classic, hands holding the bat at the very top of the handle, high backlift sweeping into the ball with immaculate precision and power. His glancing to leg and late cut were off the full face of the bat, not the jabbed snicks one sees now in one-day cricket. If one had to choose his best stroke from this catholic variety, it was his cover drive, majestic in its execution, left foot well out to the pitch of the ball so that his right pad often touched the ground.

Joe's partner in many a classic partnership or exciting finish was Reg Simpson, like Joe a batsman with a superb technique and one of the best ever players of fast bowling. I wish aspiring young cricketers could have seen those two. When they were "on song", no field could be set to contain them. Their hitting, when quick runs were needed, was not the indiscriminate slogging one sees in limited over competitions. It was audacious certainly, but controlled and stylish.

In four matches in 1949 the Notts team reached a peak of brilliance.

Against Northants, Notts scored 245 in 145 minutes for victory, Hardstaff a century in each innings. Against a Surrey attack including Bedser and Laker, Notts needed only 97 minutes to score 209. Simpson paved the way with an undefeated double century in the first innings. A week later against Hampshire, they knocked up 226 in 113 minutes. And if that was not enough for the Trent Bridge fans, they excelled this in the match against Leicester, when set to score 279 in 145 minutes, they actually hit off the runs in 107 minutes—or 156 an hour! These figures baldly stated cannot capture the manner in which the runs were made: the gauntlet thrown down accepted almost with relish; the nail-biting tension. This happened, too, in an age which many cricket writers said was a "play safe" era.

One of the Notts players of that time did "play safe" and certainly had none of the brilliance of Hardstaff or Simpson, but what he lacked in stroke-play he made up for in eccentricity and wit. Charles Bowmar Harris was his full title. Charlie Harris scored runs at the rate of about 25 an hour and was the despair of opening bowlers. With Walter Keeton, he was involved in forty-six century partnerships for the first wicket. But it is as one of the last genuine eccentrics of the game that he holds a place in cricket folklore. Harris had a favourite pastime of putting on a false moustache, dressing as a policeman and interviewing newly-arrived young members of the ground staff, hinting darkly that they were implicated in some gory murder or jewel robbery. He had a habit of putting old bloaters in the cricket bags of his colleagues, and letters would arrive with invitations to tour Borneo purporting to come from the MCC. Charlie's life was cut short at an early age by cancer. Bill Edrich and Jim Sims went to visit him in hospital in his last days. Bill said he was still playing pranks and cracking jokes to the end.

Maybe cricket has become like the age itself. There doesn't seem time for humour or characters like Charlie Harris to emerge. The game is the poorer for it. Humour is one of the few qualities that separates mankind from the animals.

My grandfather had died a couple of years before Charlie Harris. To his last days he always took an interest in the fortunes of the Notts team. He accepted that Simpson was a worthy successor to some of his earlier idols and that Harold Butler, while not being as fast as Larwood etcetera, was pretty quick, especially on a humid morning, his swing helped by the mists from the Trent.

I wish that my grandfather could have seen one other player of my early years. I think he would have approved of Bruce Dooland, whilst ignoring the fact that he was an Australian. Dooland, for four years, returned some remarkable analyses in county cricket. Apart from his stock ball which was the leg break, he had in his armoury the googly, and his "killer" ball, the flipper, which fooled batsmen into thinking it was the googly but went straight on and usually hit the stumps or achieved an lbw. In 1954, he took fifty wickets by June 1! Against Essex his figures were eight for 39 in the first innings and eight for 44 in the second, including Trevor Bailey for a duck. Not many bowlers prised Trevor out so early. For once that season there were no massive scores by Hardstaff or Simpson, and Notts struggled.

Dooland won matches on his own, finishing top of the county bowling figures with 181 wickets at an average of 14.96. The other six bowlers in the team took 199 wickets between them. Every time he bowled you expected him to get a wicket. He carried the Notts team that season from the bottom of the Championship Table to fifth position.

Heroes need a proper environment in which to parade their talents. Trent Bridge was, and continues to be, the ideal atmosphere for sterling deeds. In my youth it had even more atmosphere, before the big scoreboard was built. George Parr's tree still existed in those days. Planted in 1830, it was called "Parr's Tree" after the great nineteenth-century batsman, who regularly hit balls to leg into the branches of the large oak. Sadly the tree was destroyed in a gale five years ago. George Parr gave some worthwhile advice to the young cricketers of his day: "When you play in a match, be sure not to forget to pay a little attention to the umpire. First of all enquire after his health, then say what a fine player his father was, and finally, present him with a brace of birds or rabbits. This will give you confidence and you will probably do well." With the amount of matches the modern day Notts cricketer has to play, he would be hard pressed to accommodate all the umpires, unless he could find time to do some poaching!

Looking back on those days at Trent Bridge, I realise now that most of the time defeat or victory was unimportant. Those results in 1949 were exciting because they were a perfect culmination to the matches themselves. I could have watched Hardstaff or Simpson bat all day with no thought of whether Notts would win or not. Dooland was a joy to see even when he wasn't taking wickets. It was the style, the essence of the men themselves expressed in the way they played that stayed in the memory. It is interesting to conjecture what George Gunn or Joe Hardstaff would have made of one-day knockabout cricket. Gunn would either have carried his bat for nought not out or scored a hundred in ten overs, depending on his mood. Joe was a natural fast scorer and his cover drive would have scorched past most deep-set fields, and he would have loved the absence of slips. Like most institutions, Trent Bridge will survive all but a nuclear blast because of its great tradition. Tradition is scoffed at in some quarters but I believe without it you have no knowledge of where you have come from, and most important, you have no knowledge of where you are going. It gives a balance, a leavening and perspective to all our endeavours.

As for my grandfather, I am eternally grateful to the old devil for giving me something to believe in—a faith. Cricket parallels can be drawn in nearly every human activity.

Harold Pinter, the playwright, when asked recently about his interest in the game said that he believed cricket was the greatest thing God had invented. "Greater than sex?" asked the interviewer. "Certainly greater than sex," replied Harold. "Of course, you don't have to have two things at the same time, you can have sex before cricket or sex after cricket, but cricket has to be there at the centre of things."

If my grandfather's spirit is still abiding it is without doubt in the pavilion at Trent Bridge, perceiving some new fast bowler and saying to one of the presiding angels, "Yes, he's fast, but you should have seen Larwood!"

My heart is always at Trent Bridge and the mind is often flooded with memories of those splendid characters who paraded their talents for our lasting wonder and delight. Cricket is still to me, with all the encroachments, greed and selfishness of our present age, one of the few sane activities in an increasingly insane world.

Hampshire

John Arlott: "The Voice of Cricket." Writer, broadcaster—and twelfth man for Hampshire on a number of occasions.

Idols and Friends
John Arlott

Hampshire has long been capable of its own defence. When Winchester was the capital of the first England, King Alfred's Wessex, it was his bastion and sally-port against the Danes. When William the Conqueror came and took Winchester as his capital, the Normans were more subtly treated, Anglicised, Hampshirised, and absorbed.

That which neither the invaders nor the centuries could do, however, was done by some faceless creatures of no counties who live in Whitehall burrows. Under the Local Government Act of 1972, they lopped off the south-western corner of Hampshire and gave it to Dorset. The loss of Bournemouth may have caused little anguish, for it was a new growth; but to be robbed of Christchurch—birthplace, and still the home, of Leo Harrison—is hard indeed to bear.

Neither does Hampshire suffer alone. Yorkshire—and if its people could not prevent it, who could?—has been partly dismembered. Whole chunks of the county have been hacked off and, in a crowning indignity, renamed Humberside or Cleveland.

This is a terrifying example of bureaucratic insensitivity. County loyalties are not simply a matter of sporting support. In the most savage carnage the world has known, the First World War, hundreds of thousands of ordinary, unbelligerent Englishmen volunteered for, joined, and died in, their county regiments. Not only the naming of ships and railway engines, but the creation of county societies, conservation, preservation, the writing of their histories, centuries of topographical painting and engraving, the collection of their lore and antiquities, are testimony to the depth of feeling so unnecessarily savaged by those glass-eyed visionaries.

If a Lancastrian living in Barrow used to think Old Trafford remote, how must he feel, now that he is no longer in the county at all?—and neither is Old Trafford, which is now a spot in Greater Manchester, while Preston—not even Lancaster—is the official centre of Lancashire!

71

The authorities at Lord's have not always pleased all of us. Now, though, they have risen to the challenge and decreed that, for cricketing purposes, the boundaries of the counties shall be the same as—give or take the odd, filched rod, pole or perch—those established by the time of the Norman Conquest. That is to say, qualification will ignore the Local Government Acts of 1894 and 1972, and the Greater London Reorganisation of 1965, which obliterated Middlesex.

That will result in a certain amount of what may be called dual-countiality, which means that a man can pay his subscription to the club of the county in which he was born but in which—although he has never moved—he no longer lives. He may, by right, play for one county; and, by wrong, pay his rates to another.

Still, though—if artificially and within a limited field—the old boundary lines have been retained in minds and hearts, then, who knows, one day, by the invocation of natural justice, they may be officially re-established and the last traces of the little men's soullessness removed from the map of England.

Easy enough to argue for such devotion. Less simple to define it, harder still to explain it. Yorkshiremen, it seems, are born with it, like the divine right of kings. For the rest of us it may be acquired: and, once acquired, it remains, strong and warm, for a lifetime. Its most frequent, publicised and popular form lies in sport, especially in cricket which, strictly speaking—or at first-class level—involves only seventeen of the—now—forty-four English counties.

A county is not a single or simple unit like a town which gives its name to a football club. A county consists of so many different units, aspects and facets that it probably means something different to almost every person in it. Especially is this true of Hampshire, most polyglot of counties—naval Portsmouth, big ship Southampton, holiday trade Bournemouth, army Aldershot, air experimental Farnborough, overspill Basingstoke and Andover, railway Eastleigh, NALGO, Cathedral and College Winchester, New Forest and the Surrey-edge stockbroker belt—it has no common factor. There, too, cricket loyalties running far back divide sharply between north and south. For instance between 1914 (the year this writer was born) and 1935 (when he left Basingstoke) the county never played a match north of Southampton. Neither, in that period, did they include any player—except Bert Gibbons from Oakley, who played seven matches between 1921 and 1925—from north of Eastleigh. The big, wealthy southern towns—Portsmouth, Southampton, Bournemouth—provided most of the membership and the sadly small proportion of home-produced players.

Of course none of us could go even to Southampton—thirty miles away by train—and pay to go into the ground, even on a generous

72

eightpence a week pocket money. In those days of few privately owned motor cars and generally short domestic budgets, the boys of Basingstoke, Aldershot, Farnborough, Andover and, to an extent, Winchester, were in true cricket terms, disenfranchised. Indeed, from the start until substantially after the end of the First World War, most southern English boys never even saw a game of cricket. Soldiers posted anywhere more remote than France had effectively no home leave; and, even after the war was over, the number of troop ships available was insufficient to bring many of the soldiers from the East home for more than a year after hostilities ended.

Basingstoke then was much smaller—and far more pleasant—than it is now. It had a cricket ground, generally known as "The Folly" but properly called May's Bounty, after the wealthy, generous and bibulous local brewer and cricket enthusiast who presented it to the town club and the local grammar school, Queen Mary's. Through the war, however, it was used for military purposes and, before it could be used again for cricket, needed much attention.

Just the width of the big boys' asphalt playground away from the Folly stood—and still stands—Fairfields, a typical Victorian council school building, an angular red brick monument to Gladstone's and Forster's ideals and their fruition in the Education Act of 1870. There the end of the war found a rather tubby little boy in the "Infints" aspiring to "the big boys" and little more.

One day he peered between the lichened oak panels of the top gate to the Folly and saw men, back from work, in white flannels, engaged upon an activity he did not recognise but was, he was informed, cricket. It was all fascinating, mysterious and strangely compelling, but with few to explain it. Dogged questioning elicited information about this very odd game; further persistence produced a "cricket set" of yellow varnished bat, tiny stumps and a "compo" ball which, when it took its unpredictable, darting course off the gravel garden path, hurt the shins like the very devil.

By 1920 that long talked of, romantic stranger called "Dad" had returned, and cricket became part of that euphoria. There was, it seemed, a county team, Hants. Now, the one that played on the Folly was called BASINGSTOKEANDNORTHANTS—just like that, all run together; it was printed in dark blue on the yellow paper of the poster announcing the club's fixtures. There was, though, also a Northants whose scores were included in the index-finger-extorted information available in *The Daily Chronicle*. Bafflingly, however, their opponents were not the same; and the players were not those giants who performed on May's Bounty. All became clear when Dad—laughing with, not at—elucidated.

Basingstoke (and North Hants) was our team; but we had another, and bigger, one, out beyond. That was Hampshire, so great a team that even Mister Butler, the professional—and so far as we were concerned, presiding genius—of the Basingstoke ground and club, had not played for them. Earnest enquiry yielded the information that two pros across the town at Thorncrofts, Mister Moore and Mister Ryan (he soon joined Glamorgan as a slow left-arm bowler), had actually played for Hampshire. They instantly assumed gigantic stature. Hilaire Belloc wrote nostalgically of "The men who were boys when I was a boy"; but it was Neville Cardus who displayed cricketers, for cricketers, in all their glory as "The men who were giants when I was a boy."

Soon a school-group of six-year-old cricketing cognoscenti grew up, its discussions fuelled by those who could read the scores clearly—an immense inducement to the study of reading and arithmetic. A close watch was maintained on the doings of the side; not merely through the pages of *The Daily Chronicle*. An adult seen with the evening paper under his arm on a summer afternoon would be importuned with "How are Hampshire getting on, please, Mister?". The reply always seemed to be "A hundred and thirty for three—Mead not out sixty." Every morning the conclave subjected the Hampshire score to intensive scrutiny: indeed, from time to time they debated the dropping of the less successful members of the team. Such is the gravity of the young that the fact of none of them ever having seen Hampshire play did not make their deliberations seem unreal.

Then, all at once, we learnt that light was to be shed upon the ignorance we felt but never admitted. On July 10, 1920, a Hampshire XI would play Sixteen of Basingstoke (we swallowed the indignity with relative ease) on the Bounty. It was a grim day but not actually raining when Basingstoke were off-handedly put in to bat and all too rapidly reduced to 66 for five—and not even by a bowler we recognised. Was his name Cattmore? He never, so far as we could ascertain, played for the county; but he took three Basingstoke wickets cheaply (for 25). Philip Mead made a slip catch off him without appearing to move at all. There was time for Stuart Boyes to bowl an over before the rain closed in and play was abandoned, leaving one group of the county's juvenile supporters devoid of information, or entertainment and, to be honest, somewhat downcast.

Resentful as the young disciples were, it was, perhaps, all for the best that the fixture was so much less than the town's cricketing occasion of the year. For 1921 was Hampshire cricket's *annus mirabilis*. It was not merely that the county finished sixth in the table—with a single, one-place exception, the best they had ever achieved—but they made a considerable impact on the Test scene; and on Basingstoke.

To be sure Australia, with the legendary fast bowling pair of Gregory and McDonald, beat England all too conclusively, by three Tests to none. For Hampshire, though, it was a summer of glory. After the second Test, óur Honourable Lionel Tennyson was appointed captain of England. In the third—at Headingley—he split his hand in the field, yet, batting virtually one-handed, he scored fifty in the hour—63 and 36 in the match. He and George Brown—who kept wicket—were first and second in the English batting averages. Philip Mead, of course, was the great success of the series. He was not called in until the fourth Test, when he made 47 in his only innings. Then, in the last, at The Oval, he scored 182 not out, until then—and for seventeen years afterwards—the highest individual innings every played for England against Australia in this country.

For us, all this simply led up to the match on May's Bounty. Straight from their last fixture, in which they beat Warwickshire to take sixth place, and Mead reached 3,000 runs for the season, Hampshire came to play Fifteen of Basingstoke. In the words of Harry Lauder "It was a splendacious affair"; indeed, it was an all-day game and we took sandwiches—ham—for lunch and—jam—for tea. Even the local *Hants & Berks Gazette* described it as "some of the best cricket ever seen on the Basingstoke ground."

The visiting side called itself Hants Club and Ground but it was, with three quite important exceptions, the full county team including, again to quote the *Hants & Berks Gazette*, "the three great England players Tennyson, Mead and Brown", while "the places of two absentees were filled by local substitutes." One of those stopgaps was, to our pride, Bert Butler's son, Jim.

The ground was crowded. Old men said it had never been so crowded before; and, despite subsequent county matches there, it never has been since. Tennyson won the toss, and airily sent Basingstoke in to bat. Bert Butler and the Rev. J.B. Barker put on 69 for the first wicket before Kennedy and Newman came on and took six fairly quick wickets—but not Bert Butler's. He made 77 before, to huge local mirth, his son Jim caught him at long-on off Jack Newman. Young Arthur White scored 45, Bill Hubbard 32 and Rex Lamb, the Basingstoke captain, 22 before he boldly declared with twelve wickets down, and left Hampshire 254 to win in just over two hours.

Then, there they were—"Major the Hon L.H. Tennyson" and "Mead (P.)" as the little typed slips said—THEMSELVES. The Basingstoke bowling was soon routed. When Mead was lbw to Bert Butler—the men all round said he was not really out because he hit it—George Brown came in. He drove fiercely; Tennyson, though, was to our eyes—and, looking back, by any standards—magnificent. He was a class—probably two classes—above anyone normally seen on the Folly, and he was in immense

75

form. Cap crumpled on his head; shirt open almost to the waist; in his mighty physical prime; powerful—not so portly as he was to become—and exuberantly determined, he kindled the imagination by the sheer joyous strength of his hitting. He struck the rosy-faced, sturdy 'Erby Knowles, the local stock bowler, for two sixes, three fours and a two in a single over. Again and again the cleanly struck ball flew flat as if it had been fired from a gun; or buzzed across the grass and, as people pulled their legs away, cracked and rattled about the woodwork of the benches. The bowling was simply butchered.

Three strokes remain in the memory: a straight drive off the front foot from the Bounty Road end flew low—it hummed, and seemed to shimmer in the sun—and a young man went running and running the full length of Castle Field football pitch to fetch it. From the other end, off the back foot, he hit over the sightscreen, over Bounty road and so far into Mares' gardens that the umpire simply called for another ball. Late in his innings, he moved his left leg out of the line of a full length ball on the leg stump, simply put his bat in its place and jabbed a casual six into the allotments at square leg.

It was all so generous, so spectacular and—though it may seem an extravagant thought—so noble. The 254 runs to win were made in a bewilderingly hectic hour and twenty minutes. The county batted on to entertain the crowd, and Tennyson made 169 before he was caught from what seemed a surprisingly gentle stroke after all that had gone before. They had scored 308 by half-past six; and the little boys, their brains crammed and seething, could let the air out of their lungs.

It is a secondary, colouring, background recollection that the North Hants Iron Works band, splendid in their blue uniforms with the gold facings, played during the day; and again after the match when—to the general wonderment—the ground was lit by chains of electric lights; and there was dancing on the grass.

For one boy it was a formative experience: and remains the sharpest memory of his childhood after his Dad's return from the War.

Not all went well in the life of Lionel Hallam—later Lord—Tennyson, grandson of the Laureate. He did not always behave with a dignity befitting a peer of the realm. On the other hand, he was never mean or little; and his humour, like most of his capacities, was large.

As a captain, he was by no means a master tactician; he was idiosyncratic, erratic, hasty, at times simply and wildly reckless. Yet—or consequently—at Edgbaston in 1922, after Hampshire were put out by Warwickshire for 15 and commanded to follow on, 208 behind, he took the quite ludicrous bet—said to be a tenner at a hundred to one—that they would win the match. In the most improbable recovery in the history of cricket, they did so.

Twenty-five years afterwards, talking face to face as he sucked approvingly at a large Scotch and soda, he did not fail. "Basingstoke, wemember it distinctly, dear boy: bloody tiny little gwound, though; sixes pwetty easy. Wonderful day; gweat party afterwards; nice chaps. You there? 'Mazing; gweat summer for me, o' course; bloody ball hit the middle of the bat all the time. Always liked fast stuff, yer know; came on to the bat so damned sweet. In the Tests, too, yer know; Bwoown—great feller, no fear, yer know, no fear; hit McDonald, Gregory, weally fast fellers, back over their bloody heads like wockets. Old Mead, too; they couldn't wowwy him; when they aimed at his head he just bent slowly inside it. Just pushed 'em awound; like he always did evewyone; no bother to old Mead: just pushed 'em awound."

Club and Ground sides came to Basingstoke regularly after that, but they never matched the excitement or the effect of that 1921 game. The odd county player appeared, too, in visiting sides who came to play Basingstoke. Soon Mister Butler became mentor and counsellor to a boy who was happy to field out for his members' net practice in the hope of a few minutes in the net himself.

Mister Butler, practitioner of slow, straight-lined, near-half-volley leg-breaks, and a shrewd, dogged, legside-bias batsman, was the present influence. The county, though—the distant county—were the reality, the compulsive belief.

In the impromptu and improvised cricket matches between the few members of the urchin horde, the owner of the bat would declare, "I'm Mead". Originally the price of that aggrandisement was that he had to bat left-handed which, for a natural right-hander, was awkward, and often painful but, in terms of county pride, worth it. To general relief, right-handed Meads were eventually accepted. He never came to Basingstoke again until 1935 in a fixture with Surrey, the first Championship match played there for twenty-one years. It was no game for Hampshire, who, on a green wicket, were bowled out by Alf Gover off a short run. Historically, Andrew Sandham scored his hundredth hundred.

Meanwhile in the 1920s, for a schoolboy, Southampton was still expensively distant. The long family cycle convoy to stay with an uncle in London brought a memorable sight of The Oval Test of 1926 which brought The Ashes back to England. Other long bicycle excursions, to stay with grandmother in Eastbourne, proffered the delight of watching Sussex. They were an appealing side, with Maurice Tate a hero-figure; but the die had been cast long before, in August 1921: Hampshire had an unresisting captive supporter.

Through a second flash of good fortune, the first visit to Southampton proved as memorable as the match of 1921. In a kind of semi-coming-of-age, at fourteen, the visit, carefully planned and saved up for, was the fixture with the West Indian touring team of 1928. Everyone had been reading of the performance of the mighty Constantine who, in June, had made an instant and immense reputation when he virtually defeated Middlesex by his own efforts (one for 77; 86; seven for 57; and, at the last, 103, scored in an hour). All that and Hampshire, too: the temptation was irresistible. By yet another stroke of luck, the local stonemason, hearing of the project, remarked casually that he was going to Southampton on Wednesday and might find room in the back of his van for a couple of boys who could be up, out, and waiting at his yard by half-past seven in the morning. In the event he had to go back for half a day on Thursday to finish his work, and consented to take the same human cargo on a second journey.

Hampshire—in the person of the Hon. L.H. Tennyson—duly won the toss and took first innings. There was, though, little pleasure for their followers. In the first over, Constantine carted George Brown's off stump far back towards the wicket-keeper at quite hectic speed. He then proceeded to bowl Alec Kennedy, have Ronny Aird taken at slip, and Mead lbw; all beaten for pace; and he had taken four for 24. Alec Hosie and Jack Newman lit a glimmer of revival but soon after lunch, when Herman Griffith bowled Hosie, their score was only 88 for five.

This is no stage-managed, subjective, gloss, but the next batsman, as the scorecard categorically insisted, was "The Hon L.H. Tennyson". He was, by now, somewhat more portly than when previously seen in 1921. He was, though, again at his spirited best. Presumably the fast bowlers intended to attack him: they did. He, however, attacked them far more vehemently.

The first ball he received, bowled by Griffith, was fast, short, and outside the line of the off stump; and, to our amazement and delight, he flat-batted it through mid-off for four. Jack Newman, typical south county cricket professional, was content to hold up an end while his captain took the fight to the bowlers.

Upstandingly aggressive, glorying as he did in his best days in attacking fast bowling, Tennyson rolled out imperious strokes against the pace of Constantine and Griffith, the seam-up of Browne. Surprisingly, too, he seemed fully confident against the rolled leg-spin of Scott; though it did not appear to turn, and the bowler tended to push it through flat and fast, as if in trepidation. However that may be, "Lordship"—as the players called him—batted for the rest of the day. Some of his driving was thunderous, and he hooked more circumspectly than usual, turning the wrists and keeping the ball down. Once, though, when Griffith dropped one short, and it rose more than head high, he swatted it furiously and lofted it far and deep into the car park at long-leg. So they put on 224 that day; and, the next morning, our extra journey enabled us to see them carry the stand to 311—made in four hours—before Tennyson nicked "Sniffy" Browne's slow left-arm spin to slip. By then, scoring twice as fast as his partner, he had made 217, the highest innings of his career; at 54 an hour. He and Newman (who eventually made 118) put on 311, a stand only once exceeded for the Hampshire sixth wicket.

After our departure West Indies, too, made a long score—only 16 behind Hampshire's 429—and the match was drawn. That was no matter. Faith had not needed to be renewed; but now it was vastly increased.

With manhood, idol worship was replaced by friendship without disillusionment. Hours of net bowling; sharing the Easter coaching classes for schoolboys; eventually, the highest honour within a very ordinary club cricketer's ability, twelfth man for the county and the almost choking pride of fielding substitute in three Championship matches.

Admission to the dressing room and to the amiable condescension of such gods of youth as Philip Mead and Alec Kennedy was heady. The easy company of the retired George Brown and Jack Newman, when they came to the ground, was a warmth of history. Nothing before or since was so deeply satisfying to the dedicated supporter as to be accepted by those who for years had been of godlike stature.

After the war of 1939–45 it was often possible for a broadcaster and reporter slightly to bend the importance of fixtures in order to justify attending a Hampshire match. The players then were contemporaries who often had been team mates or opponents; who became friends; one of them, indeed, as close as any in a lifetime. With them, yet humbly and enthusiastically as ever, it was possible to suffer in defeat; glory in triumph—especially in 1961 when, that night after the defeat of Derbyshire at Bournemouth, celebrations broke out in the most unexpected of places and ended in others even more improbable.

The immediate pre-1939 period, though, was a hinge phase in one supporter's life: and in the history of the county club. It was the end of a generation of great players. Of course, the heroes of youth look greater in the eye of memory than the men of today. The post-war teams have won two County Championships, been runners-up in two more and have twice won the John Player League. On the other hand, the best positions the pre-1939 side ever achieved was fifth in 1914, and sixth twice during the twenties.

With abject apologies to those who achieved the major successes, being a supporter is a subjective matter. A man knows his contemporaries and juniors as ordinary human beings; the giants of his childhood, though, never lose the quality which established them in his imagination. They come back clear and sharp in memory when later—and perhaps more capable—players are merely blurred figures. Most men look back to a past from which time has smoothed the harsher edges. For one who was then a boy, the Hampshire teams of the 1920s remain a compelling nostalgia, even though most of their feats were shared vicariously through the newspapers or by word of mouth from a fortunate witness.

They faced some immensely powerful opposition. Certainly there were some weak counties in the table. Hampshire themselves, who only came into the competition in 1895, were often regarded as one of the lesser powers but they generally managed to hang on somewhere about halfway. That was a fair achievement for a newly built team facing such long-established opponents as the great Yorkshire, Lancashire, Surrey, Kent, Nottinghamshire and Middlesex sides of the first third of this century.

In what must now be regarded as the old-fashioned style, Hampshire had a nucleus of long-serving players who sustained them quite remarkably: and about whom a virtual mythology grew up among several generations of supporters. Those men, with their playing spans for the county were:

Lord Tennyson 1919–1933
Philip Mead 1905–1936
George Brown 1909–1933
Jack Newman 1906–1930
Alec Kennedy 1907–1936
Alec Bowell 1902–1927
Walter Livsey 1914–1929

Twenty-three years' service with a county nowadays is exceptional yet that is the average among those seven. Four of them played Test cricket: Livsey went on the South African tour of 1922–3 as first wicket-keeper but had to return home injured; while Jack Newman is one of only three cricketers who took over 2,000 wickets and never played in a Test. This is a remarkable record and accounts for those men's legendary standing over a considerable period in the county. It would be difficult to imagine a more oddly assorted group of characters, but they served Hampshire more than merely well.

Tennyson a fast bowler himself at Eton, though his bowling was never taken seriously at first-class level, was, of course, at his best as a hitter. Although he was not a consistent batsman he often turned a game by attacking bowlers—especially fast bowlers—who had taken the initiative; and he hung on to some savage catches at mid-off or mid-on. Humorous, bibulous and bold, he was one of the most colourful characters of the cricket of his, or any other, age.

Philip Mead must be numbered among the major batsmen of history. He began as a slow left-arm bowler with Surrey who released him to join Hampshire for whom, as a monumentally steady left-hand bat, he scored more runs than anyone for any team in the history of the game; and made more centuries than anyone else except Jack Hobbs, Patsy Hendren and Walter Hammond.

It was once said, perceptively, that Philip had no interest in batting, only in making runs and, over those thirty-three seasons, he averaged 47.67 an innings. He had drooping shoulders, wide hips and a rolling walk; and before every ball he received, he touched the peak of his cap three times, took three small steps up to his bat and tapped it three times in the crease. If any bowler dared to interrupt him, he drew back, stopped him, and went through the ritual again. It was a great duel when Clarrie Grimmett tried to hurry him. A splendidly sure-handed slip, he took 668 catches in his career. Dry, wry, solemn he had a weakness for backing horses; it certainly was not his strength.

Tall, wide-shouldered, muscular and immensely strong—he could tear a pack of cards across in his bare hands—George Brown had a face like that of a Red Indian chief. He was a spectacular all-round cricketer. Good enough to keep wicket for England, he did so in motor-cycling gauntlets on the grounds that, since he was not a regular wicket-keeper, he did not propose to buy gloves for the purpose. He was a left-hand bat of aggressive bent and immense power in the hook and the drive, and one who particularly relished fast bowling. He was a useful fairly fast bowler with occasional outswing; a fearless and often bewildering silly point and, according to a pre-1914 reference book "the furthest thrower in the country". Eccentric, quick-tempered, loyal, he was as lovable as he was unpredictable.

Alec Kennedy was a straight-backed, and somewhat straight-laced, serious Scot, with a facial resemblance to George Robey. A fast-medium bowler, in his absolute accuracy he was a Hampshire forerunner of Derek Shackleton. He was, too, a considerable technician; he could swing the ball both ways, was one of the first to bowl the leg-cutter and employed many subtly concealed variations of pace, length and arc. His run-up was so unvarying that, bowling for half a day on a wet ground, he stamped out his footmarks precisely to the fraction of an inch. Tireless, faithful and persistent, he took 2,874 wickets and scored 16,586 runs; five times performed the "Double", and never complained; not, that is, about work. He was a meticulous coach.

His partner in the long-lasting Kennedy and Newman operation, Jack Newman, was a lean, wiry, introverted bachelor who went to some lengths to conceal his sentimentality. In any other age his 2,032 wickets, 15,333 runs, including five "Doubles" must have made him an England all-rounder. He often opened the bowling with medium-paced outswing; but his main strength lay in his sharply spun off-breaks which he varied most skilfully, especially with an extremely well-concealed faster ball. He was a dour, sound batsman and a safe field. He backed horses even more heavily and less successfully than Philip Mead and lost his entire benefit fund to the bookies before he collected it. He was gentle, kind, sensitive, a little sad, and he made a very good umpire.

Walter Livsey kept wicket for Hampshire, acted as chauffeur-valet to Lord Tennyson, and, understandably, had occasional nervous breakdowns. Serious and sensitive, splendidly clean-handed, he was outstanding in his teens. Quite early in his career, he impressed players and critics by an amazing stumping of Jack Hobbs from a Jack Newman off-break which, off a bad pitch, turned and lifted down the leg-side. He would have kept wicket for England in South Africa in 1922–3 but for injury. He retired from cricket in 1929 through ill-health but died, last of that lengendary group, in 1978, eleven days short of his eighty-fifth birthday.

Alec Bowell, lean and dapper, oldest of them all, was a neat, stylish batsman, nimble cover-point and wise, shrewd, senior pro. The other six owed much to his knowledge and advice. He did not play far into the twenties but he was in the side at Basingstoke in 1921 as well as several subsequent Club and Ground teams there, and in his retirement in Oxford he was full of memories and wisdom.

Stuart Boyes was their junior but, bought out of the Army in 1921, he joined them and held a team place until 1939, when he was senior pro. He was an intelligent slow left-arm bowler, who could bat better than his figures, and a fine short-leg fieldsman.

Most happily, all eight of them were in the Hampshire team which, at Edgbaston on the 14th, 15th and 16th of June 1922, achieved the county's most amazing triumph. The eleven was completed by Harry Day, a stroke-making batsman and lively fieldsman who was invited to make the South African tour of 1922–3 but was refused release by the Army; W.R.—Bill—Shirley, yet another of the Hampshire Etonians and a better all-rounder than he had the chance to show in that side; and A.S. McIntyre, an occasional who, over four seasons and 45 innings, scored 493 runs at 11.46 and took no wickets for 36 runs. He had the privilege to share in a quite remarkable—all but incredible—performance.

Warwickshire won the toss, batted and made 223; then, on a perfectly good wicket, Harry Howell (six for seven) and Freddie Gough-Calthorpe (four for four) bowled Hampshire out for 15 (four extras). Mead went in at the fall of the second wicket and batted through for six not out. Freddie Gough-Calthorpe invited Hampshire to follow-on and suggested to Tennyson a round of golf on the following afternoon. Tennyson responded with his crazy—winning—bet that Hampshire would win.

The early batting was better than in the first innings, but, when the sixth second-innings wicket fell, they still needed 22 to avoid an innings defeat. Shirley and Brown put on 85; McIntyre was soon out, but the ninth wicket partnership of Brown and Livsey lifted them to 451 before Smart bowled George Brown for an heroic 172. The match had now moved into the realm of the unreal. For the last wicket, Walter Livsey, who had come in at number ten, made the first century of his career—and made it without a chance—and with Stuart Boyes (29) in a stand of 70 took the total to 521. Warwickshire now were psychologically beaten. It remained only for Kennedy (four for 47) and Newman (five for 53) to bowl them out and Hampshire had won by 155 runs. Over thirty years later, George Brown remembered the disbelief in Birmingham, the almost hysterical gaiety of the journey home, the profusion of Tennyson's champagne.

After reading the Thursday morning newspaper, that was the height of a supporter's ambition. It remains the landmark of a lifetime of devotion.

For the rest, support is a list of delights, successes and friendships; laughter, conviviality and happiness. It is the chronicle of Shack and Vic; Roy Marshall, Peter Sainsbury, Desmond Eagar and Richard Gilliat; Colin Ingleby-Mackenzie; Jimmy Gray, Butch White, Mervyn Burden, Tom Dean, Charlie Knott, Jim Bailey, Gerry Hill, Barry Reed, Henry Horton, Neville Rogers, Sam Pothecary, Arthur Holt, Trevor Jesty, "Hooky" Walker, Johnny Arnold, Bob Stephenson, Jack Andrews, Brian Timms; and, summoning him to approve it all, Leo Harrison—the friends who followed the boyhood giants.

Derbyshire

Ted Moult: Broadcaster, raconteur and Derbyshire farmer.

My Local Derby
Ted Moult

As I live on a farm some way from the village, no newspapers have been delivered since "Nipper" Decamps stopped bringing them round some fifteen years ago; and so, unless a special trip is made to the village emporium for the *Derby Evening Telegraph*, it's often the next day before I register the news. And what is the first item to be scrutinised? Well, in summer it's the County Championship matches, brought up, as I was, on three-day cricket.

The image of the first-class county, in cricket terms, is somewhat blurred; perhaps we imagine that if we have a first-class cricket team we are also first class: it sounds good, does the ego good. But why, one wonders, were some important counties left out of the prestigious list—Staffordshire, Northumberland, Cheshire, Devon; minor counties, how odd! "Once I lived in the Midlands, sodden and unkind", wrote the great G.K. Chesterton. Well that's a bit unfair, I've always thought. Derbyshire is not sodden and unkind, all Derbyshire isn't even in the Midlands!

I always think of the division between northern England and the Midlands as some imaginary line starting somewhere south of Manchester, festooning round the southern Pennines, and then following the course of the "smug and silver Trent" towards the Humber. The north of England starts somewhere near Belper, where the traditional stone houses become predominant over brick ones. Derbyshire is not an homogeneous county at all, each peripheral area being different from the next and more like its opposite district across the county border: thus the Derbyshire coalfield looks very much like a Nottinghamshire coalfield, High Peak resembles the adjacent southern Pennine moors in what was formerly the West Riding of Yorkshire, and so on.

The river Derwent is supposed to make a further division. On the left bank (that is, the eastern side), it is industrial, socialist and educationally conscious; whereas the right is more conservative and very sluggish in its attitude to learning. Most of the cricketers you have ever heard of come from the former.

Cricket for Derbyshire officially began in 1870. One of the main components in its pedigree was the South Derbyshire Club which seems to have fizzled out about four years later, but was active in 1868 when the club met, and beat by 139 runs, a team known as the Australian Aboriginals—the scorecard showing such evocative names as Bullocky, Tiger, Twopenny (who had the highest score with 33 runs), Mosquito and Dick-a-Dick.

The county went through a very deep trough in the 1880s. At the end of the 1885 season three of its top players went elsewhere. Shacklock joined Notts, Docker signed on with Lancashire and Frank Sugg, who discovered that he had not been born where he thought, but somewhere in Smethwick, felt obliged to go and play for Warwickshire! With the loss of these three, the performance declined to such a low level that, in 1887, only three of the other first-class counties, Yorkshire, Surrey and Lancashire, agreed to play Derbyshire. The county played six games against these clubs and lost them all. Following this debacle and due to some agitation in the press, Derbyshire were relegated to second-class status. It is interesting to note that other clubs in later years, notably Northants and Somerset, did not suffer the same fate when going through their extended periods of misery.

One of the main reasons for Derbyshire's return to first-class cricket was the demon fast bowler from Australia, F.R. Spofforth. He had married a girl from Breadsall in 1886 and lived in the county for three years. Although the Derbyshire committee amended the rules to allow him to play, such was the adherence to the native principle that the County Cricket Council put it to each of Derbyshire's opponents to test their reaction to his participation. Only Yorkshire agreed to his inclusion without condition, and Notts and Surrey condescended to play an outfit described as "Derbyshire plus Mr Spofforth". He played only nine games in all but his influence was, as captain, significant in Derbyshire's recovery.

In 1894 it was agreed that Derbyshire, Warwickshire, Leicestershire and Essex should join the existing nine first-class clubs, Hampshire being added to the list later that year. Thus the competition for the County Championship was between fourteen clubs. In the end this number was increased by the inclusion of Worcestershire in 1899, Northamptonshire in 1905 and Glamorgan in 1921.

Derbyshire has long had its headquarters at the Nottingham Road ground in Derby, at the southern end of the old racecourse. Horse racing finished in the late thirties, stopped, it is said, because the borough council considered that the sport of kings brought undesirable elements into the town. What they would have thought of modern soccer hooliganism is a matter for conjecture. The playing area has advanced northwards over the years to where the racing stables used to stand, and is now big enough for another match to take place at the same time. Six local clubs use the ground in addition to the county side. Mind you, indulging in cricket in open spaces with several matches going on simultaneously can be extremely hazardous; it is not unknown for a player to be struck on the back of the head from a hefty on-drive from another game!

The new area utilises part of the original grandstand (former Mecca of the punters), for the members of the Club. The other part houses the regional offices of the Agricultural Advisory Service, so for me it is possible to obtain advice and entertainment from the same place. Very handy. Apart from this, any sufferer from agoraphobia would be advised to go to Edgbaston or Trent Bridge where the buildings surround the boundary. The County Ground is undoubtedly the most bleak in England, unpopular with the Aussies and as recently stated in the *Guardian* "not entirely unconvincing as an opening set for *Macbeth*". (Chesterfield, on the other hand, can claim to have one of the loveliest grounds in the country.) Maybe more trees will provide the answer. There is no check on the Gate: getting into the ground is like a burglar bursting into a child's money-box. Nevertheless, nearly all the cricket takes place there.

I have only played once at the County Ground; it was in a game organised by Fred Rumsey between his eleven and another from Nottingham Forest, captained by cricket enthusiast Brian Clough. It was in aid of battered wives and we did manage to raise a few pounds, enough to buy more than a few tins of Elastoplast, I should think. I remember several who took part, in particular J.P.R. Williams, wicket-keeper who married a Buxton girl; John Taylor, also a Welsh international rugby captain; and Phillip Whitehead, local MP and cricket nut.

There is no doubt that Derbyshire has been one of the least fashionable of cricketing counties; maybe the grounds have put visitors off. Although much of the country is cloaked in scenery of unrivalled beauty—like the Peak National Park—the game of cricket has been mostly associated with grimy coal mines, Victorian railways and unattractive industrial villages reminiscent of D.H. Lawrence's novels. Even so, there are enough natural features to make one wonder how different these areas would have been if their assets had been exploited in the 19th century with the benefit of modern technology and sense of conservation. The dark satanic mills (although I believe Blake had the Universities in mind), as popularly considered, were never very far from the stumps in the early days. Even in south Derbyshire, round

87

Swadlincote where I live, most men are either "down the pit" or "on the bank" (digging clay for the pipe works and ceramics). Nevertheless the mines produced the pace men: it used to be said that if you shouted down a mineshaft up would come a fast bowler. The famous Derbyshire names—Mycroft, Bestwick, Copson, Jackson and Gladwin—were all associated with the Black Diamonds.

People tend to forget the economic advantages of becoming a county player pre-1939. Although the pay of cricketers, indeed all sports persons, was derisory by present day standards, the step up from a collier's wages was significant. Sport was one avenue of escape from the muck and dust to a better life. This difference was not maintained in later years when a miner would probably earn more than the average cricketer, especially in the pre-Packer period. In the thirties the professionals received £4 a week for Derbyshire, plus match money: £7 for a home game, £9 away. Out of this they had to pay their own hotel bill.

In former days there was less social acceptability between the gentlemen and the players, the players being mainly miners or quarry men and all possessing that rugged independence of spirit that denotes such callings. They were sometimes insulated from the amateurs even within their own county. Furthermore it is thought that many of Derbyshire's best performers were denied national recognition because of an uncouth demeanour, or through the absence of a university or public school background.

Such local dialect as was spoken is amply illustrated in the local publication "Eye Up Me Duck", showing the colourful nature of the patois of the Erewash valley. I recall a village game where I live: at the crease was one George Woodward, tall and ungainly, described as an awkward kidney bean pole. For several balls he played a sort of forward defensive stroke without full commitment, as though his bat was fastened to the stumps by invisible elastic bands. Finally he made contact and set off like a galloping rhinoceros for the other end, only to crash into the umpire, one Walter Holmes, knocking him to the ground. "Ow wor ah?" asked the batsman. "Ow wor yer?" cried Walter, dusting himself down. "Out, yer gret tom fule, off yer go to th'pavilion."

Even in the periods when Derbyshire were doing well, it was thought that a player had to be twice as good as one in a more fashionable county to make it into a Test series, or be selected for an MCC tour. In periods of lesser achievement by the county, it was almost impossible. It is easy to display brilliance if you are brilliant in a good team, which is why footballers move to better clubs—well, one of the reasons, apart from the money. Would we have heard so much about Kevin Keegan if he had spent all his career at Scunthorpe, for example? Likewise if you come in to bat at No 4 or 5 with a 100 or more on the scoreboard, you have a better chance of showing your ability than when your side is struggling all the time.

Of course, every team requires a captain and the first Derbyshire one I can remember is Arthur Richardson from Quarndon, who was involved with the leather industry in the district. That was in the thirties. Then there was Robin Buckston from Sutton-on-the-Hill and the equally popular Eddie Gothard, well known in Burton-on-Trent club cricket circles, who had the distinction of a hat-trick against Middlesex and of bowling out Bradman on his last tour in 1948. Gilbert Hodgkinson, Old Derbeian and cavalier batsman, had two seasons with the county; his business interests included Rowleys "high class" flower shop—presumably they were busy with bouquets when Stan Worthington deputised for him as captain. David Skinner comes to mind as being prominent in the period of reconstruction after the war, for then the pre-war favourites were becoming a bit long in the tooth. One season the captaincy was shared between Pat Vaulkhard and Guy Willatt; however Willatt broke his left hand in the first game against Warwickshire, so Vaulkhard took over for the rest of the season. I remember well his barn-storming approach to the game. Not hit and miss like me, but hit and hit! He was noted for driving fast bowlers back over long-on for six.

Another notable and erstwhile young England hope, later to become prominent in the Tony Greig/Packer controversy as one of the game's top administrators, was Donald Carr. Having been appointed vice-captain of England in India in 1951–2, he became the first Derbyshire player to captain the national team. Unfair omissions are certain to occur when one attempts to pick out star performers, but no chapter on Derbyshire would be complete without referring to the achievements of fast bowlers Les Jackson and Cliff Gladwin.

The Gladwin and Jackson opening attack was reminiscent of the pre-war partnership of Copson and Pope, and was reckoned by many to be the best in the land. Les, from Whitwell colliery, was called upon to play for England against the Australians only once. He used to bowl length and line, making the batsmen play each delivery, and would never waste a new ball by bowling wide of the off stump or down the leg-side; unlike many modern players who seem to have an unaccountable faith in negative bowling wide of the stumps.

Cliff Gladwin, from Glapwell, specialised in the "in-ducker", having three short legs (usually Carr, Alan Revill and Derek Morgan, who was another good captain) in close attendance. For me Cliff is immortalised by the famous incident in South Africa during the 1948–9 tour. It was the Durban Test, and one run was needed off the last ball to win the match. Gladwin went to Alec Bedser, who was batting at the other end, and said, "Cometh the hour, cometh the Man"—before proceeding to engineer the winning leg-bye.

Harold Rhodes was another good fast bowler, who through no fault of his own was no-balled many times for throwing; the films eventually cleared him, but it was still a very unhappy incident about what, he and we knew, was his natural action. A good chap to have on your side was wicket-keeper Dawkes, who came from Leicestershire, a good hitter and probably on the edge of promotion to the national side if it had not been for Godfrey Evans. Wicket-keepers last a long time and Bob Taylor is no exception; the most amiable of men, dedicated and an absolute sportsman. Bob holds the world record for wicket-keeping and has been unfortunate to be somewhat in the shadow of Alan Knott. He is no mug with the bat either as his fighting Test innings of 99 on the last Australian tour showed. In 1981 Bob scored his maiden first-class century.

It is perhaps fitting that the time that I was first associated with the county side was, like 1981, a year of high achievement. It was in 1936 when I was a small boy and would walk down the canal bank under the trees with my grandfather, or by way of contrast be taken to the ground by my Uncle Alf in his car. My grandfather was a retired butcher and had plenty of time; my uncle was an active businessman and used to snatch opportunities between meetings—he was always having meetings. He was also on the Club Committee so we sat in the old pavilion. One of the highlights was when the West Indians came. Learie, later Lord, Constantine was my favourite—a very long run up, then an athletic leap into the air before delivery. It must have been an awe-inspiring sight to any batsman; I think my eyes would have been riveted on his flashing white teeth. On one occasion a group of West Indians, staying overnight in a small hotel, demonstrated their fielding ability by practising with the landlady's Crown Derby china cups and saucers, nearly causing their hostess a cardiac arrest.

I suppose the year 1936, when Derbyshire won the County Championship, is inscribed in the minds of cricket lovers of the Peak county because it is, up to now, the only time they have come top of the list. Being adjacent to Yorkshire with about thirty Championships under its belt, Derbyshire, although it had several seasons in the top bracket, were sometimes described by unkind northerners as "Derbyshire Tups", or "strong in the arm wik i th'ead". I believe, however, that students of philology will confirm that "wik" does not mean weak, but "sharp and astute"! The thirties were after all the period of Yorkshire greatness; nevertheless Derbyshire had run them close for a few seasons.

The players in Derbyshire's vintage year were—and I can still remember them as though it were yesterday—A. E. Alderman; Denis Smith, a left-hand batsman from Somercotes who still holds the highest batting record for the county; T. S. Worthington, who on the day that his son was born scored a century in each innings in a match with Notts, batting against the bowling of Bill Voce and Harold Larwood; Leslie Townsend, a great all-rounder who was worth an England place; Harry Storer, a gritty unyielding player; Charlie Elliott who eventually became a Test selector; Harry Elliott, wicket-keeper; Alf Pope, one of the famous brothers, the other being George; Tommy Mitchell from Cresswell who wore spectacles and always bowled with his sleeves down; and ginger-haired Bill Copson who my grandfather said would have been unstoppable if his health and strength could have equalled his spirit. The captain was Arthur Richardson, the only amateur in the side.

Three of the team are still at the County Ground, for the ashes of Harry Storer, Stan Worthington and Denis Smith have been scattered over the wicket.

The main reason for the county's success was team work, effective bowling and the astute captaincy of Arthur Richardson, who after all had done the job for six years. An important factor was that the professionals played all the time: the practice of selecting pros for the distant away matches and then dropping them for the more convenient home games, to make room for gifted amateurs, was not employed. Derbyshire had been third in the Championship in 1934 and second in 1935. Now, in the glorious year of 1936, they were first.

Copson was the most colourful of the bowlers and took the most wickets in the season: 160. Only Larwood and Hedley Verity exceeded the figure that year. Alf Pope took 99 and Mitchell, of the cleverly varied leg-breaks and googlies, took 121. Tommy finished up in the Bradford League and my grandfather said he could have been an equal success on the stage or music hall had he chosen to go in that direction. No doubt the famous George Pope would have had his share of bowling triumphs had he not suffered a cartilage injury in the spring of 1936, which prevented him from playing after May.

The batting wasn't as good as the bowling, and although adequate for the year, no records were broken. Even Denis Smith went through a loss of form until quite late in the summer. But all the players knew their job and had confidence in each other; there were few team changes in that season, nobody wanting to muck about with a winning combination.

*   *   *

Looking back over the last twenty years, 1981 will probably go down as the golden year of cricket in the memory of lovers of the game: and without doubt the most thrilling. The weather, always a vital factor, looked like being fairly vile in what was probably the wettest spring and early summer for years. Spring corn certainly needs water; if any batsman makes a thousand runs in May, it usually means a poor look-out for my barley. This time though the wet was overdone; in June, when the farmers who choose to make silage for their winter feeding requirements were going about it, an onlooker might have imagined that they were combining the job with ploughing, such was the mess in the fields. However in July the climate recovered, giving us the chance to gather the hay, strawberries and corn, and to enable the whole nation to appreciate the finest exposition of cricket entertainment.

There isn't space here to discuss the merits of the three-day game nor to make odorous comparisons with the limited over variety. Let's just agree that they are two different games played with the same tackle. But it is always remarkable to me that even in a five-day Test match, after all those runs and all those words by Johnston, Bailey, Trueman and company, you can still have a nail-biting finish. But for a series of real tension, pressure and close finishes, future writers will need to look no further than the inaugural year of the Nat West Trophy and its first custodian, Derbyshire. The county had not been without its moments in one-day competitions and had previously been to the final of the Gillette Cup—abandoned by the sponsors, it is said, because so many cricketers were sporting facial fungus—but had never won anything.

In the early rounds of the new competition, Derbyshire had a bye and then met and beat Scotland. In the quarter-finals they had a very satisfying victory over local rivals Nottinghamshire, who were having their best season for fifty years and went on to win the County Championship. In the semi-final, which turned out to be a two-day affair, they drew Essex, captained by the talented Keith Fletcher.

The first day was a mixture of cutting wind and glowering skies which seemed to blow down the Derwent valley from the high moors. Even the "mini-hill"—that meagre earthwork which represents the Committee's idea of a windbreak—failed to reduce the Aeolian effect. Essex were put into bat and were bowled out for 149. At one point they were 98 for eight, but by then Wood had used up all his quick bowlers on this green and difficult pitch and in the last six overs of spin, Norbert Phillip, who has a taste for such fare, helped Essex advance the score to 144 for nine. He was finally out to a stumping by Bob Taylor, his sixth victim of the innings and a record for 60-overs cricket. Earlier, young Paul Newman, whose coolness at the very end of the game was as yet unforeseen, had made in-roads into the Essex batting by removing Gooch and Fletcher.

Nearby Aiton's factory chimney belched vigorously, making the sky even darker, and after the players had been driven off for bad light for the fourth time, the home side reflected on the dismissal of their two batting stars, Kirsten and Wright—both out lbw. Incidentally, I always found the laws on leg before wicket easier to understand in the old days when the ball had to be pitched on a line, wicket to wicket. It doesn't seem to make much sense that batsmen are now given out lbw when the ball pitches outside the off stump, but not when it's on the leg stump.

The next day the weather brightened, Derbyshire continuing their innings with the pitch looking more shaved than some of the players! Steele and Miller had gone in and come out again before I arrived; Hill was bottling up at one end with the bright hope Kim Barnett at the other. Hill, who finished up with 21 runs off forty overs, began to get me worried. At lunch the sand in the egg-timer was three-quarters gone, but wickets, I was told by some of the old hands, were as good as runs. But the run rate was worse than that of Essex.

Forty runs were still needed from the last eight overs when Fletcher reintroduced his pacemen, Lever and Phillip. Wood, in spite of strapped-up ribs, managed 18 runs. Barnett stood back to Phillip in an attempt to reach the Cattle Market and was bowled. Colin Tunnicliffe (earmarked for posterity in the final) came and went, although encouraged by his aunt, the Mayor of the city, Councillor Flo Tunnicliffe. Seventeen were needed from the last two overs.

Finally the two men at the crease were the faithful Taylor and the young-hopeful Newman. Essex still looked odds on to win. Fletcher posted all his men near the boundary, mainly on the leg-side, and as Phillip began to bowl the final over, ten runs were still required. Scrambling two from the first ball, and then a single, Taylor, not known for his big hitting, opened the account. Newman got another run from the third ball and yet another single from the fourth. A mid-wicket conference now held our attention: no doubt Taylor was making sure that Newman understood that it was necessary only to *equal* the score of Essex, since Derbyshire, in the event of a tie, would win, having lost fewer wickets.

Two more balls. Phillip bowled a short one on the leg, which Newman sent straight to the long-leg boundary for four. Only one more needed for success. The field closed in to breathe down our young hero's neck. Newman pushed the ball back to the bowler and set off in desperation; Phillip scooped it up, turned, shied at the stumps, and missed. I am one of the people who wishes that spectators would stay behind the ropes after a game is over; I always get cross when people stand up and leave the cinema before you have had a chance to read the credits. However, I suppose the euphoria this time was justified, and amid the cavorting of the spectators, the waving of bats and general back slapping, I noticed one very thoughtful gesture: Keith Fletcher putting his arm round the unhappy Norbert Phillip. Such is cricket.

Almost as soon as the news was out, the final at Lord's was a sell-out. Down in the Derby Wholesale Fruit Market, a well-known cadre of support, you couldn't get a ticket for ten crates of blood oranges. On the fine September morning, we heard Don Mosey, in his usual incisive and articulate style, describe the match as the battle of the two Cinderellas. Of the two least fashionable clubs, Northants had the edge on batting while Derbyshire had a better chance of bowling their opponents out. However, it depended very much on whether the overseas pair, John Wright from New Zealand and Peter Kirsten from South Africa, would succeed on this important day.

Northants must have been particularly grateful to Barry Wood for his decision to take the field, for Cook and Larkins put on 99 before the latter was caught on the mid-wicket boundary by Miller on the run. Then followed, what was to me, the best catch of the season: the one which dismissed Williams. Alan Hill fielding deep, after initially losing track of the ball in the air, made a two-handed catch whilst completely airborne. This prompted Robin Marlar to speculate on whether Rudolf Nureyev had joined the coaching department! Three men were run out: Lamb, to the groans of the Northants supporters, through a brilliant piece of fielding by Miller; Willey, despatched in a similar way by Wood; and Yardley by Tunnicliffe, who was actually standing in front of the stumps when he did the trick. The same man disposed of Cook after a fine captain's innings of 111.

The Northamptonshire innings ended with 235 runs on the board, certainly short of the 260 or so which seemed a possibility earlier in the game. Derbyshire started comfortably enough; after fifteen overs they were 41 for no wicket. Then a ball from the blond Mallinder removed Hill's bail. Derbyshire started the innings needing a little under four runs per over, which looked easy on a lovely batting wicket; but although Wright and Kirsten seemed to be going well, uncomfortable thoughts on the run rate began to loom in the back of the mind. Did the two batsmen think they were in a three-day match, I wondered?

When Steve Oldham, who was not fully fit and therefore not playing, brought a new bat out to John Wright, he walked about twenty yards towards the wicket with him, no doubt as a courier from the Derbyshire HQ on the balcony. Two decisive balls in the forty-eighth over produced ten runs. From a short delivery from Mallinder, Wright smashed a glorious six into the crowd; and the next ball produced four byes, deceiving wicket-keeper George Sharp and nipping down the leg-side. Derby were in with a chance of winning.

Then Wright was out lbw; and shortly after Kirsten followed him, dismissed in the same manner. Mallinder's revenge! Wood tried to raise the game and was bowled by a fine ball from Sarfraz, and the score was 189 for four. The veteran Steele was bowled for a duck by Griffiths, one of Northants' heroes in the semi-final. When Miller came in Derbyshire had required 38 runs to win in 4.4 overs; now the run rate had risen alarmingly to 8.14 per over! Sarfraz obligingly bowled a full toss to Miller who hit it for a huge six, reducing the target to 24 runs off 18 balls: back to 8 runs per over. Minutes later Kim Barnett was narrowly run out, struggling for the second run and having to manoeuvre round Geoff Miller. Nineteen runs needed off the last two overs in the September twilight. In comes cool Colin Tunnicliffe and off the first ball from Sarfraz, slices a four on the off-side boundary. He takes thirteen off this, the next to last over.

Now it's the final over. The first ball from Griffiths (what a responsibility for him) produces two runs. Five runs to win off five balls, and it's getting darker all the time. Second ball, a single to Miller. Four runs off four balls. Tunnicliffe faces Griffiths—ah horrors—he just hits it back to the bowler. Now four runs are needed from three balls—although three runs would be enough, for at this stage there are only six wickets down and Derby would win on that basis.

Tunnicliffe cops another single. The penultimate ball: one to Miller on the leg-side. The entire Northants team converges on the two Derbyshire batsmen. One run to tie and victory. All depends on the last ball; it's a re-run of the semi-final. Griffiths is on his way and in the gathering gloom Tunnicliffe waits for him. Everybody in the Derbyshire camp is praying that he is not going to be bowled. Tunnicliffe makes contact with his pad and Miller charges down the pitch like a rocket and hurls himself over the crease.

Cook, having no short-leg, has to come in from silly mid-on to gather the ball and break the wicket; but too late, the scores are level and Derbyshire has won. A voice is heard from a man whose head has been under his coat for the last two overs. "Have they done it yet?" They had. They had won something for the first time since 1936.

Credit must be paid to the captain, Barry Wood, who as Geoff Cook said after the match, had transformed the team since he had taken over. Mesmerising his opponents, who never knew whether his tooth was in or not, this product of Ossett—via Lancashire—must have savoured his finest moment with the Club. Winning at any cost does not appeal to any true sportsman, but as Snoopy (my favourite philosopher) said, "It doesn't matter whether you win or lose until you lose!"

Lancashire

Bill Tidy: Cartoonist, writer and broadcaster, creator of *The Cloggies*.

Birth of the Cricket Crowd
Bill Tidy

I'll tell you later why I'm writing this in total darkness.

My county, like most others, is a one cricket-centre area. The side lives at Old Trafford and only occasionally makes mystery tours to outposts like Liverpool where I would wait as a lad, banana sandwiches in hand, hoping for a glimpse of Washbrook.

To compound the felony, they nearly always timed such sorties to Aigburth to correspond with the man's selection for England, so I don't think I ever saw him. Perhaps they didn't like the name Aigburth, an address more associated in my mind with two-way Forces Family Favourites in those days than cricket; but in the end the decision of the Lancashire committee led me to an inescapable conclusion. Much as I loved the game, I found it impossibly boring to watch. To play, and to listen to, yes, but the prospect of sitting through a three-day county game or a five-day Test was more than I could bear, and I still feel the same today.

I played a bit and listened a bit, and as Test match commentaries outnumbered Lancashire commentaries by 5−1 at least, I slowly lost contact with the county. Surrey didn't help matters much by burying the Championship for seven years, and although interest would glow a little with Hilton and Tattersall turning teams over twice in a day, I honestly can't remember a thing about Lancashire for years. They became like *Coronation Street*, just a result to look for on the back page but not one to remember. The truth is that I would have gradually forgotten what colour rose to clench between my teeth in moments of stress, had it not been for an amazing event in 1970: namely the revolutionary invention of the now famous English Cricket Crowd at Old Trafford.

Cricket audiences had existed for many years and, apart from minor changes in the peaks of members' caps, looked much the same as they did in Grace's day. Deck-chairs don't alter much either, and I defy even Professor Desmond Morris to detect any evolutionary difference between the gentle snoring of, say, 1870 and that of a century later.

Elsewhere on the cricket globe, under the influence of sun, or alcohol, spectators at games had been known to fall from trees or even remove their ties, but here nothing had changed; and who could forget '44—or was it '43?—when the cries of shocked anger which greeted a flying bomb passing Lord's occasioned a dozen members to be cautioned about their conduct and general demeanour.

No mammoth ever committed suicide by flinging itself into a block of ice just to look good even when long dead, but the cricket authority may well have toyed with the idea. Appearance seemed the thing, and that attitude would have gone on for ever had it not been for a chance mating of Lancashire, Gloucestershire, Old Trafford, King Gillette, 80,000 pints of Wilson's and the ordered movement of the sun. Who could possibly have imagined that Old Man Gillette, after insulting W.G. Grace with the throwaway safety razor and dismissing beards into limbo for half a century, should suddenly feel remorse and insist that instead of setting up a poker or baseball cup, he would provide a cricket trophy instead? Well, he did, and nothing much happened until a madness night in Manchester, Thursday, June 8, 1970, when Old Trafford in a mighty convulsion gave birth to the cricket crowd.

Previous to this happy event, watchers of the English game had been referred to as cricket lovers or spectators (see *fig.* 1), but instantly, overnight, they became a "crowd". (See *fig.* 2.) The unthinkable had happened and beer cans at Bath, bare torsos at Lord's, and streakers and men in gorilla suits at Test level were the dread but logical progression. Where it will end is anyone's guess, but there's no doubt that it started in Lancashire, at Old Trafford, on a day and night when cricket became football without the pavilion being wrecked or (another first) policemen on horses watching the game!

How many members rose stiffly from their seats to throw themselves into the ship canal or onto the track at Warwick Road Station is immaterial, for before the Gloucester game attendance at the ground had been of the Southport beach in mid-December variety, and cricket in general was in decline. Clubs like Warwickshire seemed superbly organised with money coming in from many sources and were staving off dangerous days, but I fear that had not some errant Man. United supporters, heavily *Wilsonned*, wandered into the ground that day, Lancashire could well have been just another county staggering along on Bingo and supporters' clubs crutches. They may well be today, but they must be comforted by the thought that in time of need, cometh the hour, cometh the crowd, as it did in 1970.

One-day cricket, like the illegitimate offspring of a Victorian household, was looking for a home, and hearing the racket as far away as Salford, naturally was left on the doorstep at Old Trafford. The crowd and

98

The birth of a cricket crowd: June 8, 1970

Instead of clapping and shouting "good shot", these Lancashire supporters have taken to the air. This is the first time in cricket history that a heavier-than-air watcher has left the ground. The coloured objects waved or held between the hands and shaken horizontally side to side are scarves, never before seen on a cricket ground. Prior to these gymnastics, it was generally thought impossible to wave anything with one hand and not spill a drop from the glass in the other. The terraces of Old Trafford were still wet next morning; but it wasn't beer.

Cricket Lovers, or Spectators

Note ignored fly, sleeping gent and man eating pork pie very quietly. Only four seats are occupied, although seat marked "X" may belong to man with worried expression hurrying off left of picture.

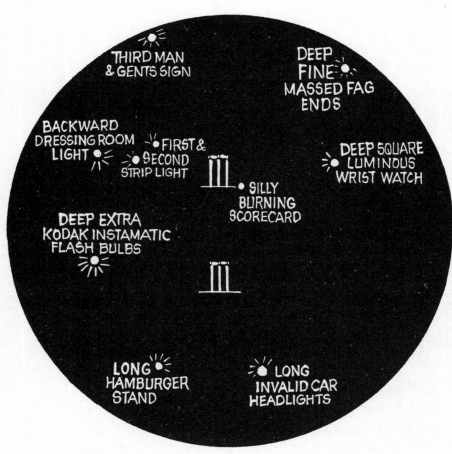

Procter's amazing sky-at-night field placing, 9:55 pm, June 8, 1970.

the game were now together, and the gods could sit back and watch something new. Nothing more seemed necessary to make Lancashire Hotpot Supreme—yet even this mixture was to pick up another ingredient by accident.

It has been the practice even back to Hambledon to play the game in daylight, bright sunshine being considered the best possible condition by players and watchers alike. When the light failed it was always due to inclement weather, and curiously enough Old Trafford earned a vile reputation for bad light, rain, and any other cosmic disturbance.

In the same way that fish in dark pot-hole pools lose their eyes but learn to sense the world around them, so the Red Rose generations evolved. It was natural that light would eventually become secondary to sound, feeling and smell.

Kerry Packer's night-time cricket series was hailed or despised as novelty, but for sheer daring it couldn't hold a floodlight to Lancashire's attempt at cricket in almost total darkness. Who could forget Gloucester captain Mike Procter's memorable sky-at-night field setting at 9.55 that evening, or his, and the side's sportsmanship in carrying on in the twilight.

I could lay out the facts and figures of the game, but they are insignificant when compared to the cosmic shift in cricket attitudes after that night's battle. If Michelangelo was better known for beating the Pope at climbing up the ladder than for painting the ceiling, then I'd say that Procter bowled and batted at lightning speed and that David Hughes belted 2×6, 2×4, 2×2 off a vital over.

Great! Gripping stuff but all repeatable, especially with Botham popping up in every department these days, but that crowd-burst was close to an immaculate conception, with no one to blame but all to rejoice in. Alas, Lancashire seem to have gone off the boil again, and I'll probably lose interest and then they'll come up with a black sightscreen or something to pull me back into the fold, but this time I'll be ready when it happens . . . which is why I'm writing with my eyes closed.

Warwickshire

Donald Trelford: Editor of the *Observer*.

Memoirs of a Stowaway
Donald Trelford

These days the train from Coventry to Birmingham is an Inter-City that glides through villages with Shakespearean names like Hampton-in-Arden, past cows and horses and hedgerows and redbrick farms with white picket fencing and an XJS in the drive. At the time I first remember it—immediately after the war—it was a very different journey. The line jerked more slowly through the coalfields and urban sprawl of north Warwickshire—stopping at places like Foleshill, where we scrambled aboard, 10-year-old stowaways, our Dad's Army haversacks laden with pop, crisps, spam and our sacred cricket scorebooks; on through George Eliot country—Bedworth, Nuneaton, Stockingford, Arley, Water Orton—then through the smoke of Castle Bromwich, Bromford Bridge, and into a bomb-scarred New Street station.

For a small boy from Coventry in the late 1940s the route to Edgbaston was more than a journey: it was an education. From the top of the 48 bus through Birmingham you caught your first sight of coloured immigrants in the crowded street-stalls of Balsall Heath, all fruit, noise and vegetables; as you neared the County Ground you glimpsed, through neat hedges and trees, the suburban villas of middle-class Moseley—not so much two nations as two worlds. Strangely, perhaps, it wasn't the contrast between poverty and wealth that most impinged on a young boy's mind—that came later—it was the contrast between teeming, almost frightening commotion and an elegant, unmatchable repose.

The ground itself—at the time I'm thinking of—had something of the same Edwardian serenity. In fact, I find the faded sepia turn-of-the-century pictures in the pavilion more familiar than the shops, bars and ballrooms of today. This isn't so surprising really, since the stadium can hardly have changed much in the first half of this century; the "improvements" came later. The ground on which A.C.S. Glover gave his celebrated leap for joy at dismissing W.G. Grace in 1895 was recognisably the same as the one on which I saw his fellow leg-spinner,

Eric Hollies, rejoice after bowling Bradman in 1948 (a feat he repeated ten days later in Bradman's last Test). This same Glover, evidently an emotional man, once hurled the ball into the crowd—*while captain*—in response to an insult, and injured an elderly couple.

Looking towards the pavilion from the scoreboard at the other end, you had a double-decker stand on the right and open raked concrete seating on the left. All gone now, like the Balsall Heath slums, but the pavilion bell-tower is still reassuringly there, along with the raspberry brick Victorian terrace over long-off and the church spire over long-on. So is the Committee room under the bell-tower, affording what H.S. Altham has described as the best view of cricket in the world. But we didn't know about Committee rooms, nor the inside of pavilions, at the time I first saw the ground.

Edgbaston's urbanity struck us all the more forcibly after the Courtaulds ground in Coventry, where the county sometimes played. This was redolent of the dour atmosphere of works league cricket, of asphalt, coke, corrugated iron fencing and the smell of the textile factory.

But first you had to get into Edgbaston. We sometimes forget that locked gates and crowds spilling over the boundary ropes are not just a product of the limited over game. Warwickshire's record crowds were achieved in the 1950s and will never be beaten now. There were enormous queues outside the ground for the visit of the Australians in 1948—many of whom were too late to catch the quaint sight of Bradman going out for the toss in a three-piece suit and a trilby hat. The ground always seemed to be full in those days—for which my mates and I were duly grateful as we collected abandoned pop bottles from under seats and returned them at twopence a time to recoup the entrance fee.

I remember the season of 1946 because my closest pal's father, an all-rounder called Jim Melville, played a few games for the county. He later achieved even greater celebrity as the man who stopped the pavilion clock at Courtaulds with a six over square leg. His son and I used to practise behind the scorebox when Hollies, Hazell of Somerset or Peter Smith of Essex were bowling endless maidens.

I must have seen the county in 1947, too, because I can clearly recall the bustling action of Vic Cannings, an opening bowler who returned to Hampshire and now coaches cricket at Eton. I also saw a bulky-looking Walter Hammond, a ghost haunting his own legend, walk back in a painful silence after scoring seven laborious singles. A happier sight was the dashing Peter Cranmer, the pre-war rugby hero, a cravat at his neck, hitting huge sixes into the gardens round the Courtaulds ground—64 runs in half an hour, if I remember right.

But 1948 was the year it all came together. That was the year we planned our stowaway trips to Birmingham, waiting for the train to slow down at a signals halt outside Foleshill station, then clambering in on a bend where the guard couldn't see us. I still have a flattened thumb-nail which came from banging the door too fast on one of these excursions. How we got out of New Street station without a ticket I can't quite recall; but we were extremely small, quick and cunning, and the crowd round the barrier was extremely dense.

That year it began to come together for Warwickshire cricket too. Some of the pre-war players had given way to the new generation—Dick Spooner, Alan Townsend, Bert Wolton and, above all in my memory, the New Zealander Tom Pritchard. Pritch was the first truly fast bowler I ever saw and he is the one against whom I have come to measure all fast bowlers. By this standard the bald Charlie Grove at the other end was a trundling medium pace, though he could move the ball about a bit in the mornings.

I've heard it said since by experts, including *Wisden*, that Pritchard wasn't really one of the fastest because he hadn't enough body in his action, not enough "back", to make the ball work for him. Mind you, none of these experts had faced him at the other end. He looked pretty quick to me and truly intimidating for the first few overs of an innings. He took 166 wickets at an average of 15 in 1948. I saw nobody quicker in English county cricket before Trueman, Statham and Tyson in the early 1950s. Pritchard created an exciting sense of danger, the mark of the authentic fast bowler. My father remembers the Australian, McDonald, creating the same kind of expectation in a North-country crowd in 1921; he also remembers him knocking a stump most of the way to the boundary.

Memory can play tricks with speed, of course. In the Edgbaston pavilion there is a photograph of the legendary Kortright in the moment of releasing the ball in 1896. The whole field is shown, with the wicket-keeper standing upright and half-way back, second slip in a daydream and mid-off barely interested. There is certainly no sense of urgency or danger there. This may not mean he wasn't fast. The lesson may simply be that, while standards of batting and bowling haven't changed all that much over eighty years—at least among good players—standards of fielding have been revolutionised. Standards of umpiring too: Alan Smith, the Warwickshire Secretary, points out that in this picture the umpire isn't even standing behind the stumps, which must have made lbw even more of a lottery than in India.

Assumptions about the idea of progress in cricket, culminating in the notional supremacy of the modern game, can be facile. We should never forget that Wilfred Rhodes was in the same England side as W.G. Grace, yet went on to play Test cricket until 1931, by which time giants like Bradman and Hammond had begun to make their mark—and both of them were still around after World War Two to play with "moderns" such as Compton, Bedser and Bailey.

Warwickshire, it has to be noted, had turned down "W. Rhodes of Huddersfield" when he applied to join the Edgbaston ground staff in 1897. But why pick a Yorkshireman to demonstrate cricket's long-term continuity when there's Willie Quaife, Warwickshire's own W.G., who first turned out for the county in 1893 (the year before they joined the County Championship) and hung up his pads, reluctantly, with a century in his farewell match at the age of 56? Over 33,000 runs in as many years, plus nearly a thousand wickets (including that of W.G. Grace, clean-bowled on two occasions), saving the sweetest of his 72 hundreds to the very last—to prove his point to the club committee, a fitting end to the career of a lifelong rebel.

Quaife, according to *Wisden*, "was one of the shortest men who ever figured largely in important cricket". The most correct of players, always unhurried, he anchored the Warwickshire batting for a quarter of a century. His brother Walter topped the national averages in 1897, and his son Bernard also played for the county, but W.G.—a stern, nut-like man in the pictures—outlasted them all.

By the time Quaife retired in 1928, R.E.S. Wyatt was launched on the great all-round career that was to bring him the captaincy of county and country in quick succession. Known as the most brittle of players because he broke so many bones, Wyatt (who always kept count of his score, as if he didn't trust the scoreboard) dominated Warwickshire cricket in the pre-war period. To me, however, Wyatt will always be associated with Worcestershire, his adopted county after the war. The name that personified Warwickshire cricket was Tom Dollery, who started in 1932 and became the county's first professional captain in 1948. To me, he *was* the bear with the ragged staff, the county's emblem. At the time I could never understand why Dollery wasn't an automatic choice for England—though looking back, it was clearly a vintage period for batsmen, with Hutton, Washbrook, Compton, Bill Edrich and Simpson in full flow. I am surprised that Dollery's career average was only 38, though he doubtless suffered from always batting at number five: it's openers and number threes who generally get into the record books.

I can see Dollery batting now: a strong, assured-looking figure, sleeves rolled up, his bat as broad as a barn door. He played the "professional" shots with great ease—the leg glance, the trickle to third man with angled bat off the front foot, the push off the pads in front of square leg. He timed his innings patiently: a slow start, the gathering of singles and twos, mostly to leg, then, when he was properly set, opening his chest for the cover drive and pull over mid-wicket into the crowd. His bat sounded sweet, like that of the great stroke-players, Graveney,

Cowdrey or Gooch.

He had the air of a man wholly at ease with himself, a true yeoman, a natural leader. I remember a great innings of 173 against Somerset in 1953, when he overhauled Fred Gardner in no time after giving him several hours' start: they put on over 200 together.

Dollery's great comrade-in-arms was Eric Hollies, whose career also straddled the war, and to whom he sometimes kept wicket. Hollies took 2,200 wickets for the county at an average of 20; and 100 wickets in a season fourteen times. Although his leg-spin didn't "take" overseas, he could be devastating against tourists in England—never more so than against Bradman's Australians in 1948. Leslie Duckworth, the historian of Warwickshire cricket, has described Hollies's bowling in that match as the finest of his career; others recall his ten for 49 against Notts in the same season, which he achieved without the help of fieldsmen. Duckworth's description bears repeating: "Flighting the ball beautifully, varying his pace and spin and apparently able to pitch the ball where he wanted at will, Hollies soon had both Bradman and Hassett playing with the light of acute and uneasy speculation in their eyes."

On that occasion Hollies bowled Bradman with a top-spinner. More important, the great man didn't seem to have spotted Hollies's googly—or so Hollies and Dollery thought. When Bradman came out for his last Test innings shortly afterwards at the Oval, Hollies bowled him a googly second ball—with the famous result that Bradman got a duck and thereby ended his career with a Test average of 99.9 instead of 100. That evening Hollies rang Dollery to report triumphantly: "He never saw it, Tom!"

Eric Hollies (even the name, like Tom Dollery, sounds quintessentially English) was a stocky, fair-haired man from the Black Country, cheerful and ever-eager to bowl. He was one of the most naggingly accurate bowlers of all time—for a leg-spinner, bowling out of the back of the hand, quite remarkably so. He came up to the wicket with a hop and a skip of which I can still do a fair imitation, and flighted the ball more than a modern bowler would dare. When he had trouble with his knee or his ankle, as he often did towards the end, he could do without a run-up at all.

Whenever I read Alan Ross's poem, "Watching Benaud Bowl"—one of the few really good poems among the many bad ones about cricket—I mentally rename it, "Watching Hollies Bowl":

> *Leg-spinners pose problems much like love,*
> *Requiring commitment, the taking of a chance.*
> *Half-way deludes; the bold advance.*
>
> *Right back, there's time to watch*

Developments, though maybe too late.
It's not spectacular, but can conciliate.

Instinctively romantics move towards,
Preventing complexities by their embrace,
Batsman and lover embarked as overlords.

Hollies got far more wickets than runs in his career—a rare feat. His batting was a friendly joke in which the whole county shared (though he never saw the joke himself). I remember the ironic cheers that greeted every successful attempt to put bat on ball: a run was a riot (there weren't many of these, however: his career average was 4.94, assisted by 258 not-outs!).

Dollery and Hollies were the backbone of the Championship squad of 1951—that "extraordinary team of ordinary players", as the skipper later described it. They didn't seem ordinary to me. Not Pritchard. Not Spooner, the left-handed opener who was also a *stumper* in the old sense, actually stumping batsmen out (157 of them, mostly off Hollies). He had a brisk walk between overs, hurrying with his body bent forward, his peaked cap and his big nose to the fore, gloved hands behind his back. He also had a classic cover drive, forcing the pace when Fred Gardner was in one of his catatonic moods.

Nor Alan Townsend, surely one of the safest post-war slip fielders, to be compared with Sharpe of Yorkshire; the catches stuck to him like glue. He also had a knack of breaking long stands with a nippy medium-pace off the pitch, using a lot of shoulder like Dexter or D'Oliveira. Nor Bert Wolton, a handsome upright batsman with jet-black hair who drove very straight, often over the top, and a brilliant cover point.

Other names from this period are Jimmy Ord, a tiny batsman with nimble feet and a slashing square cut; J.R. Thompson, a Marlborough schoolmaster who hit a stylish hundred in the summer holidays; A.H. Kardar, the elegant Oxford all-rounder who played for both India and Pakistan; Fred Gardner, the apotheosis of works league cricket, the most stolid and slowest of openers, his wide face like an unsmiling Bob Hope, though he beamed as he took a hundred off Hassett's Australians in 1953.

A little later came Ray Hitchcock, a punchy left-handed hitter from New Zealand; I once saw him drop a catch on the boundary then throw the batsman out in his rage. Jim Stewart was the county's biggest hitter since J.H. Parsons—17 sixes, a world record, at Blackpool in 1959; he came close to playing for England at both cricket and rugby, and lost a big toe in mid-career. Norman Horner was a busy opener, always eager to press on, who scored a cracking double-century at the Oval in an unbroken stand of 377 with Billy Ibadulla. Ibadulla created another record with 166 on his Test debut for Pakistan against Australia in 1964.

Three quick bowlers who toiled with some success on the ungiving Edgbaston turf were Roly Thompson, Jack Bannister and Ossie Wheatley, a big blond character who had broken all records at Cambridge and later captained Glamorgan. Bannister, who changed his style completely after a back specialist told him to give up the game, once took all ten wickets in an innings—and was dropped for the next match.

Tom Cartwright was in a special category, an injury-prone swing bowler who was sometimes unplayable in English conditions. I once faced him at soccer when he was outside-right for Foxford school in Coventry, so I followed his early career very closely and wished him towards a hundred in his first game for the county in 1952—he was out for 82. It was another ten years before he fulfilled his early promise as a batsman with 210 against Middlesex.

Random memories of opponents come flooding back too. Dickie Dodds of Essex, a tall, thin opening bat, characteristically driving four boundaries in the first over and getting out for 20; an elegant 96 by L.B. Fishlock, the great Surrey opener; another stylish left-hander, M.P. Donnelly, the New Zealander, promising much but scoring little when I was watching; "Writer" P.B.H. May, in the Navy on his National Service, scoring a precocious 98; G.H.G. Doggart looking in disbelief at the Courtaulds turf as the ball jumped over his hands in front of the sightscreen; Keith Miller swinging his bat jauntily as he walked out to the wicket with his side hundreds of runs ahead, a wild swing at the first ball, a six off the second, then out, swinging his bat all the way back to the pavilion.

The best game I saw in the 1950s, perhaps the greatest in Edgbaston's history—*Wisden* called it "one of the most remarkable matches of all time"—was England v. West Indies in 1957, which brought Test cricket back to the county after a gap of thirty years (though Botham's Test last summer must run it close for excitement). The sun was so strong on the Saturday that it burned one side of this spectator's face and not the other. It was pretty hot on the field, too, with Ramadhin (seven for 49) bowling England out for 186. The West Indies scored 474, thanks largely to 161 by Collie Smith, a powerful striker who later died in a car accident. As we trailed home on the Saturday night, with England 102 for two in the second innings, our only faint hope had been lit by two defiant cover-drives from Peter May just before the close.

The rest is history: May 285 not out, Cowdrey 154, after a partnership of 411, England's highest ever. I saw every ball of the first four days, including the best of the English fight-back, which carried an extra symbolic load, as sport often does, in the year after the Suez disaster. But I missed the last day because I had to report back to the RAF for an athletics meet. We heard it all on the radio, however, as a demoralised West Indies slipped to 72 for seven, with Laker and Lock on the rampage. The criticism of May which followed—for not declaring earlier—was incomprehensible to anyone who had seen him hold England together by his own tenacious mixture of technique and temperament. Ramadhin's performance under pressure—two for 179 in 98 overs (a record)—also deserves a mention in history's despatches.

Towards the end of the fifties came the mighty Smiths—A.C. and M.J.K.—both of whom have made a powerful imprint on the county's history. Mike's *annus mirabilis* was 1959, that glorious summer, when he scored over 3,000 runs, most of them steered round the leg-side. Before that he had scored 2,000 runs for four successive seasons. For all his dazzling sporting triumphs—he also played fly-half for Oxford and England and captained the country at cricket—Mike Smith always remained something of an anti-hero, a tall spidery figure in glasses, the school swot, playing down the glamour and the drama, getting on with the job. Curiously, for a man with less than perfect eyesight, his secret seemed to be in the eye—or in that vital junction where eye, hand and brain move together. He was a brilliant short-leg catcher, breaking all county records; an odd sporting phenomenon, with a built-in radar system of his own.

Alan Smith was a golden boy from Birmingham who won cricket and soccer blues at Oxford. He was a natural athlete with cricket in his bones. His batting was a frequent disappointment—to himself above all— except in the limited over game, where he twice made the winning hit for the county in its only Gillette Cup victories. He played for England as a wicket-keeper, but always preferred to be bowling with his whirling windmill action, and once stripped off the gloves to take a hat-trick against Essex—Fletcher and Bailey were among his victims that day. He also led Warwickshire undefeated to the Championship in 1972. He was a skilful captain, with a profound love of cricket and a pleasing personality, and is now one of the game's leading administrators.

One of his greatest coups for the county was to sign up Rohan Kanhai, the son of a Guyanese cane-cutter, on a trip to the West Indies (he had actually gone out to look at another player). In his period at Edgbaston Kanhai averaged well over 50, which makes him the county's most successful batsman ever, ahead of Mike Smith, Amiss, Barber, Dollery, Wyatt, Parsons, the Quaifes, the Santalls, Bates, Kilner, Groom, Kinneir, Foster or the improbably named Julius Caesar, who appears in the club's earliest records.

Kanhai learned his early cricket without pads or gloves, which may account for his strength at cutting and hooking, skills exercised away from the body. An unsublimated anger in Kanhai's batting has prompted the sombre thought in more than one observer that the real, the symbolic point about cricket is to assert the power of bat over ball, of man over nature, life over death. Lance Gibbs, Deryck Murray and Alvin Kallicharran were other successful Caribbean imports to the county.

Alan Smith's Championship side of 1972 had Kanhai in his best season, Kallicharran in his first, Mike Smith in his "second coming", Amiss emerging into full flower, the young Whitehouse bursting on the scene, a Jameson who sadly couldn't recapture his incomparable stroke-making of the year before, plus Gibbs, McVicker and David Brown, the long-serving England fast bowler who is now the county's cricket manager. Alan Smith himself led the bowling averages, having put Murray behind the stumps.

Willis didn't qualify until the July of that season, having been vetted over dinner at the Carlton Tower by Alan Smith and the chairman, the late Edmund King, who liked to ensure that Warwickshire's recruits were decent chaps off the field as well as good performers on it—perhaps a key to the county's comparatively peaceful dressing-room morale over the years. But the rangy Willis made a vital contribution to the title by bowling out Derbyshire with eight for 44, including a hat-trick. He went on to become the county's—and indeed the country's—leading fast bowler throughout the seventies, his great heart pushing him on even after his huge body had started to feel the strain.

Dennis Amiss, born in Birmingham, is also worth a special mention in any account of Warwickshire cricket. I first heard of him over twenty years ago from a friend—the same one I had practised with as a child—who had played with him in county youth games. Already Amiss's short-arm technique had made him almost impregnable. His problem later was his lack of confidence: once he realised how good he was, he became a formidable player. In my view, and that of many others, England discarded him just as he reached his full maturity as a batsman. He was the best possible partner to Boycott.

The victory in 1972 was Warwickshire's third county title, the others going to Dollery's team in 1951 and to F.R. Foster's side in 1911. Which was the best? In 1972 they won most convincingly by 36 points, but the class of 1911 had some great stars, including the two Warwickshire players I would most like to have seen—Foster himself and the Rev. J.H. Parsons.

F.R. Foster was a flamboyant character whose flame burned brightly for just a few seasons before the First World War. For those few seasons he was the most dashing player in the game, winning matches single-handed, Botham-style, with bat or ball. He was quite unreliable. After being appointed Warwickshire captain at the age of 22, he immediately announced his retirement from cricket because of a romantic attachment, then reappeared for the next match. He was often on what he called "binges" the night before a match, even while on tour for England. On one occasion he had to be sobered up at 7.00 am, fed steak and beer for breakfast, then sent onto the field to open the bowling.

He bowled fastish left-arm over the wicket and formed a deadly attack with S.F. Barnes in Australia in 1912; they took 66 wickets between them in the Tests. (Barnes's family had his ashes buried at Edgbaston, marked by a wicket gate, even though he took only three wickets for Warwickshire at the start of his long and distinguished career.) Foster had that rare gift of picking up more speed off the wicket than he had through the air, and swung the ball about prodigiously. Only E.J. "Tiger" Smith, who followed the great A.A. Lilley behind the stumps for both Warwickshire and England, could keep to him without conceding numerous byes.

Foster's philosophy was that "The bat should always beat the clock." He obeyed his own precept most memorably against Worcestershire at Dudley in 1914, when he hit 305 not out in four hours ten minutes, still a county record. He joined the Royal Flying Corps, injured a foot badly in a motorcycle accident in 1915, and never played cricket again, retiring to the family clothing chain. A great career all over by the age of 26.

Another Warwickshire career cut off tragically young was that of Percy Jeeves, an all-rounder killed in Flanders in 1916. P.G. Wodehouse saw him play at Cheltenham in 1913 and borrowed the name for Bertie Wooster's manservant, as he admits in a letter to the club. Wodehouse also wrote much later from his exile in America to say: "I never wear any tie except the Warwickshire."

J.H. Parsons was not so much a Wodehouse character as a hero from Kipling or a Buchan adventure yarn. His father was chef at Brasenose College, Oxford, and later ran a pub in Birmingham. Parsons himself was working as a car-tester in the new motor industry in Coventry when he was invited to play for Warwickshire Seconds. He scored 200 on his first appearance and soon found himself a pro in the county side that won the Championship.

When war came in 1914 he fought at Gallipoli, was commissioned in the field and won an MC in the last British cavalry charge at Huj, which led to the capture of Jerusalem. Having acquired a taste for soldiering, he stayed on in the Indian Army, serving five years on the North West Frontier.

He was away from county cricket, except for occasional leaves, for ten years—from the age of 24 to 34—which must be the main reason why he never played for England. He did, however, play for both the Gentlemen and the Players and toured with the MCC in India, causing a stir by insisting on going to church during Sunday matches.

He was a powerful driver off the front foot, disdaining deflections. Two of his finest innings were 161 against the visiting West Indies in 1928 and 190 against New Zealand three years later. He hit the West Indian bowler Scott for four straight sixes before being brilliantly caught on the boundary by Learie Constantine. At the age of 70 he hit 65 in 43 minutes, including four sixes, against Solihull School, making the boys' hands tingle at his driving.

He was ordained in 1929 after the Archdeacon of Coventry had talked him into it between innings at Edgbaston. He was later a Canon at Truro Cathedral and a Chaplain in the Second World War. It is said that on Saturdays he used to be excused from the slips so that he could prepare his sermons while fielding in the deep.

Parsons described his early days with Warwickshire thus: "The old pros were grand fellows. They all, either consciously or unconsciously, played according to the principles of the game." For Parsons "the principles of the game" included a straight bat and hard driving. But he also meant something more—a concern for values that go wider than cricket and yet are an essential part of it. That was what a small boy dimly sensed at the club all those years ago. It is why being top of the table isn't the only thing that matters to Warwickshire—nor being bottom either!

Kent

Colin Cowdrey: Oxford University, Kent and England. Skippered Kent from 1957-71, equalling Lord Harris's record of fifteen years as captain.

The White Horse Rampant
Colin Cowdrey

I drew back the curtains and was relieved to find a hazy blue sky, the August sun of 1948 bursting through to dispense the mist in time for an 11.30 start on the St Lawrence Ground at Canterbury. To a fifteen-year-old, invited to play there for the first time, it was a traumatic occasion; an honour of course, but certainly an ordeal. I was so anxious to do well that my excitement was tempered with a nervous tension we call butterflies. The time would not pass by, and the hours between waking and bowling the first ball seemed something of a prison sentence.

This was the start of a week's cricket for schoolboys, a series of three two-day matches against Sussex, Middlesex and Surrey. No spectators as such, just a few dutiful members of family in support, yet the atmosphere was quite overwhelming. Here I was walking out to bat where all the greats had trod. I could scarcely believe it was happening to me.

Most young lads with a passion for cricket have read their *Wisden* and have become familiar with all the names. I knew every Kent name, many of their deeds too, but it was the initials that really stuck with me. Did Leslie Ames really have the initials LEG? Whenever I meet someone with the name of Wright, he is always DVP in my mind; yet Freeman was never AP, always Tich. The captains who I idolised were JRM, APF, and BHV. Mason, Chapman and Valentine, each having a tremendous influence upon the character and style of Kent cricket.

Strangely, I first came to have a feel for Kent in the air-raid shelters in 1940–1. My best friend, being slightly older than I was, bagged Surrey and I was always Kent, as we played our dot cricket using the dice and a proper scorebook, meticulously kept. The games were hard fought, and I recall becoming grumpy on more than one occasion when Surrey got into a strong position. We played two-innings matches, home and away. The Oval and Rectory Field, Blackheath, in the traditional fashion. It was here I came to identify the names: Fagg, Todd, Ames and Valentine leading the batting; Harding, Watt and Wright shouldering the bowling.

Now, here in this schoolboys' cricket week, I was hanging my clothes on Arthur Fagg's peg; and it used to be Bill Ashdown's before him. It is a lovely thing about cricket that the players seem to home back to the same peg, or chair or corner, year after year. On most of the grounds in England, I could walk in and know where I had changed. I could visualise my locker and peg at Sydney and Melbourne, Barbados and Port of Spain. In my early matches, the youngsters were always careful to see that the old 'uns were settled in before putting down their bag, or hanging their coat on a peg. It was Johnny Wardle who threw my jacket off a peg in Capetown—"My lucky spot here"—and then went on to take twelve wickets to win the Test match. Conversely: "Who'll swop," cried Geoff Pullar, "I got nought and one and dropped a 'percher' at mid-on last visit—don't want that peg again." These superstitious touches in search of that little extra luck are all part of the game.

In fact my first meeting of the Kent players was at Grace Road, Leicester. I was rising fourteen, in August 1946, having just made the First Eleven at Tonbridge. I was on holiday on a farm in Leicestershire and Ewart Astill, the Leicester and England all-rounder, who had been our coach during the term, had promised to take me to my first county match. By an extraordinary coincidence the only day that fitted was the occasion of Kent's visit. I was taken into the Leicester dressing room to meet Leslie Berry and Maurice Tompkin, then to the Kent dressing room. There was the astonishing sight of Leslie Ames wearing nothing but his Kent cap. In a moment or two, he had slipped a singlet and pants on and there we stood for several minutes in conversation, the great idol LEG being kind enough to ask me all about my summer term's cricket at Tonbridge. But I came to discover that his first act of changing every day was to fish out the Kent cap and put it on.

I spent an hour or so sitting with the Kent players as they struggled to cope with the vagaries of Jack Walsh, the Australian-born slow left-arm Chinaman and googly bowler. He was a superb bowler who spun the ball prodigiously both ways, with two googlies, one less hidden than the other. There were very few batsmen who could hold their hand on their heart and honestly declare that they had him under control. We were all sitting behind the line that morning with a clear view of every ball that Jack bowled: the Kent players would be shouting out which they thought it was. We had a lot of fun, as not many balls went by without a diversity of opinion. Then there would be an argument when the batsman had successfully smothered the spin as to whether it had been a Chinaman or googly, judging the spin of the ball as it glanced off the bat. It was much easier from the pavilion, too!

I left the Kent dressing room with a deep impression of the fun that they were having. With the financial stakes in low key, as they were in my early years, it was easier to keep the humour as high priority. He was a dull captain who did not keep his team laughing and in good spirits. Now, of course, winning means so much, not just in prestige but to the individual pocket, that a player who smiles could be viewed as lacking dedication. It is one of those myths that have developed and it is going to be hard to alter.

I like to think that the Kent cricketer, and playing in Kent, has been known for the fun and good humour engendered. Over the years, countless cricketers have said to me how lucky we are to play on so many lovely grounds, amid such pleasant countryside. Unsophisticated grounds too, but not primitive; most importantly, we have been able to play more amongst trees than concrete stands and soulless terraces. It was a cruel blow to us when the ground at Canterbury, our proud jewel, so noted for its tree surround (and a tree within the boundary no less), was savaged by Dutch Elm disease. Every tree has been replaced, but slowly, so slowly, the effectiveness and beauty of the screen emerges.

In a strange sort of way this was the story of my own experience with Kent. Once my Oxford days finished and I was able to play full time with the county, I found that most of the household names had disappeared from view. Arthur Fagg and Douglas Wright were in their final years, although Godfrey Evans was still in prime form, earning his England place. For some ten years, we were a team of young elms doing our best to replace our mature and distinguished predecessors. So often when the wind got up, we were not strong enough to hold firm. It was a frustrating, tantalising period. I was fortunate that Leslie Ames was appointed Cricket Manager to be at my elbow, and he became just as permanent and vital as the famous tree within the boundary.

After a few years in the wilderness, the young players began to acquire a taste for the challenge again. Out of the blue, Derek Underwood and Alan Knott climbed onto the stage to take leading parts, although still tender in years. John Shepherd was drawn from the lovely cricket haven in Barbados to make his life and home in Canterbury. How could we have won without his remarkable all-round prowess, and more important, his enchanting personality? Then, one day, with Pakistan our guests at Canterbury, a beautiful sylph-figured athlete by the name of Asif Iqbal caught our eye with his running in the outfield and his incisive stroke-play; everything he did accompanied by a delightful smile. He developed an attraction for Kent cricket and has played a huge part in our successes. Asif, and John Shepherd too, embodied the spirit of attack which lifted our cricket out of the ordinary.

We were fortunate also to meet with Michael Denness from Ayr, a beautiful strokeplayer and glorious fielder. He set up a superb partnership with the rocklike Brian Luckhurst. It was fitting that both Luckhurst and

Denness won England caps and toured Australia, Denness as captain. As my support and vice-captain, Alan Dixon made an invaluable contribution which has been much underrated. He had known the days of our agonising struggles and was able to bring a calm philosophical approach in our more heady days, grateful for the turn in the wheel of fortune.

The excitement began in 1967. For a while it looked as if we could win the County Championship. It was a traumatic finish to the season as we ended runners-up to Yorkshire, winning eleven matches to their twelve. By way of compensation, Kent beat Somerset in the final of the Gillette Cup at Lord's. We then had to wait for a week to find out whether Yorkshire could beat Gloucestershire at Harrogate for the Championship. It would have been a distinguished double for us if they hadn't; but alas, the rain-affected uncovered wicket at Harrogate proved too much for Gloucestershire, who were beaten by an innings and 76 runs inside two days. So—and we had realised that rain was our best chance—our hopes were dashed, but we could be pleased with a good season.

We were proud, too, that at Bradford earlier in the year we had bowled Yorkshire out for 40. Rain deprived us of following this through to a result, but fast-bowler Norman Graham will always remember his six for 14; a match notable for Geoffrey Boycott falling to him for a pair. In the return match in Canterbury Week, we had to take them on during a Test at Trent Bridge: Boycott and Close out of the Yorkshire team, Knott, Underwood and myself from Kent. The gates were closed on each of the first two days, more than forty thousand people cramming in to see the game. Alan Dixon had a superb match as Kent captain and the capacity crowds enjoyed the sight of Godfrey Evans making a return to county cricket, deputising for Knott in his forty-eighth year, eight years after his official retirement. He kept wicket brilliantly. Kent held their own for two days, but eventually went down by six wickets in a memorable match.

In 1968, we built upon the successes of the previous year. This time, Kent won twelve matches out of the twenty-eight and Yorkshire only eleven, yet once again we came second in the table. A new bonus points incentive scheme had been introduced, and as we licked our wounds, we had to concede that in experience Yorkshire had the edge over us.

In 1969, we hoped for so much. Now we really did begin to feel as if we had sufficient experience. Denness, Luckhurst, Asif, Cowdrey, Johnson, Ealham, Knott, Shepherd, Dixon, Underwood, Brown, Dye, Graham. Leary was in reserve, a fine games player with a wise head. Nicholls played a valuable part as reserve wicket-keeper and pugnacious left-handed batsman, and young Bob Woolmer was showing his great potential.

It was my thirteenth year as captain but nothing went right, although we looked a good side and played a lot of good cricket in front of feverishly excited and expectant crowds in Kent. Mid-season, I broke an Achilles tendon and played no part in July and August. Our supporters could hardly bear it as we sank to tenth place. Had the bubble burst?

Happily, 1970 came to be our year: the first Championship win since our years of domination in 1906, 1909, 1910, 1913. Yet, and I shudder as I recollect our gloom at the time, Kent stood bottom of the table on June 30.

It all began at Harlow against Essex. While I was away at a Test match, Mike Denness led us to a fine win, having scored 167 himself on the opening day. He captained the side to victory over Hampshire at Maidstone; then I had the satisfaction of being back in the saddle when Underwood helped us to beat Somerset at Weston-super-Mare, Denness making another fine hundred.

The matches against Gloucestershire at Cheltenham and Surrey at Blackheath were both cliffhangers. On the last day at Cheltenham, with the ball spinning, Kent chased 340 and got them with a wicket to spare. In the first innings, we had escaped the follow-on by a single run. Gloucestershire looked certain to win, especially as we were without four Test players, Knott, Luckhurst, Shepherd and myself. Denness and Asif put on 105 in ninety-five minutes, Denness finishing with 97 and Asif 109; two remarkable innings. But we must salute the cool, calm Stuart Leary, making a rare appearance, who found himself with number eleven John Dye needing just two runs to win, and managed to squeeze them out.

If this match was not enough, who will forget Graham Johnson's fine bowling at Blackheath against Surrey. He took twelve wickets in the game, which ended with a great catch by Asif. Once again the latter had produced a delightful attacking hundred. Surrey were left 263 to win; then with just two balls remaining and the light fading, they needed twelve. Graham Johnson tossed up a slow, well-flighted, tempting half-volley to Pat Pocock, Surrey tail-ender but no mean striker of a cricket ball. He moved into it well and drove it high over mid-off, apparently a certain six. Asif was stationed at deep long-on, although he could hardly be seen from the middle against the backcloth of the crowd underneath the dark football stand. As the ball rose above the skyline, Asif set off at full sprint in the general direction; as he neared the line of the ball, he caught sight of it again, leapt high and caught it, just as it was soaring over the boundary and into the crowd for six. Once again, we had snatched a dramatic victory.

It was only now we felt that we had just an outside chance of the Championship. It had been a very open year; the even nature of the counties shown by the fact that seven at one time or another headed the table, some on more than one occasion. Whilst Kent were languishing near the foot of the table, Northamptonshire set the early pace but were soon overtaken by Lancashire, then Sussex and the eventual challengers Glamorgan. Sussex went ahead again, and Surrey came to the fore. Lancashire had a good run and went neck and neck with Surrey. Suddenly a new challenger, Derbyshire, came to the top of the table, but were promptly overtaken by Glamorgan.

Amid all this excitement, our position had been strengthening in the middle of the pack. It was all going to hinge on Folkestone Week with games against Nottinghamshire and Leicestershire, with a final match, which could prove the decider, against Surrey at The Oval.

The weather at Folkestone was gloriously sunny, but the pitch was almost too perfect as we looked for two definite results. Twice in the first match against Notts we had the mortification of being put to the sword by Garfield Sobers at his glorious best. Bowlers and fielders just stood around as pawns when Sobers was in full flow, and the Kent crowd watched in admiration, but rather forlornly, as their hopes appeared to be swept away. On the final afternoon, we were left 282 runs to win in three hours; just 94 an hour. Denness and Luckhurst gave us a superb start. Asif scored 56 in fifty minutes, and coming to the last twenty overs we needed 112 to win. In a tight finish Alan Knott suddenly wafted three remarkable boundaries, with extraordinary innovation, and we had won with an over to spare. By an standards, it had been a splendid cricket match, but in the context of our chase for the Championship, this victory came as a gift from the gods and a priceless fillip.

As we celebrated in the Folkestone Cricket Club tent we reminded ourselves of our good luck, for at one point on the second morning with the ball moving about in the early heat haze before the sun broke through, we had slumped to 27 for five and the follow-on loomed large in the face of Nottinghamshire's total of 376. David Halfyard, old Kentish warhorse now turned adversary, took three for eight in nine overs and almost punctured our title hopes. But Brian Luckhurst held firm, and his 156 was one of the most important innings of his career. Alan Ealham has always enjoyed Folkestone and he has never played better than his 57 that day. John Shepherd weighed in with a valuable 47. Now we were top of the table and if we could beat Leicestershire, we really would hold the whip hand.

Leicester won the toss on a good wicket and at 119 for three just after lunch, they seemed to be on their way. Then, quite unexpectedly, the ball began to swing. John Shepherd, ably supported by young Bob Woolmer, had an inspired spell, taking four wickets for nine runs in 21 balls. It was a lovely piece of bowling on a good wicket, and the kind of performance which John had been able to pull out of the hat on so many occasions over the years.

Once again, and appropriately, it was Denness and Luckhurst who gave us the solid start we needed with an opening stand of 98. Asif tore the Leicestershire bowling apart, and this was followed by some devastating stroke-play from Graham Johnson (108) and John Shepherd (37).

After a week under a hot sun, the Folkestone wicket became responsive to spin and as Leicestershire began their second innings 269 runs behind, it was Derek Underwood who carved out victory with six wickets. We won the match by an innings and forty runs, and this result with its array of bonus points took us seventeen points clear at the head of the Championship Table, with only Glamorgan having a chance of catching up.

We moved to the Oval, knowing that if we could gather four or five points we were out of range. I won the toss on a grey, murky morning when the ball was likely to move around, and put Surrey in. It was vital that we should pick up whatever bowling points we could. And so on September 9, 1970, with Surrey 150 for nine through some very good bowling from Shepherd and Woolmer, the latter giving notice of his enormous promise with five for 40, we had secured four of the vital points. Next day, we scored 291, and I had the fun of taking a hundred off Surrey, to the delight of a large Kent crowd who had made the journey to the Oval. Frank Day and his family, farmers from Marden in the heart of Kent and lifelong supporters of Kent cricket, filled several cars with drapes of hops, and the players balcony and much of the pavilion were duly decorated for the occasion. Edward Heath, Prime Minister and distinguished Kentish sportsman in his own right, having won the Sydney-Hobart ocean yacht race earlier that year, had cheered us on through the month of August. He now chose to break away from No. 10 for an hour to share a glass of champagne with us.

For Leslie Ames and me it was an unforgettable occasion. We had come together in 1957, and it had taken us fourteen seasons as a partnership. There were many times that the hurdles appeared too high to jump. When Yorkshire swept the board, we admired their professionalism and wished that we had flourishing league cricket to feed us with reserves. When Surrey dominated, we felt that the club centred on a big city had a much wider field from which to choose its players. We pondered the disadvantages associated with playing on so many different county grounds, never our home pitch.

In the end, of course, it was the tremendous club loyalty, the devotion of our members and public across the country, inspired with our special history and love for the game of cricket, that pushed us on and kept us going through so many disappointments.

It was my privilege and fun to lead a fine team, most of whom were to go on and climb higher peaks. Mike Denness was to prove to be a very good captain, taking the Club on to fresh triumphs. He was a fine batsman and a brilliant athlete, always a superb example in the field. As the years go by and the history is written of that team of the seventies, which Leslie Ames and I had fought so hard and for so long to produce (and not just us but a host of devoted coaches and helpers too), it will be compared favourably I imagine with J.R. Mason's teams in the early part of the century. But we were short of two things. There was no Frank Woolley and there was no Tich Freeman. Indeed, I cannot match either of them in any teams that I played in. But who could? Only Garfield Sobers in my lifetime could compare with Woolley. And I know of no executioner so completely effective as was Tich Freeman. With either one of them alongside me in 1970, the Championship would have been won early in August. Had I had both at my disposal, the other sixteen counties would have been competing for the silver medal, leaving Kent so soundly gold as to be unbeatable.

Yet having said that, I would not swap any of my team. After all Denness and Luckhurst as a partnership would have been a match for Ashdown and Hardinge or Fagg and Todd, the stars of my dot cricket days. Asif batted as excitingly as any of the amateurs between the wars, I dare say. Has Kent ever had a better all-rounder than John Shepherd, Frank Woolley apart? Has anyone caught the public imagination like that superb fielder Alan Ealham, for the way he could throw the wicket down in full flight? Could you really put any spin bowler ahead of Derek Underwood? In fact the name of Underwood would appear in most people's best Kent team of all time. And what of the wicket-keepers, for it seems that Kent has the right to provide the best England wicket-keeper of the day? When I played with Godfrey Evans, I was quite convinced that he was the finest keeper that I had ever seen and that I would never see his like again. Within five years, Alan Knott had emerged to become every bit as good. I have no idea how you could separate them, argue as long as you like about their different techniques.

In Bob Woolmer and Graham Johnson, I had two highly promising all-round cricketers, both playing a match-winning part on a number of occasions. There had been another all-rounder, Alan Dixon, a superb cover point, who announced his retirement at the end of 1970 after twenty years of devoted service to Kent cricket. He had been a thoughtful and most loyal vice-captain, before handing over to Michael Denness. In this category, too, I must mention Stuart Leary, brilliant footballer with Charlton in the days when they held their head high in the first Division, and a much underrated, shrewd all-round cricketer. Leary was a useful leg-spinner and, as I look back, I regret that I did not call on him to bowl more regularly. In John Dye, Norman Graham and Alan Brown, we had three attacking fast bowlers who each had their day and whose individual contribution was vital. All in all, it was a splendid team of some seventeen players. Everyone was desperately excited during that final run in to the Championship and it was a job to contain them and play sensible cricket, taking each day as it came.

On reflection, I have to concede that only four of the players might qualify for the best Kent team of all time; but there is no lessening of respect for any of them for that. The selectors sitting down to choose that illustrious team would have Underwood and Knott high on their lists, and they could hardly leave Asif and Shepherd out of their considerations. Leslie Ames must win a place for his batting alone, for let me remind you that of his hundred hundreds, only one or two were scored in *more* than three hours; a remarkable achievement. Knott and Godfrey Evans may have to play in alternate matches. Underwood could play alongside Blythe and Freeman, although Frank Woolley, an automatic first selection, would be grumbling that he had to wait so long for a chance to bowl. There are thirty-five batsmen to fill five places! With regard to the captaincy, there are three possible contenders: J.R. Mason, A.P.F. Chapman and B.H. Valentine, each one of them blessed with infinite humour and charm, and all Test players in their own right. Under each one's leadership, the Kent team was tremendously happy and successful.

This has been my experience of Kent cricket. But a final tribute should be paid to the Kent supporters; the enormous, patient following who, over the years, expected us to give all that we had, who rejoiced when we were successful, and when the fun we had spilled over so that they could share it, whose cup overflowed.

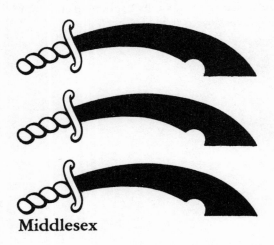

Middlesex

Barry Norman: Writer, broadcaster and guide to the Hollywood Greats.

The Last Days of August
Barry Norman

On the second day of the final Test between England and Australia I turned up at Lord's about ten minutes before the start of play. Yes, yes I know the Test match was at the Oval, but that game was already headed for a draw—Australia 251 for four with Border 51 not out and Botham reduced to human shape, having temporarily exhausted his stock of miracles.

Nothing there, I thought as I drove through the early autumnal mists of the A1 before emerging into the warm but hazy sunshine of Hendon, to stir the emotions. The game at Lord's, however, was another matter: the third day of Middlesex v. Yorkshire and Middlesex still in with a faint chance of retaining the County Championship.

Well, all right—a *very* faint chance, depending really on Middlesex gaining maximum points from every remaining match while God obligingly visited some frightful curse on the players of Notts, Sussex and Somerset. To a Middlesex supporter this seemed the very least that God might be expected to do.

In any event the position vis-à-vis Yorkshire was extremely promising: the visitors 264 for nine declared and 4 for no wicket; Middlesex 366 for nine declared. Let others go to the Oval with nothing more stirring to look forward to than the breathless adventure of Boycott batting with Tavare; at Lord's there was a result in prospect and an eminently satisfactory result at that.

So there I was outside the Tavern as the bar opened and the first over was bowled and Sharp swung at Daniel and was promptly dropped by Hughes, running in from deep fine-leg like a man who hadn't quite got his mind on the job yet. His team mates turned away from him rather coldly as he tossed the ball in and shuffled back to the boundary, staring fixedly at his boots as if he had never seen such things before and was trying to work out what they were.

At the ringside we, the cognoscenti, offered him a few mild insults,

127

sucked the froth off our pints and pondered, at our leisure, where best to sit to watch the inevitable slaughter of Yorkshire.

I love Lord's in late August when the season is drawing to a close and it's the last day of a county match and there's hardly anyone in the ground but me. The queue for beer is comfortably short and on the counter behind the bar the Scotch eggs lie like old cricket balls, the shine long since worn off them. Even Selvey, you reflect observing them closely, couldn't get those to swing, nor could Emburey make them turn. Nothing much you could do with them at all except send them down at a brisk military medium, seam up, and hope for the best.

I love Lord's at any time really and that, initially, is why I became a Middlesex supporter. By rights I should have been a Surrey man because I was born in Surrey and so were my parents and my uncles and my aunts. Not that the aunts matter too much because none of them ever knew the first thing about cricket. But my father was a Surrey man and so was my uncle Alf, who still kept wicket and opened the batting in good club cricket until he was nearly sixty. And my maternal grandfather, the first to talk to me of the mysteries and legends of the loveliest game in the world, the first to make me realise that cricket was the most glorious way of wasting time ever devised by man, spent most of his adult life no farther from the Oval than the Elephant and Castle.

His tales were all of Surrey men, unaspirated giants of the game— 'Ayward and 'Obbs and 'Itch. So when first I packed my satchel with sandwiches and Tizer and set off for the cricket it was to the Oval that I should have gone, but instead I went to Lord's, for by then I lived at Edgware and Lord's was but a couple of bus rides away while the Oval was on the far side of London, south of the river in "Here be dragons" country.

Now this was in August, 1945, and England were playing the Australian Services in the fourth Victory Test match, and Hammond made 83 and Bill Edrich 73 not out and Cyril Washbrook scored 112 and was thus the first person I ever saw reach a century. Keith Miller, that Errol Flynn among cricketers, opened the Australian bowling and I had never imagined that anyone could be so incredibly quick or so unpredictable. High, wide and handsome was Miller and so, that day, was much of his bowling, though it all came alike to Hammond and Edrich and Washbrook. It was the only time I ever saw Hammond bat but I still remember his cover drives, the ball pursuing a kind of scorched earth policy as it sped, faster than light, from the middle of the blade to the fence. It's my belief that Einstein formed the Theory of Relativity after watching Hammond hit a cover drive.

And yet it's Edrich whom I remember best from that first day at Lord's. He came perkily down the pavilion steps with the confident aggression of the small man. David he was to Miller's Goliath and though, on this occasion, it was Goliath who had the slingshot, David hooked the missiles with amazing power to the boundary. Edrich's batting was always a thing of guts and belligerence; watching him facing a fast bowler was like watching some unexpectedly tough little kid walking up to the school bully and kicking him smartly in the shins. I saw him once, bareheaded and fearless, nip down the pitch to Tom Pritchard, a pretty swiftish New Zealander then playing for Warwickshire, and hit him straight back over his head into the pavilion at Lord's. It was a mighty drive but it was more than that; it was the declaration of an apparent six-stone weakling that nobody was going to kick sand in *his* face.

I admired Bill Edrich immensely. I admired him even more than Denis Compton but Denis didn't enter my life until a year later and then I only saw him bowling, and to see Denis bowling was never to see him at his best. It may have been to see him at his most amusing but it was not to see him at his best. The occasion was Middlesex v. Kent and though Compton bowled Leslie Todd for 162, it wasn't a happy day for a prospective Middlesex supporter. Todd and Jack Davies scored 219 for Kent's first wicket and Todd and Leslie Ames added 171 for the second.

I looked it up the other day in *Wisden* and was struck by the fact that the Middlesex bowling was opened by the fast-medium stuff of Laurie Gray and the orthodox slow left-arm spin of Jack Young. When, may I ask, was the last time you remember seeing the bowling opened on the first day of a county match by a left-arm spinner?

Had I been older, more knowledgeable and as romantic as I have since become, I think the sight of Young being introduced immediately into the attack would have won me over to the Middlesex cause there and then. But I was only twelve and read no significance into what I saw. After all, in those days no county side would have turned out without at least two specialist spinners, any more than a soccer team would have taken the field without a pair of wingers. It wasn't until much later that the time and motion study men took over and determined that an attack consisting of five fast bowlers, delivering thirteen overs an hour, was the most efficient—not to say the most boring—way to dismiss the opposition.

But that game against Kent, that was the first time I ever saw Middlesex play and I wasn't greatly impressed. I suppose in those days I was a Lord's supporter most of all, and indeed I didn't see first-class cricket anywhere else until twelve months later when my father took me to the Oval for the last day of the fifth Test between England and South Africa. All I can truly remember about this is a monumental and exceedingly dull innings by Bruce Mitchell who scored 189 not out (his second century of the match) and so saved, and almost won, the game for his country. South Africa, needing 451 to win, ended the day on 423 for seven.

129

My father and I watched Mitchell's epic performance with admiration but not great pleasure. "Marvellous innings for his country," we said, "but thank God English batsmen don't play like that." (Of course Geoffrey Boycott wasn't quite seven years old then and Chris Tavare hadn't even been born.)

I rather took to the Oval that day. There's a pleasing mateyness about the place, the warmth of the old school muffler, perhaps, rather than the coolness of the old school tie at Lord's. Nevertheless Lord's has a raciness and a sophistication that set it above all other cricket grounds and that, I think, has much to do with its location.

In the days when there were such things and men could afford them, mistresses were kept in St John's Wood and I've often thought, wistfully, how nice it must have been in the pre-war days to be a well-to-do man about town, dropping into the club for a mid-morning snifter, taking a cab to St John's Wood for lunch and a bit of hanky-panky with the mistress, and then rounding off the afternoon in the most satisfying way possible by watching Hendren complete his hundred at Lord's. The cricketing male chauvinist pig's dream.

Anyway, Lord's is a worldly, knowing sort of ground and a county such as Middlesex—and I speak now of the geographical area, not the cricket team—hardly deserves so romantic a headquarters. Middlesex is a sort of unscheduled disaster of a place, the only county in the land that consists entirely of suburbs.

Some people, when asked where they come from, might reply with modest pride Derbyshire or Notts or Sussex or even Hertfordshire which, though but a Minor County to be sure, did once trounce Essex in the Benson and Hedges Cup, thanks to that horny-handed son of the English soil, Dilip Doshi.

But nobody, faced with the same question, would ever reply "Middlesex", except possibly as a joke. For while the names of all other counties conjure up images of dales and downs and country pubs and softly-rustling fields of wheat, the name of Middlesex produces in the mind's eye only an endless vista of Tescos. Well, all right—a Fine Fare or two, perhaps, the occasional Sainsbury, the distant glimpse of a shy Woolworth . . . But in Middlesex the open country is that patch of green up ahead there with the sign saying "Keep off the Grass".

In short, nobody could possibly feel any loyalty or sentimental attachment to Middlesex the geographical area, were it not for the fact that it does have Lord's and Lord's houses the Middlesex cricket team and the Middlesex cricket team used to contain one R.W.V. Robins.

Now R.W.V. Robins may not today mean a great deal to the average Middlesex supporter but he means quite a lot to me, and not simply because he played nineteen times for England and captained his county in the miraculous year of 1947, when Compton and Edrich scored more runs in a season than anyone before or since and Middlesex always seemed to declare at tea-time on the first day with the score at 420 for six and won the County Championship for the first time in a quarter of a century.

No, his true significance lies in the fact that he was the most famous old boy of Highgate School where, in 1947, I was pretty much a new boy, having barely begun a five-year stretch with no remission for good conduct.

Sporting heroes were not too common among Old Cholmeleians and we clung fiercely to those we had. So, Robins being the greatest of these, we were all perforce Middlesex supporters and even though the man himself betrayed us by sending his own son to Eton, we remained steadfast in our loyalty—in my case not only because it was incumbent upon me as a Highgate boy but also because R.W.V. was a leg-spinner.

I've always had a soft spot for leg-spinners, having for twenty years (before I gave it up in favour of off-break bowling) tried to be one. Leg-spinners are the tortured intellectuals of cricket, natural masochists who have chosen to ply their trade in the most complicated way possible in the most complicated game of all.

And that's another reason why Middlesex has an unshakeable grip on my affections. In the post-war years, before leg-spinners followed the Dodo into oblivion, Middlesex was the home of those brooding contortionists who wilfully turned their wrists and arms inside out to make the ball spin from leg, when it would have been so much easier and more comfortable to make it spin from the off.

In that Championship season of 1947 Middlesex played not one but three leg-break bowlers—Robins, the youthful and tragically short-lived Ian Bedford and Jim Sims. And of these the one I loved most deeply was Sims. He was 43 years old then and looked every day of it—a grey-haired, grey-visaged veteran with round shoulders and the mournful expression of a man upon whom fate has just played a rather nasty trick and who is expecting another one any minute now.

In the field he was not so much inactive as virtually motionless. Fielding, he gave you to understand, was none of his business and he was merely among those present as a favour to his captain who found it more convenient to have eleven rather than ten people dotted about the pitch. This is not to say, however, that Jim Sims took no interest in fielding. Indeed, I can see him still, standing somewhere in the vicinity of mid-wicket, watching with quite considerable curiosity as a slowly-rolling on-drive passed close to his right ankle, to be retrieved on the boundary by somebody else.

But then, after a few overs of immobility, the ball would be tossed to him and with a heavy sigh he would begin the true work of the day. A word or two with his captain, a slight readjustment of the field, a thoughtful glance up at the sky, not the confident glance of one asking celestial help but the less hopeful glance of one seeking no more than celestial neutrality. And then he would lurch a few paces to the wicket to start the long, slow, devious process of luring some batsman to his doom.

Of course, Robins and Bedford were also splendid leg-spinners but to me they never really looked the part. They were brisk, cheerful men, optimists who seemed faintly surprised when any ball failed to take a wicket. An optimistic leg-spinner is a contradiction in terms, almost an affront to nature. Jim Sims was what a leg-spinner ought to look like—lugubrious, deeply and pessimistically philosophical, an Eeyore among bowlers. I grieved with him every time he recovered his cap at the end of an over and shuffled back to his place in the field with two fours struck off him and not a wicket to his name. And I rejoiced even more than he did in those blissful moments when the magic did its work, and the batsman played at a ball that wasn't quite where he thought it was and there was a sharp click and a bail fell and for a moment a small, sad grin twitched at the corner of old Jim's mouth.

Perhaps it was perverse of me to develop a special affection for Sims and Edrich when every other schoolboy in the county admired Denis Compton to the point of idolatry. But Compton, especially in 1947, was almost too good to be true—lithe, handsome, prodigally gifted and almost infallible except, of course, in the matter of running between the wickets.

Quite enough has already been said about Compton's eccentric system of calling, in which "Yes" or "No" could mean anything from "Maybe" to "Don't bother me now, I'm thinking", and in which, having struck the ball, he was quite likely to shout "Wait!" while already standing beside his partner at the bowler's end. The most famous example of it was when he ran his brother out for a duck in Leslie's benefit match, an event which I witnessed. I seem to recall, as the shattered beneficiary trailed forlornly back to the pavilion, a desperate Denis trying to persuade a Sussex team clutching its collective sides with mirth that this was the kind of thing that could have happened to anybody.

It couldn't, of course; it could only have happened to him, which is why every schoolboy adored him. Well, you had to, really. You couldn't profess to be a lover of cricket and not thrill with anticipation as Denis strode bouncily to the wicket, ready to play every shot known to man and a few known only to himself—as, for example, for Middlesex against The Rest at the Oval in 1947 when he swept a ball from Tom Goddard (he who took 238 wickets that year) and sent it to the boundary while simultaneously falling flat on his face.

But Compton, like Sims, was a-typical. Middlesex Man is much more closely represented by Robins or Edrich—smallish, chunky, compact, confident, cheerfully belligerent, neat in dress and gesture, brisk and businesslike.

From that mould, or one very similar, have emerged through the ages stalwarts such as F.G. Mann, Jack Young, Don Bennett, Fred Titmus, John Murray, Peter Parfitt, Clive Radley and, give or take the beards, Mike Gatting and the Messianic Brearley himself.

Around men of such physical stamp are Middlesex teams traditionally constructed, though others of different, rangier builds have also played their considerable parts—men like Alan Moss, whose first, fast over for the county, watched with amazement by me, consisted almost exclusively of wides; or the vast, black and explosive Wayne Daniel or, for the one marvellous season of 1980 when Middlesex won both the County Championship and the Gillette Cup, the bald and professorial Vincent van der Bijl who, with his great height and prodigious swing, did for Middlesex what Joel Garner does for the West Indies and Somerset.

Which reminds me: there was a time when the school loyalties might have fluctuated between Middlesex and Somerset, for the latter county was captained briefly by another Old Cholmeleian, S.S. Rogers. But those were the days when Somerset was a joke county for whom almost anybody could play simply by turning up at the Taunton ground and announcing that he had nothing better to do for the next three days. So we didn't really take Somerset too seriously but merely wished them well whenever they weren't playing Middlesex.

Essentially it was the Lord's team, the "league o' nations side" as Yorkshiremen used to sneer derisively in the days when Yorkshire could lay claim to a decent eleven, that we supported with passion and continued to support long after we had left school. What one has learned to love in childhood one tends to love forever and so, whenever my work takes me abroad for lengthy spells, upon my return to England I gravitate towards Lord's and Middlesex like one going home. And beside the Tavern with a pint in my hand I study the heroes of today and compare them, sometimes favourably, sometimes not, with the great ones of my particular Golden Age of the late 1940s.

I like this present lot—the pugnacious Gatting, the dashing Butcher, Barlow swooping about in the covers with a speed and energy the very contemplation of which would have caused cardiac arrest in old Jim Sims, Emburey with his lazy trot to the wicket and the ball tossed high, the way off-spinners always used to do it before one-day cricket turned them into slow-medium stock bowlers, Radley with that idiosyncratic, slithering turn for the second run, swooping into the crease as if about to inflict a sliding tackle on the umpire . . .

The Middlesex team of the last few years, led by the guru Brearley, is probably the most efficient the county has ever had but ... Is it simply nostalgia that makes me wonder whether, in thirty years' time, the twelve-year-olds of today will remember Gatting and Butcher with the same wonder and delight that I remember Edrich and Compton? Will they ever be able to think back upon an opening batsman worthy of being mentioned in the same breath as Jack Robertson, of the hawklike profile and the wrists of steel?

Now there was a Master—a man who never played an inelegant shot in his life, who never had to scamper for a run, who never looked less than immaculate, who relied on sweet timing rather than brute strength but who still scored his runs fast enough to make 331 not out in a single day against Worcestershire. When Jack Robertson retired he took the secret of late-cutting with him, for nobody has ever played the shot—save by accident—since he left the scene. No fast bowler, dull enough of imagination to bowl outside the off stump to Jack Robertson, could expect the now traditional nervous flick of the bat and a thin edge to first slip. Instead he would see the great man lean gracefully across his wicket and, with a deft movement of the wrists, send the ball scudding away out of everyone's reach to the boundary. The duty of third man when Jack Robertson was batting was merely to retrieve the ball from the crowd and lob it back to the bowler.

When in 1980 I first turned out for the Lord's Taverners, Robertson was also in the side. He was 63 years old, silver-haired by then but trim and lean as ever. As Jack went out to open our innings Jim Standen, the captain that day, beckoned me to the dressing-room door. "If you want to learn anything about batting," he said, "just watch this fellow. He's got it all, even now." And so he has; and so he always had. Ludicrous that he played only eleven times for England.

It was Cyril Washbrook mostly who kept him out of the Test team but was Washbrook really a better batsman than Robertson? In 1948 when England, inexplicably, dropped Hutton for one match was George Emmett of Gloucestershire truly a safer bet as replacement than the great Middlesex stylist? They say, you know, that Middlesex players have a better chance than anyone else of being picked for England, simply because Lord's is their home ground. I don't believe it. Only twice—on the West Indian tour in the winter of 1947, when he scored 390 runs at an average of 55.71 in the Tests, and again in India in 1951—was Robertson given an extended run in the Test team. Born out of his time, that was his trouble. If he was around now, the question the selectors would have to grapple with would be whether Boycott or Gooch was the more suitable prospect as Jack Robertson's opening partner.

John Murray was another Middlesex man who received less than his due from the Test selectors. He was always an infinitely superior wicket-keeper to Jim Parks, but it was the Sussex man who won 46 caps for England while J.T., during the same period, got only 21.

I saw J.T.'s last match for Middlesex at Lord's. Against Lancashire it was and, as I remembered it, Murray brought the match and his county career to a perfect conclusion by stumping the last Lancashire batsman off John Emburey. A few years later at a cocktail party I told this tale to J.T. himself, and he denied that it had ever happened. He hadn't stumped anybody, he said; not that day he hadn't. Well, I suppose he knows best, but my version of the events is far more satisfying than his and if it isn't true it ought to be.

Whatever actually happened, it all took place on another day in late August, and the game was over just before lunch with only a few of us there come to say goodbye to J.T. as he trotted up the pavilion steps to a gentle round of applause. Another splendid pro, neat and stylish in everything he did; the world's most successful wicket-keeper with 1,527 dismissals to his credit. There should have been thousands at Lord's to bid him farewell with a standing ovation, instead of barely enough of us to fill a phone booth.

Strange, though, that continuing link between me and Middlesex and the last days of August. All my strongest memories seem to be connected with the end of summer and the end of the season. Nothing ends with quite the same finality as the cricket season. Soccer, grim, earnest and uninspired, drags on somehow, somewhere through every month of the year, but cricket comes and briefly flourishes and then stops. Not too surprising perhaps that in those final days of the season one takes a keener interest in the play, storing up memories for the winter months.

Well, whatever. As Murray vanished into the pavilion never to appear again in a Middlesex team, I found myself thinking back to another wicket-keeper on another August day twenty-seven years earlier. Mickey Laws was his name and he was playing his first innings for Middlesex against Warwickshire and a right botch he made of it, too. For a long while his fruitless attempts to lay bat to ball were greeted with deep and contented chuckles by the assembled populace, and when eventually he managed to score his first (and, as it transpired, his last) run before being bowled by Tom Pritchard—that same Pritchard who, earlier, had been driven violently for six by Bill Edrich—the wild cheering with which a small group of us greeted the achievement must have sounded to him like heavy sarcasm. How was he to know, lonely and desperate out there in the middle, that we, too, wore the colours of his old school?

I never saw Laws play for the county again. He could only have had a few games anyway, and those as substitute, for Leslie Compton was the regular keeper and when he retired J.T. Murray took over. Nevertheless, Laws was part of Highgate School's intermittent connection with

135

Middlesex, a connection that for me was most significant a few years later when a fellow I actually knew at school won his Middlesex cap at the age of 19 or so.

Bill Knightley-Smith his name was; a left-handed bat who was filling in the summer before going up to Cambridge. He was one of those multi-gifted athletes: school sprint champion, football captain, fives captain, cricket captain and a most gentle, modest and amiable fellow withall.

Poor Bill. In that golden, youthful summer he was named by the London *Evening News* as one of the most promising young cricketers of the year. But thereafter it all went wrong. He won his Blue once, as a Freshman, but only once. Middlesex lost interest in him and though, after university, he went to Gloucestershire, he was never again able to establish himself in the first-class game. After the 1957 season he retired from cricket and went back to Highgate as a teacher. Five years later, one day short of his thirtieth birthday, he died of heart trouble.

Once, a year or so before his death, somebody asked him what had happened to blight all that early potential. I'm not entirely sure that Bill knew himself but the problem, he said, was that he had been too orthodox a player; after watching him in action once or twice opposing captains and bowlers had his measure, and knew precisely how to set their fields to him. "I went on batting as well as I'd ever done," he said, "but they stopped me scoring any runs."

Ironically, at just about the time that Bill died another Old Cholmeleian, Colin Drybrough, was winning his Middlesex cap. I remembered this Drybrough, too, from school but only vaguely—a small and very junior squirt he had been when I was a rather distinguished sixth former. It seemed astonishing to me, being older than he was, that of all post-war Highgate boys C.D. Drybrough should be the most successful—captain of Oxford in 1961 and 1962, captain of Middlesex in 1963 and 1964. True, they were a couple of undistinguished years for the county but that was not his fault. He was an extremely useful all-rounder, a hard-hitting batsman and a left-arm spinner, who did the hat-trick and altogether took four wickets in five balls against Northants in 1964. If Middlesex could climb no higher than sixth in the Championship under Drybrough, they did a lot worse during the fifties and sixties under other captains. These were not in any way glorious decades for Middlesex. Indeed, it was only when Brearley came along as skipper in 1971 that things began to look up . . .

But on that August day last summer when Middlesex played Yorkshire and the butterfingered Hughes bowled the second over and, with pleasing irony, saw Lumb dropped at slip—hard to tell by whom; one of the several Middlesex blonds anyway—Brearley was otherwise engaged, leading England at the Oval. The unique Phillippe Henri

Edmonds (surely the only Zambian-born left-arm spinner of part-Belgian extraction ever to play for England) skippered the side in his absence. And a workmanlike job he did, too.

All those Yorkshire batsmen of exciting early promise—Lumb and Sharp, Athey and Love—who should, by now, be vying with each other for places in the Test side but who, somehow, have never turned out to be that good, came and briefly looked interesting and went and Edmonds himself and Monteith, the Irish spinner who fills in when Emburey is on England duty, took a few wickets each and soon after lunch Middlesex were left needing 66 to win.

The uncapped Hartley who, for reasons best known to the management, leads Yorkshire when the regular captain, Chilly Old, is playing in Tests or suffering from a cold or a strain or a headache or some mysterious and debilitating ailment to which he alone is prey, opened the bowling with himself and Athey—hardly the most alarming new ball attack in the history of county cricket.

It seemed at first that Yorkshire were simply intent on catching the next train home but this was to misjudge Hartley, for all of a sudden 66 began to appear a rather difficult total to reach. Slack was caught at slip off Hartley with a stroke that made one wonder whether the batsman's play was inspired by his name or his name by his play. Quite soon thereafter, Slack's opening partner Barlow, having apparently decided that ten was an extremely respectable score beyond which it would be over-ambitious and even greedy to aspire, and having consequently remained on that figure for what seemed to Middlesex supporters like a week or two, leapt impulsively to 12 and, stricken with remorse, promptly got himself out. After that, facing Carrick and Whiteley—quite possibly the weakest spin attack in the entire world—Middlesex struggled.

C.R. Cook, the new boy, looked likely to go at any moment and finally went caught at silly mid-off by Hartley off Whiteley—though only after deep consultation between both umpires, the venerable Derek Shackleton and the magisterial Don Oslear. Ultimately banished by these austere arbiters young Cook sloped reluctantly away, expressing clearly in a subtle pantomime that Marcel Marceau would have envied his firm conviction that he had been ripped off.

But then, happily, the industrious Radley took over: here a dab, there a nibble, a straight four off Whiteley, a sliding tackle or two on Shackleton and Oslear and the game was over. Middlesex had, as we had all expected, won handsomely.

It was a pleasing end to the season though we knew, secretly, that the victory had no significance. Notts or Somerset or Sussex would win the County Championship and, looking at it dispassionately, it was time one of them did. Middlesex, over the past few years, had done very well indeed, winning two Championships and two Gillette Cups. Middlesex in 1981, deprived frequently because of Test match demands of the services of Gatting, Emburey, Brearley and—once—Downton, had looked a pretty ordinary side, certainly not one that had any kind of divine right to the County Championship.

Realistic Middlesex supporters knew that the county's major contribution to the 1981 season would be the retention of the Ashes for England. And on that Friday evening of August 28, as Boycott and Tavare spent several days batting out the last hour at the Oval, we knew Middlesex had done it.

Romantics and sentimentalists might claim that England's success was due to the rejuvenation of Ian Botham but Middlesex men knew that his miraculous return, Lazarus-like, from the Test match scrapheap was thanks entirely to Mike Brearley. Brearley is probably the only true intellectual ever to captain England (or any other Test side for that matter) and he undoubtedly stands alongside the saturnine Douglas Jardine as the best, hardest and most effective skipper the country ever had. As a player he was probably never more than half a Test match batsman but what did that matter when, in the last four crucial games of the series, he could turn the previously dispirited Botham from Clark Kent into Superman?

To put it another way, Brearley was Butch Cassidy to Botham's Sundance Kid—"Keep thinking, Butch. It's what you're good at." Butch Brearley kept thinking, Sundance Botham kept shooting from the hip, and England beat the Aussies out of sight.

Such reflections went through my mind as the victorious Middlesex batsmen and the defeated Yorkshire fielders trooped together off the field, and the shutters came down on the bar. And I sat for a while looking out at the dusty, deserted square and remembering the small boy who had sat in much the same spot thirty-odd years before watching Denis Compton run out his own brother in his benefit match and I thought, as that small boy had done, that there was no place like Lord's and no team like Middlesex and I thought that, given a bit of luck, we'd win the Championship again next year . . .

Northamptonshire

Frank Tyson: Northants and England, now Director of Coaching for the Victorian Cricket Association in Australia.

Northamptonshire Revisited
Frank Tyson

Northamptonshire! That small English midland county, 14,000 miles from my Melbourne home, is, for me, synonymous with the inner spirit, as well as the external trappings of county cricket. The mere mention of its name is enough to wind back the clock of my memory twenty years to the time when I last trod the Wantage Road ground as a player. To quote the poet, Wordsworth, whose verse I was supposed to recite whilst walking back to the end of my twenty-seven yard run, those times are now:

> Apparelled in celestial light
> The glory and the freshness of a dream!

Let's play the word association game: "Tell me the first thing which comes into your mind when I mention Northamptonshire." I see the slow-moving river Nene in its shallow valley, fishermen perched along its banks at the Billing Aquadrome, waving to the passengers in the passing trains. I envisage the partially excavated site of Northampton's ancient castle, hard by the station, the traces of a Roman camp at Duston, the earthen walls of an Iron Age fort at Hardingstone, Delapre Abbey with its lawns sloping down towards the river, on the banks of which the forces of Henry VI were trapped and vanquished in the Battle of Northampton during the Wars of the Roses.

The word "Northampton" conjures up memories of the County Cricket Ground on Wantage Road. It is the recollection of a rather barren heath, ringed by members' cars, the Western Stand and, on the popular side of the oval, over ground hacked into unevenness by the studs of Northampton Town footballers during the winter months, by improvised seats of long planks supported on upturned boxes. The Members'

Pavilion, a red-brick dinosaur from a bygone Victorian era, was a double-storeyed structure situated almost behind the bowler's arm. Indeed, when the wickets were pitched too much to one side of the square, batsmen in the middle would stop Northants players from moving around in their dressing room directly behind the bowler because it distracted them. The building contained the bare essentials for the conduct of the game: two offices on the upper level, a committee room, a bar and two dressing rooms with bathrooms reminiscent of those in a nineteenth-century Australian country pub. At the back of each dressing room, steps descended to a sinister subterranean chamber which some said was a drying room for damp clothes. The heating of the building was central: one coal fire in the visitors' dressing room!

The scoreboard, its white facade boards gaping, had seen better days. On the ground floor it housed a primitive printing press, which, at sporadic intervals during a match day, emitted clanking sounds and spat out up-to-date scorecards which were marketed around the ground by a character wearing a white coat and a baseballer's cap in Northampton's colours of maroon and gold. On the first floor lurked the scoreboard attendants who lived in a mixed atmosphere of fear and ignorance: fear that the structure in which they worked would eventually fail to bear the weight of the numbers they posted, let alone their own: and ignorance of the true state of the game, since the scorers were posted on the opposite side of the ground to them. The scorers were housed in a sort of elevated dog-box which was cheek by jowl with the Western Stand, and positioned at right angles to the pitch, thus preventing them from guessing what was going on in the middle. This spartan accommodation the scorers shared with the representatives of the Northampton press, the *Chronicle* and *Echo*, and, more often than not, a reporter from the local paper of the team opposed to Northamptonshire.

Northamptonshire; there's that word again. After a match at the County Ground, there was time for a succulent grill at the Black Boy Hotel, and then it was on to the New Theatre, with complimentary tickets, to witness the last rites of the English music hall. Sometimes we were lucky to see and hear one or two of the old-time stars, not yet claimed by television. More often than not, however, the stars of the day's sporting entertainment at Wantage Road comprised most of the mid-week theatre audience and were regaled by such spectacles as Les Girls in "We've Got Nothing On Tonight" or "Strip, Strip, Hooray!".

The Northamptonshire cricketer's amusements in the fifties, however, were not confined to the fleshpots, escapism and low comedy.

There were other more edifying experiences to be enjoyed. Open-air Shakespearean productions in Abington Park were the amateur counterparts of excellent theatre to be savoured on the Northampton Repertory

142

Theatre stage which, over the years, had produced so many leading lights of the thespian world. I used to relish my annual visit to Rothwell church, the acoustics of which rounded beautifully the tonality of the London Symphony Orchestra. It was an eerie experience to sit in the Rothwell pews, listening to Mozart or Mahler, knowing that in the crypt beneath one's feet lay thousands of skeletons in a charnel house: the reputed relics of either a plague or the Civil War Battle of Naseby, fought nearby in 1645.

Northampton cricketers in my time were very much like their counterparts today. They liked a glass of beer. One could choose between Northampton Ale or Phipps. It could be sipped in the sedate and pleasant atmosphere of the Plough Hotel whilst listening to the Liverpuddlian accents of Syd Emery, the landlord, describing the Australian sides who had stayed in his house; or it could be gulped in livelier fashion at the rowdier pub, the Cross Keys, where Frank, the host, had lurid memories of the days of the American servicemen in Northampton.

At the opposite and upper end of the social scale, Northampton players, each spring, enjoyed the hospitality of the roller bearing firm of British Timpken and its managing director, Sir John Pascoe, while he was alive and active in the company. Sir John was never loth to recruit the county side as the backbone of his Timpken Eleven, which clashed with Cambridge University on the firm's admirable Duston ground, at the beginning of each summer. The champagne lunches, which were an accepted feature of these games, were eagerly anticipated and long discussed after the event by the Northants pros, though it must be added, they did little for the standard of cricket after the midday interval.

One of the strange sentimental associations which Northamptonshire has for me is that unusual connection which links it to the hamlet of Hallett in the back-blocks of South Australia. It is in this small bush settlement, just outside the town of Clare, that Jack Manning is the local publican. Jack "Tanglefoot" Manning was a highly successful orthodox slow left-arm bowler who was one of the dynamic forces in the Northamptonshire team of the fifties. No less a contributor to the Northamptonshire cause of those days was George Tribe. George now lives in the same city as me, Melbourne; he is, in fact, one of the leading coaches in the system which I, as Director of Coaching for Victoria, helped to establish. George was a wizard of left-arm wrist spin and a dogged batsman to boot; he was a friend of the late Des Fitzmaurice, the former delegate of the South Melbourne Club to the Victorian Cricket Association, an ex-Lancashire League professional, and coincidentally, a spectator of the incident which led to my playing county cricket with Northamptonshire.

The event took place at the ground of the North Staffordshire club of

Knypersley in 1951. At the time it appeared that my hopes of making the grade in first-class cricket were in tatters. At the ripe old age of twenty-one, after having played several games for Lancashire Second Eleven while I was in the army, I had been told by my native county that there was no opportunity for me at Old Trafford, since I had decided to go to university and would be too old for county cricket when I came down at the age of twenty-four. Anyway, rumour had it that, since I had broken down with a back injury while playing in a minor county game against Northumberland, I was injury-prone. So it was that I found myself playing as Saturday afternoon professional for Knypersley, and agreeing to participate in a Sunday game against George Duckworth's Commonwealth Eleven in order to raise money for charity.

In those days the Commonwealth team had the individualistic habit of allowing its players to decide the order in which they would like to bat in friendly games. When they saw that I was to open the bowling for the Knypersley eleven, Worrell, Tribe and Fitzmaurice, all of whom I had played against in the league at one time or another, immediately determined to enjoy a restful Sabbath and put their names down for the numbers nine, ten and eleven berths in the batting order. It was thanks to their thoughtfulness that I was allowed to bowl at Jock Livingston, the former New South Wales batsman and, at that time, a recruiting officer for his newly-adopted county of Northamptonshire. A short, sharp spell and I was invited for a trial at the Northamptonshire nets.

So it was that in the spring of 1952, I left the confines of Hatfield College and took a train from Durham station, high on the viaduct spanning the valley of the Wear, bound for a Northampton examination and a chance to prove my mettle as a potential county cricketer. I arrived late at my destination, only to discover that I was expected to play in a practice game at a ground some ten miles distant, and that the bus transporting the team had already left. I was two hours late getting there and the opposition were batting. I changed hurriedly and rushed on to the ground where I was immediately called upon to bowl. The blasé band of professionals who were to be my future colleagues assumed their positions in the field, expecting the normal run-of-the-mill medium-pace bowler. Even to my modest eyes, the slips seemed a little close. The first ball pitched just short of a length, clipped the edge of the opposing tentative bat and sped to second slip where it struck Freddie Jakeman on the shins before he could even make a token gesture of bending towards the catch. A howl of pain rent the air as the stocky Yorkshireman clutched his leg and fell to the ground.

His fellow slip fieldsmen carried Fred to the pavilion, returned to the scene of the tragedy and, with many a covert and suspicious glance in my direction, advanced another five yards to the rear. It required only that one ball in Northamptonshire to make my reputation! I was dubbed "definitely fast" and an invitation to join the county groundstaff followed as a matter of course. I was offered the princely salary of £200 per annum, which I accepted with alacrity.

In my first months at the Club, I was introduced to its history and traditions. The memorial board in the Members' Pavilion told me of R.P. Nelson, the young Cambridge educated captain, whose promise was cruelly cut short by the Second World War. Older members spoke to me in reverent tones of George Thompson, Northamptonshire's first great professional captain, who played in representative games against the mighty Australians of 1902 and 1909, toured New Zealand, and was the driving force behind the Northants team which gained first-class status in 1905. They praised C.J.T. Poole, one of the county's first notable left-handed amateur batsmen, who achieved a W.G. Grace or Jack Hobbs status with the naming of the Wantage Road ground's main gates after him—as I recall, much to the annoyance of one of my left-handed contemporaries in the Northants side who estimated that he had scored four times the number of runs as Poole without even a turnstile being given his name!

It was as he was entering the ground through the C.J.T. Poole gates that I first met Ted "Nobby" Clark, Northamptonshire's and England's fearsome left-handed fast bowler of the late twenties and early thirties. An irascible soul in his heyday, Nobby was known, while bowling on a perfect wicket, to have shouted to a skylark singing above his head to shut up, since there was nothing to sing about that day. His rather testy nature was being put to the proof when I first encountered him, for he was being prevented from driving his car into the ground by a gateman who, ignorant of Nobby's identity, was demanding either payment or a member's ticket before admitting him. "Get out of my way, before I run you down," hissed Nobby, "those fellows up there"—and here he illustrated his remark with a wave towards the Northants Committee Room—"owe me thousands."

That remark was very close to the truth, for rumour had it that when Clark was given his benefit match, it was ruined by rain and he lost over £600, which in those days was a lot of money. When asked by a compassionate committeeman whether he would like to have another benefit game to make good his losses, the cynical fast bowler retorted: "No thanks, I don't think I can afford it!"

Northamptonshire had two representatives in the England team which met the West Indies and India in 1933—4: Clark and A.H. Bakewell. Bakewell's story is a tragic chapter in Northamptonshire folklore which was to be repeated in later years, in the instance of Colin Milburn. In 1933 Bakewell scored a century in the Oval Test against

145

G.C. Grant's West Indians. He was twenty-four and on the brink of a distinguished international career as an opening batsman. Two years later, with an average of 45 to his credit in eight Tests, Bakewell was forced to retire from not only the international but also the first-class game, as a result of a motor accident which occurred while he was returning from an away game at Chesterfield and which permanently damaged his arm. Thirty-four years later another big man in Northamptonshire cricket, Colin Milburn, was also cut down in his cricketing prime, only two months after scoring 139 in the riot-disrupted Test against Pakistan in Karachi, by a car crash which caused the loss of his left eye. It was ironic that lightning struck Northamptonshire twice in the same spot. After the Bakewell affair—a misfortune which killed the amateur, R.P. Northway—Northamptonshire players were forbidden to travel to away games by car; yet tragedy contrived to strike again, this time on home ground, in spite of all the precautions taken. During my time with Northamptonshire, no one was allowed to forget the dangers of the road; each time the coach bearing the county players to and from Northampton went over the hump-backed bridge just outside the town of Market Harborough, someone aboard was sure to say: "There's the bridge where Northway and Bakewell ran off the road in '35."

The administration of the Club in the early fifties was firm on such matters as travelling arrangements; but it was far from autocratic. The Secretary was Colonel St George Coldwell: a gentle, genteel personage, redolent of the Indian Army, pukka sahibs and chota pegs. His lines of communication with the more earthy of the professional staff were tenuous but cordial; it did, however, try even the Colonel's patience when he had to explain to a fractious band of improvident pros, freshly returned from an expensive away game, that merely because there were cheques in their cheque books did not necessarily infer that there were funds in their accounts. Much of the administrative hard labour of those years devolved on the shoulders of the diligent Assistant Secretary, Ken Turner. It was he who, especially after his appointment to the secretaryship in 1958, led Northamptonshire out of the administrative middle ages. Solvency was no longer a perennial problem; new stands, indoor nets and supporters' clubs sprang into being, accompanied by such fund-raising activities as discotheques and football pools. Financial security led to well-backed recruitment campaigns and, long after my departure from Wantage Road, the county could afford to attract the talents of such players as Mushtaq Mohammad and Bishen Bedi—and pay them much more than the starting salary which I received!

My first field commander at Northampton was the England skipper of the time, Freddie Brown. In build and temperament "F.R." was a big man and the renaissance of the county side can be traced back to the early fifties when he gave the Club a new vitality and purpose. Freddie did not brook opposition to his views gladly; he would not infrequently go into a selection committee meeting with a pre-compiled team list, lay the names on the table before his fellow selectors together with the statement that these were the players he would like to lead in the next game—and walk out! His autocratic attitude did not win him many friends amongst the game's hierarchy, but it gained him respect for his judgement amongst the players and, importantly, it won matches. Moreover "F.R.'s" authoritarianism extended to his players and was based on the premise that he never instructed anyone to do something he would not do. Over after over he bowled on-the-spot leg-spinners, his face becoming redder above the kerchief which he invariably wore around his neck; then, with scarcely a pause, he would sieze the new ball, when it became due, and send down another dozen overs of swingers and seamers. A man of decided views, he had his firm likes and dislikes. On hot, enervating days in the field, he was not above taking something stronger than cordial when the drink break came. I know from personal experience that the twelfth man forgot the "tissue restorer" at his own peril.

Freddie Brown's lieutenant during his captaincy term was Dennis Brookes, his senior professional. Silver-haired, even at the age of thirty-seven when I first met him, Dennis lived up to his outward appearance by being one of the old school of senior pros. His judgement in cricket matters was in keeping with his character: serene, considered and composed. I never saw him ruffled or discountenanced, although the spectators at the United Services Ground in Portsmouth came very close to disturbing his composure on one occasion, when they threw their seat cushions at the Northamptonshire captain because of what they considered an inequitable declaration. It was rarely that Dennis gave any cricket supporters the slightest grounds for such criticism. He was as impeccable a judge of declarations and the art of keeping the opposition in the game, as he was a ruthless destroyer of any bowling which fell short of the highest class. Upright and poised in his batting stance, he gave the almost audible impression of physically thinking out his strokes before he played them. This control and composure brought him 30,874 runs and seventy-one centuries against every county in the Championship in twenty-five seasons of first-class cricket. He only failed in eight of those summers to reach the professional's milestone of a 1,000 runs. His appearances for England were limited to a single occasion against the West Indies in Barbados in 1947. Later in the tour he broke a finger, and when the doctor treating the injury strapped the injured member to its neighbour rather than a splint, he caused a serious infection which necessitated Brookes returning to England post-haste.

Dennis' sang-froid now serves him well in his capacity as a JP on the

Northampton bench; he is also Assistant Secretary of the County Club. His equanimity was learned the hard way, for he was a member of the long-suffering Northamptonshire side which played from May 1935 to May 1939 without winning a single game. Those were the days when the stronger county teams visiting Northampton only booked hotel accommodation for two of the three days of the game, in the expectation that they would conclude matters long before the scheduled time. When the long awaited victory eventually came Northamptonshire's way, it was said that the whole side went out and got drunk—even the teetotallers! And who could blame them? Four years is a long time between drinks.

Dennis Brookes was captain of Northamptonshire in 1957 when the county ended the season runners-up in the Championship to the mighty Surrey combination. That performance was, at the time, the apogee of Northamptonshire's achievements. It was certainly a far cry from the dark days of the late thirties and the success was due in no small measure to the feats of the team's triumvirate of left-handed spinners: Tribe, Manning and Allen. Between them the spin triplets captured no fewer than 305 wickets, predominantly on home pitches which were not unsympathetic to the slow bowler's wiles. The bare surfaces at Wantage Road at that time were far removed from the well-grassed, ideal batting wickets prepared by groundsman Ron Johnson in 1954, when twenty of Northamptonshire's thirty-one games failed to yield a result. Ron was, like Dennis Brookes, one of the old school. He was a perfectionist in his job and refused to work by the clock. At any time of day or night it was not unusual to see him on his beloved wicket, puddling in tons of his favourite fertilizer, which was certainly organic and highly pungent. It was an amusing experience to watch the facial expressions of visiting spin bowlers who were unwise enough to rub their hands in the dust of the pitch to gain a better purchase on the ball, and then lick their fingers! Such a slip of the tongue was enough to turn the strongest stomachs against eating lunch.

Jack Mercer, Glamorgan's former medium-pace bowler, held sway over the pencils and book in the scorers' box. Jack was quite a character, a superlative conjurer with whom it was positively dangerous to play cards and a leading member of the Magic Circle. His sense of humour was infinite and he always appeared to be laughing so hard that he was compelled to keep a handkerchief in his hand to wipe away the tears which streamed endlessly from one eye. At the luncheon and tea intervals and at close of play, when Northants were bowling, Jack would materialise in the home dressing room, always in his Glamorgan blazer and bearing a slip of paper from which he would read in a monotone: "Tyson thirty-five overs, five maidens, eighty-five runs, three-wickets—well bowled." Each set of figures was invariably suffixed by those words "well bowled".

During his days with his Welsh county, Jack built up a reputation for himself as a hitter of enormous sixes into the blocks of tall flats which surrounded the Cardiff Arms Park ground. On one occasion he hit a ball straight at an open window at which a man was spending a leisurely and cheap afternoon watching Glamorgan play. The man was jerked from his reverie by the sight of the approaching ball—and promptly closed the window for protection!

The Northants supernumerary staff included the team's trainer, physiotherapist and father-confessor, Jack Jennings. Jack was in charge of the Northamptonshire pre-season fitness preparation. The first week after Easter always saw the unenthusiastic ground staff assembled at the County Ground, ready for a series of five mile runs against the chill spring winds as far as the Kettering Road Golf Club and back again. Grumbling and cold, the group embarked upon its marathon ordeal, urged on by the vociferous Jennings from his perch on the saddle of an antique bicycle. As the run progressed, it developed into a battle of wits between the task master and two notable recalcitrants, Des Barrick and Bob Clarke. The two reluctant athletes pursued their mandatory path with many a backward glance at their tormentor, ever ready to duck down a side alley until Jack pedalled past, before catching a bus back to the ground.

Bob "Nobby" Clarke was one of the few Northamptonshire-born players to command a regular place in the county side. Blond, barrel-chested and immensely strong, Bob was an indefatigable left-handed medium-pace bowler without any great knowledge of the skills with which nature had endowed him. I recall Freddie Brown talking to Nobby like a Dutch uncle one day and saying: "Now Nobby, if you hold the ball like this and bowl it like this, it will swing in." Bob's reply was a simple, uncomprehending: "Oh, aar. Do it?"

Two other locals in the Northamptonshire side of the 1950s were the Davis brothers, Percy and Ted. Percy was a batsman of great correctitude and a peerless coach who regularly migrated to spend more than twenty English winters instructing South African schoolboys. He was extremely superstitious and always insisted on donning his Northamptonshire cap as his first item of apparel when changing for a game. It was not unusual when entering the Northants dressing room to find Percy stripped to the buff, naked but adorned, in the middle of his pre-match preparations.

Other Northamptonshire natives were in the eleven from time to time: Alan Liddell, John Wild and Brian "Waddy" Reynolds; but for the most part, the side was not indigenous. Yorkshire was represented by Dennis Brookes, Fred Jakeman, Des Barrick and Doug Greasley, whilst Lancashire was reflected in the accents of Keith Andrew, "Buddy" Oldfield, Albert Nutter, Vince Broderick and Sid Starkie. George Tribe, Jock Livingston and Ray Hogan were the dinkie-die Aussies in the team, whilst the Land of the Long White Cloud was represented by "Kiwi" Arnold and John Guy. John Fellowes-Smith, a South African, played unconcernedly side by side with Don Ramsamooj, a West Indian, and their team mates included Surreyites, Raman Subba Row, Harry Kelleher, the Shropshire Lad Bert Lightfoot, and, from the county of Durham and its neighbouring palatinate of Northumberland, Gus Williamson and Lewis McGibbon. Rumour at the time had it that Northamptonshire's next recruit would be an Eskimo!

The diverse origins of my Northamptonshire colleagues militated against a unifying force within the eleven. It was with the purpose of fostering team-spirit that Keith Andrew and I founded the Cosmo Club amongst the Northamptonshire players upon our return from the Australian tour of 1954–5. The concept was to hold team meetings on the eve of away games, to "get the boys together" and to discuss tactics for the following day. During club meetings fines were imposed for such aberrations as swearing and when a member expressed his intention of not "bloody well paying", it cost him another bob! The proceeds of the meetings were channelled into the funding of a slap-up dinner at the end of the season at a delightful country pub, the Falcon at Castle Ashby. The funny thing about this rather infantile idea was that it worked, and Yorkshiremen, Australians, New Zealanders and Lancastrians alike forgot their birth-places momentarily to become Cosmo members and North-amptonshire players. The club created a genuine sense of team entity which contributed immensely to Northamptonshire's playing successes in the fifties.

The range of the Cosmos' activities was boundless and embraced golf days, arranging barbecues for touring teams, end-of-season functions and even fishing expeditions! The most memorable piscatorial escapade, organised by myself, took place in Bournemouth during an away game against Hampshire—and proved distinctly less than successful! The preliminaries were efficiently completed: the lines were purchased, the bait supplied and a compulsory five o'clock call placed at our hotel reception desk for every member of the team. The morning was still dark when the whole of the Northamptonshire side made their way to the end of the Bournemouth pier, baited their hooks and heaved their lines over the side. Instead of the expected splashes as twelve paternosters hit the seas, the Northamptonians heard only a dozen thuds as their lines sank into soft sand. The tide was out! And the name of Tyson was Bournemouth mud for the rest of that match.

A slightly more successful fishing excursion was mounted by my fellow-founder of the Cosmos, the Northants wicket-keeper, Keith Andrew, during one very wet weekend in Worcester. After spending two days watching the rain fall and the nearby River Severn rise, to the accompaniment of tall stories from the local citizenry about how the New Road ground was the only one in England on which a salmon had been caught during a flood, Keith decided to suit his actions to the mood of the moment. When the Northants players arrived at the Worcester ground on the third morning, the wicket-keeper was discovered, rod in hand, fishing in the pouring rain, in an enormous pool of water which had gathered in the outfield. Laughter turned to incredulity when Keith suddenly tugged on his line and hauled a huge fish out of the depths! The fact that it turned out to be a kipper, purchased at the local fish shop en route to the ground, took some time to dawn in the minds of the ingenuous onlookers.

Pranks such as that played by Keith Andrew were mere devices for easing the pressures which inevitably built up during the endless summer round of travel and cricket tension. No one was more adept at sparking off laughter than the plump, pipe-smoking all-rounder, Des Barrick; his gifts were infinite, for not only could he have earned a living as a comedian, but his cricketing talents included those of a number five batsman, a leg- and off-spinner, seam bowler and a nonpareil cover-point fieldsman. His selection in the modern day England side would have been automatic. It would also have been remarkable, for it was said that Barrick did not "laike" at cricket in his native Yorkshire until he was in his late teens. His pipes came in two sizes: the small when he was smoking his own tobacco, and the large when other people gave him a fill.

Once, while I was restoring the tissues in a hot tub after a hard day in the field, Des entered the bathroom and poured a jugful of icy water over my shocked body. Since he knew full well my rather volatile and vengeful temperament, I was rather surprised to find him seated fully dressed in the changing room when I entered, armed with a bucketful of cold water which I proceeded to pour over his passive head without his uttering a word. It was only when the bucket was empty that I learned that Des was wearing *my* street clothes, which he had donned in expectation of retribution!

Bert Lightfoot came to Northamptonshire from Woore, just outside Crewe. He was very much an unsophisticated country boy with a surprisingly sophisticated talent for batting left-handed and bowling right-handed medium-pace swingers. His nose was his salient facial feature and an eloquent expressor of his frequent surprise at this new strange world of cricket in which he found himself. He registered his amazement by slowly elevating his proboscis heavenwards: a gesture which he had the opportunity of executing after his first ball in county cricket, which Harold Gimblett hit completely out of Somerset's Taunton Ground over long-on and into a nearby timber yard! To this day I am not sure whether Albert was airing his mortification at the fate suffered by his bowling or was simply following the towering flight of the ball.

151

In the mid-fifties, the Northamptonshire left-handed spinning firm of Tribe and Manning was widely known as one of the most lethal combinations in English county cricket. The South Australian, Jack Manning, was an orthodox spin bowler who employed unorthodox methods to turn the ball from leg. He used a baseball grip to spin the ball, which literally buzzed as he propelled it down the wicket with a rather round-arm action. His baseball twist communicated an alarming dip and inward curve to the ball, which bit and turned viciously if there was even a modicum of assistance in the wicket for the slow bowler. For Jack, in bowling, as in life, it was all or nothing. He wanted to bowl the best of all possible deliveries; just as, during the fat, financial times of the cricket season he enjoyed the best of all possible lives, only to return to more menial days and labouring during the winter. In 1954 Jack captured 116 wickets in county cricket and it was a tragedy for both himself and Northampton when torn cartileges cut short his prospering fortunes.

George Tribe marked his Northamptonshire debut against the touring South Africans in 1951 by taking six for 53 against a Test batting line-up. In his first full season with his adopted county George captured 126 wickets, and the message flashed around the dressing rooms of Northamptonshire's sixteen regular opponents: "Watch this fellow Tribe, he spins the ball like a top." Such was George's acumen, however, that in the following season he still ensnared 108 batsmen in county games, many of them with balls which did *not* turn and trapped them lbw! George, with his three different types of Chinamen, two varieties of wrong-uns and his infinite selection of top-spinners and flippers, was the bane of batsmen but the delight of wicket-keeper, Keith Andrew, who revelled in solving the mysteries of the left-hander's spin. It was not unusual for Keith to chuckle audibly behind the stumps when he detected another subtle variation in George's wrist movements. The Yorkshire batsman, Brian Close, however, was far from amused when he was twice bowled by Tribe in a county game behind his legs, as he mistook the direction of the ball's spin and padded up! It is not widely recognised, particularly in Australia, that Tribe was an accomplished and determined batsman as well as a skilful bowler; in his eight years with Northamptonshire he seven times completed the "Double" of a thousand runs and a hundred wickets—and still failed to command the attention of the Australian selectors more than once!

By modern standards, the Northamptonshire number three batsman of the fifties, the left-handed New South Welshman, Jock Livingston, was clearly of international calibre. Indeed, even in the halcyon days of Barnes, Morris, Bradman, Harvey and Miller, Jock must have been very close to selection in the Australian side. He was a superb player of spin, endowed with the footwork of a prima ballerina, and an ebullient and irrepressible stroke-maker. A mathematical genius to boot, Jock could work out his current batting average to the third decimal point before returning to the pavilion after being dismissed. In all modesty, I must also confess to the opinion that Jock was a fine judge of a player—especially fast bowlers!

It is an interesting experience to look back on the Northamptonshire side of my active cricket days and to try to work out why we were comparatively successful. In five summers between 1954 and 1958, Northamptonshire never dropped beneath seventh position in the Championship ladder. In the 1957 season the county was runner-up to the omnipotent Surrey eleven which clinched its sixth successive Championship under its new leader, Peter May. Surrey were undoubtedly the team which dominated the fifties and almost monopolised the first-class premiership. The strange facet of that domination, in the context of the relationship between Surrey and Northamptonshire, was that while the London county were the most consistent team in the competition, day in, day out, they seldom succeeded in beating Northamptonshire. The midland county's win over the Champions at the Oval in 1957 was the fourth occasion on which they achieved the feat in that era.

The strength of the Northamptonshire eleven of the fifties was, in my estimation, contained in the individual abilities of its members. In batting it was competent and at times brilliant; its spinners were among the best in the land and, while it lacked a full complement of a brace of fast bowlers, it possessed one who was genuinely fast.

Northamptonshire! The word means what Wilf Wooller called me when I hit him on the head with a bouncer at Ebbw Vale. It brings to mind the time that the groundsman had to sweep snow off the pitch at Oakham before play could start in an early season friendly between Leicestershire and Northamptonshire.

Northamptonshire! The word conjures up the picture of Gloucester off-spinner, Bomber Wells, bowling to George Tribe and being halted at the top of his action, because George was not ready. "Are you ready now, George?" asked Bomber after a moment, and when George said "Yes", he carried on with the delivery from the point at which he had frozen. The name of the county evokes recollections of crisp winter Saturday afternoons, when I used to play inside-centre for the Northampton Men's Own rugby fifteen, alongside the slightly speedier, eighteen stone Colin Milburn.

What's in the name? Memories of skittle games in cosy pubs; the doorstep from Dr W.G. Grace's house, acquired by one enterprising Wellingborough cricket fan and placed at the gate of the local grammar school's cricket pavilion.

Is it still there, I wonder?

Northamptonshire!

153

Worcestershire

Rev. Hugh Pickles: Vicar of Blewbury in Oxfordshire and a fully paid-up member of the cricketing clergy. He has played for Worcestershire Club & Ground, coaches cricket at two Midlands schools, and over the years has written regularly for the Worcestershire C.C.C. yearbook and *The Cricketer* magazine.

Pears, Pearmains, Plums and Peerless Pitches
Reverend Hugh Pickles

Worcestershire—the green and pleasant Midland shire about which the writer boasts, and of which he is proud to be a county cousin, with its uniquely situated ground standing out like a jewel (perchance an emerald—Worcester green!), incomparably where county cricket is concerned. Certainly there can be few more picturesque grounds, surmounted as it is by the Cathedral on the banks of the river Severn to the east, and to the west the distant Malvern Hills.

The scene as one looks at old photographs—like that of W.G. Grace approaching the pavilion gates after scoring a century in 1899 at the age of 51; or again, that of the Worcestershire players led by the burly H.K. Foster talking to the slighter Australian batsman, the great Victor Trumper, coming in after fielding in 1902—has altered little since the turn of the century.

The playing area is beautifully level; the pitches flat, comparatively fast and true, described by former captain Don Kenyon as "good cricket wickets". One batsman who clearly enjoyed playing on them was Don Bradman; he scored 235 in 1930; 206 in 1934; 258 in 1938; and 107 in 1948. Reg Perks used to say that he had never bowled to anyone who saw the ball so early and played it so late as did the Don.

Thus a deep and lasting debt of gratitude is due, initially, to that pioneer of groundsmen, Fred Hunt, a native of Aldworth, still a thriving cricketing village on the Berkshire downland. Fred, with his team of groundsmen, virtually created the County Ground, accompanied by his dog and aided, above all, by his horse, who until old age pulled the heavy roller for hours over the turf. The weeding, it is reputed, was carried out by Fred's own hand with the aid of his pocketknife. So came into being one of the best county grounds, then as now. No doubt the periodical flooding of the ground when the Severn overflows has helped, too!

Worcestershire became a first-class county in 1899, thirty-three years after its inception, largely due to the pertinacity and efficiency of the then Secretary, Paul Foley; a determined and dedicated character, one of a number in the annals of the country's history.

Let it be said, in spite of the old but debatable dictum that the game is greater than the player, there would be no game without individual players and administrators. Furthermore, the history of cricket is essentially a saga of cricket characters without whom there would be no statistics (with apologies to Bill Frindall, whom I first met on the Worcester ground some years ago when we were introduced by Brian Johnston outside the commentary box. Brian had initially greeted me as an "old ram". Now, simply, "the Rev"!).

Like neighbouring Gloucestershire with her Graces, Worcestershire cricket was greatly influenced in its formative years at the turn of the century by the brothers Foster, hence the nickname "Fostershire". One recalls another photograph of the Reverend H. Foster with his seven sons, standing outside their house at Malvern. Of the brothers, H.K., as captain and batsman, exercised the greatest influence over the early years of the county; while his brother R.E., nicknamed "Tip", became one of the most renowned and gifted batsmen, not only of Worcestershire but of England, during that era before 1914 known as the Golden Age of cricket.

Some other cricketers of this pre-war period come to mind. George Simpson-Hayward, another amateur and captain in 1911–2, was one of the best and last of underarm spin bowlers, and also played for England. Among the professionals were such men as Fred Bowley, a consistent batsman likened to the later champion Don Kenyon; Dick Pearson, an all-rounder; and Ted Arnold, a tall, upstanding batsman and medium-pace bowler who played in several Tests.

The pace bowlers were principally G.A. Wilson, round-arm slinger; W.B. Burns, fast; and the burly R.D. Burrows, a somewhat erratic fast bowler but a typical professional of the period. Fred Hunt, besides being groundsman, was also a professional stock bowler. In later years, H.K. Foster recalled that Fred used to prepare three pitches for each match but on one occasion chose the wrong pitch so that a vast score was made by the opposition. Fred's bowling suffered accordingly!

Mention, too, must be made of Frank Chester, a very promising young cricketer who at the age of seventeen scored a century for the county, the youngest to do so. He, tragically, lost an arm in the Great War, which ended his playing career. He will, however, be long remembered as one of the best of Test match umpires.

During the years between the wars a number of characters stand out in Worcestershire cricket: Major M.F.S. Jewell, an admirable captain in the

156

twenties, and Gilbert Ashton, one of the triumvirate of talented Cambridge brothers. Once when Gilbert, with other players, was staying with Col. Billy Taylor (another captain in the twenties) he was woken up at 6 o'clock in the morning by the sound of Taylor shouting at his son who was throwing stones outside his sister's bedroom window, exclaiming that the boy should be practising inswingers! On another occasion Gilbert, who was headmaster at Abberley Hall School, was asked at short notice to play in a three-day county match, but being unavailable sent a deputy— one of the masters—A.W. Carr, who promptly scored a maiden century!

It is reputed that Fred Root—famous for his inswing leg-theory bowling with an arc of fielders behind the bat on the leg side—always insisted on being photographed in a cap because of his bald head. In his early years as an apprentice with the county, he used to bowl for hours on end in a barn during the winter months with a highly-polished ball, to master the art of inswing bowling.

In the early thirties, "Doc" (so called because of his black bag), H.H. Gibbons, formed with C.F. Walters—the most elegant of contemporary batsmen—a highly successful opening partnership. The latter also opened for England and once, in 1934, captained the Test side against the Australians.

Among the bowlers, most significantly, was the arrival of Reg Perks in 1928. He served Worcestershire nobly and well as a fast-medium bowler for over twenty-five years, taking 100 wickets in a season sixteen times. Originally from Hereford, tall, well-built, a magnanimous man always with a pleasant, cheerful expression and ready smile, he was never happier than when bowling over after over, come what may. He marked the beginning of his long, successful and honourable career when, in his first Championship match for the county in May 1930, his initial victim was the great Jack Hobbs. He played for England in 1939 at the Oval against the West Indies, and in the unfinished 10-day Test in South Africa on the 1938–9 tour.

Reg will be remembered not only for his marathon bowling achievements, but also for his hurricane hitting. I recall in one match a succession of sixes hit massively to the northeast corner of the ground near the Severn Bar, reminiscent of another left-hander, Gary Sobers, on that historic occasion of 6 sixes in an over against Glamorgan. Reg, himself, claimed a record never likely to be broken when he hit a six which soared out of the Worcester ground and carried all the way to Birmingham—the ball having lodged in a passing lorry!

The Hon. Charles Lyttleton was another personality of the period; a hard-hitting batsman who captained the side in 1936–9, and later as Lord Cobham was a distinguished President. It is said that when he was captain the county was well-supported by a number of young ladies, who were attracted not so much by the cricket or cricketers but by the colourful language that issued forth from the mouth of the skipper! On one occasion the Hon. Charles threw away his bat in disgust as not being fit to use—after a mishit from which he was caught on the boundary—and declared that any so-and-so could have it, whereupon Reg Perks took possession of the bat and used it for the rest of his days!

My own connection with Worcestershire began shortly after the Second World War, when I went with some local farmers from around Woodstock to the then indoor nets in Britannia Square, Worcester, with matting on a wooden floor normally used for a bowling alley. Reg Perks was in charge, assisted by that other fine professional Roley Jenkins, and a young lad, Martin Horton; both were later to make it into the England team.

So began the cousin-by-adoption relationship with Worcester so much appreciated and enjoyed ever since. In those days Brigadier Michael Green, as Secretary, was in charge of operations, along with Grace, his aide, who has happily been the efficient and helpful assistant of each succeeding secretary. Reg Perks and Norman Whiting, another assistant coach and good post-war batsman, remembered how the "Brig" would appear most weekends at the nets in Britannia Square, driving up in his vintage car with a different young girl each time, whom he would introduce as his "niece"!

The county was then fortunate in having a succession of amateur captains, each of whom fitted the role required at the right time: A.P. (Sandy) Singleton, extrovert, Oxford Blue; R.E.S. Wyatt, ex-Warwickshire and England, experienced old campaigner; A.F.T. White, Uppingham and Cambridge Blue, affable and bluff; R.E. Bird, Worcester farmer, rather more taciturn; all good batsmen and leaders.

Another talented amateur of this period was C.H. Palmer, the Bromsgrove schoolmaster, an accomplished all-rounder who played for England. He later joined Leicestershire as captain and secretary. Yet another was George Chesterton, an Oxford Blue and master at Malvern, an excellent medium-fast bowler, who if he had not been a schoolmaster would regularly have taken a hundred wickets a season. One of the leading professionals was Dick Howarth, the first player to complete the "Double" post-war: a left-arm spinner and batsman, who played for England against South Africa in 1947. A Lancastrian by birth, Howarth wore his green cap at a jaunty angle; dapper, square-shouldered, sporting a Douglas Fairbanks-like moustache—and indeed looking like that famous filmstar—he wheeled away with his left-arm bowling in a deceptively easy fashion, and was a determined batsman.

Then there was Roley Jenkins, a great character with a rolling gait and crab-like run up, who became an expert leg-spinner, batsman and outfielder. The stories about, and by, Roley are legendary and most of them true. For example in a match against Scotland he bowled, in his own words, "three beautiful overs" to the Rev. J. Aitchison, a leading Scottish batsman, "beating the bat about ten times." Twice Aitchison shouldered arms to the "wrong 'un" and lbw appeals were turned down. Roley apologised to the umpire for appealing and said: "I forgot we were playing under Scottish law!" He then ambled up the wicket and addressed the batsman: "I'm told that you are a parson?" The latter replied: "Yes, that's right. I am." Whereupon Roley retorted: "If I had your b..... luck, I would be the Archbishop of Canterbury!" It was in this match, incidentally, that wicket-keeper Hugo Yarnold claimed seven victims, including six stumped—a world record for stumpings in a single innings!

A similar incident occurred when the Rev. David Sheppard was batting for Sussex, and Roley had him playing and missing. The bowler uttered a few choice expletives! When he later apologised, the Rev. forgave him. On the following Sunday David Sheppard preached a sermon in which he compared Christianity with batting against Roley Jenkins' leg breaks and googlies. "If you decide to go forward, you must go all the way—not halfway!" Quite a good theme and a lot of truth in it!

Another Jenkins' story concerns the time when Middlesex batsman Jack Robertson scored 331 not out at Worcester. Again, Roley was one of the sufferers. After the match, Robertson discovered that one of his car tyres was flat and implied that a certain leg-break bowler might have been the culprit. The alleged culprit, however, assures me that he was not.

1949 was Worcestershire's Jubilee Year in first-class cricket and the county enjoyed its best season since 1907, finishing third and coming near to winning the Championship. Eddie Cooper and Don Kenyon formed a successful opening pair, and Reg Perks broke Root's record of 123 wickets for the county; while Hugo Yarnold claimed 110 victims behind the stumps. Roley Jenkins completed the "Double" (as he did again in 1952), and took a hat-trick in each innings against Surrey.

The fifties saw the arrival of several stalwart newcomers: Laddie Outschoorn from Ceylon, George Dews from Yorkshire, and Bob Broadbent from Middlesex; all proved reliable batsmen and excellent fielders. Future England players Peter Richardson, of farming stock from Hereford, an adventurous young left-handed opening batsman (and a noted leg puller!), and Martin Horton, the local all-rounder, also arrived on the scene.

Don Kenyon played for England against Australia in 1953 as an opening batsman. He had a keen eye, wrists of steel, powerful forearms and was a fine timer of the ball. In his day one of the best openers in the country, but whilst a very good county player, he was not so successful for England. I saw him playing in his first Test at Trent Bridge, facing

159

Lindwall and Miller in poor light at their fastest and most dangerous—a true baptism by fire! Later in the evening, at the Black Boy, I met Don, still dazed by that torrid experience in his first innings for England and not altogether happy about his initiation into Test cricket!

In 1955 Reg Perks became the county's first professional captain, but retired at the end of the season, aged 43. As one great career ended another got off to a good start: Martin Horton, still only 21, achieving the "Double" of 1,000 runs and 100 wickets in his first full season.

Peter Richardson succeeded as captain, and he and his younger brother Dick, another left-hander, made history by playing together for England against the West Indies in 1957. Len Coldwell and Jack Flavell, later to become such a successful tandem of quick bowlers for Worcestershire and England, came into the side; and Roy Booth, always so smartly groomed, moved down from Yorkshire to replace the plucky Hugo Yarnold as wicket-keeper.

In 1961 Worcestershire, now skippered by the shrewd Don Kenyon, came their closest to winning the Championship for the first time, only to be pipped at the post by Yorkshire. With the advent of Tom Graveney, who had severed his ties with Gloucestershire, the side was one of the best in the country. In 1962, his first full season, Graveney scored five centuries, heading the batting with 1,500 runs. Gloucestershire's loss was Worcestershire's gain. Here was an experienced and skilled batsman of the highest class, a magnificent strokemaker and prolific run-scorer. Of all post-war batsmen he was the peer in grace and artistry. To have seen him produce one of his glorious cover- or off-drives was an aesthetic treat indeed.

In describing Tom Graveney playing in a match towards the end of a sunny season, *The Times* cricket correspondent once delightfully depicted him as looking like "a ripe chestnut"—an apt description. Always a picture of health, he could be distinguished by his splendid long-peaked green cap, and that characteristic touch in assurance. The pride of Worcestershire in his heyday, he was, among modern batsmen, seemingly comparable to the immortal Victor Trumper of the Golden Age, and there can surely be no greater compliment.

The year 1961 was also notable in that four Worcestershire bowlers each took 100 wickets—Flavell, Coldwell, Gifford and Horton—for only the second time, and probably the last, in the history of the Club; the previous occasion being in 1937. As before, it was two fast-medium bowlers, a left-arm spinner and an off-spinner who were involved.

In 1964 the goal was reached. Worcestershire deservedly became County Champions. It had been a close race with Warwickshire right up to the end of August. I was lucky enough to be present on this momentous occasion, August 25, 1964, watching and waiting with

Henry Blofeld—an entertaining character never at a loss for words, aptly nicknamed "Blowers"—whom I had met for the first time that day, and I remember well the excitement as Worcestershire beat Gloucestershire by an innings. Then (though the players were already celebrating with champagne) the agonising suspense, waiting over two hours to hear that Hampshire had beaten Warwickshire at Southampton. Only then, and with great relief, did we know for certain that the Championship was assured and the celebrations justified.

Certainly this was a finely balanced side, and probably the best Worcester team in the history of the Club. The captain, Don Kenyon, must undoubtedly take the credit for his astute tactical skill, his fine example as a consistent opening batsman, and, above all, his qualities as a much respected leader, exercising quiet but firm authority.

The highest praise must also be given to Tom Graveney for the splendid part he played in the Championship matches, scoring over 2,000 runs with five centuries and an average of 55. He reached a personal milestone during the season in recording his 100th century in first-class cricket.

Don Kenyon, Ron Headley, Dick Richardson and Martin Horton each scored 1,000 runs in the season, and played a considerable part in the team's success. But, ultimately, excellent bowling, splendid catching and fine fielding were prime factors in the winning of the Championship. Jack Flavell and Len Coldwell formed the spearhead of the attack. They were well supported by the medium pace of Jim Standen and the left-arm spin of Norman Gifford, while Bob Carter and Brian Brain both performed capably as reserve pace bowlers; as did Doug Slade and Martin Horton as spinners.

Dick Richardson and Ron Headley were outstanding as close fielders, each holding fifty catches apiece; behind the stumps the immaculate Roy Booth claimed 100 wickets as the leading wicket-keeper in the country.

Worcestershire began their campaign in 1965, their centenary year, with the Championship pennant flying proudly over the County Ground. And to crown the celebrations, they became County Champions for the second year running.

After a poor start to the season, having won only three matches up to the end of July, the county went from strength to strength. Three batsmen stood out as giants. Once again Tom Graveney excelled; so, too, did Headley, who in the latter part of the season became a reliable, attacking opening batsman.

The third was Basil D'Oliveira, destined to become a notable figure for both Worcestershire and England. Originally, D'Oliveira was encouraged to come from South Africa to play county cricket by John Arlott. Then Tom Graveney introduced him to Worcestershire, where he quickly made his mark in his first season for the Club. He was a batsman of tremendous natural ability with strong forearms and wrists, a very good eye and power of stroke, particularly off the back foot. He was also a capable and useful stock bowler either at medium pace or off-spin, with an exemplary high, rhythmical action. A man of great personal charm, he had above all determination and application as a player. Basil or "Dolly", as he is affectionately known, will continue to be remembered not only as a great cricketer, but also as one of the finer characters of cricket history. Not least, his quiet dignity and impeccable behaviour over the wretched apartheid controversy in which he was involved has stamped him as a good sportsman and a true gentleman of the game he has graced so well. The mystery still remains, however, as to Basil's true age!

Another young player who emerged as a promising middle order batsman was Alan Ormrod. Later in his career he was to become a very fine opening batsman in the classical mould, with a Graveney-like style; and, as a sheet anchor, offset his partner-to-be, the more cavalier Glen Turner, in launching the innings.

Don Kenyon, though still captain, missed a number of matches as he had now become a Test selector. Nevertheless, he continued to play an important part as leader of the side. When he was absent Tom Graveney proved a capable deputy.

Again it was the bowlers who contributed principally to the county's success, with Jack Flavell, as before, the leading wicket taker. Roy Booth, who kept wicket with his usual efficiency, played several useful innings with the bat, particularly in the last vital match versus Sussex at Hove. When Worcestershire with five wickets down for 70 still needed 132 for victory, he, in partnership with Dick Richardson, steered the county home to win the game and clinch the Championship.

One game in particular I remember from this year was Gloucestershire v. Worcestershire, at Cheltenham: John Mortimore's benefit match. On a spinner's wicket, as so often at Cheltenham, we watched a fascinating duel between two highly skilled batsmen, Tom Graveney and Basil D'Oliveira, and two equally skilled off-spinners, David Allen and John Mortimore. In their different styles the two batsmen defended effectively or drove the ball off front and back foot with precise timing on the one hand and immense power on the other.

For the record, Graveney scored 47 and D'Oliveira 81, with a century partnership in the first innings. In the second innings each scored a splendid 50 not out to win the match for Worcestershire by seven wickets. A nostalgic memory in these days of pace and seam, of crash helmets, of batsmen playing away from the body and improvised shots across the line of the ball. Those were the days!

Memories of a different sort came when I was invited to go with the

Worcestershire team as County Champions on their tour of Jamaica in March 1966. Being a cleric, as a matter of courtesy, I sought approval from the then Bishop of Oxford. Having stated that I had been invited to go to Jamaica, the Bishop asked, "In what capacity?" thinking, no doubt, of a call to the Mission field! When told, the Bishop said: "Ah, of course, I should have known that it was to do with cricket! You must certainly go!" (This was, incidentally, in the season of Lent!)

And off I went. It was a wonderful trip and a memorable tour. The flight via New York; the ascent and view from the top of the Empire State Building; the exploration of the "Island in the Sun"; the rum; the calypsos; practising in the nets with the players at Sabina Park; the stay at the Sheraton in Kingston; the matches against the Parish XIs among the sugar canes at Monymusk; the bauxite at Mandeville; among the American tourists at Ochio Rios; and, finally, at Montego Bay. Here we enjoyed the delights of sea-bathing and watched—like "mad dogs and Englishmen out in the midday sun"—an exciting game in which Gary Sobers, as a guest player, scored a splendid century for the Jamaica XI, and Basil D'Oliveira, not to be outdone, did likewise for Worcestershire. The cricket played against the Parishes was of county standard and keenly contested, while the friendship among players and followers is something I shall always remember—especially the dedicated Ross Slater.

In 1968, Glen Turner, the young New Zealand opening batsman, appeared on the scene. Even then, when still a youngster, he had tremendous powers of application and intense concentration. Fair, slim built, boyish-looking, nimble on his feet and strong in the wrist, he reminds one of a whippet straining on his leash, eager and anxious to be after the ball, batting or fielding. At first he was a dour and painstakingly slow batsman à la Boycott (and one or two others nearer home!)—as in the 1969 Test match at Lord's when he carried his bat in making a century for New Zealand. However, with experience and more confidence, he completely changed his approach to batting. During the seventies, he became a very fine attacking player, in spite of having his top left hand too far round the back of the bat handle, rather like John Edrich. Nevertheless, or perhaps as a result, he plays very straight always with fine timing and splendid strokes, particularly driving to off and on. He also has a rare ability to drive the ball short of length "on the up" off the front foot. In 1970 Turner scored ten centuries in the season, a county record. Three years later he became one of that élite group of batsmen who have succeeded in scoring 1,000 runs before the end of May.

Since the retirement of Tom Graveney (who had taken over the captaincy in 1968) at the end of 1970, Worcestershire have been led by Norman Gifford, who has proved himself a shrewd and capable captain, well liked and respected. His first success was in 1971 when the county became John Player League Champions, as much due to his inspired leadership as his performance on the field. Like his left-arm predecessor, Dick Howarth, Gifford is a Lancastrian—stocky, well-built, a pleasant, agreeable but determined character. He is a genuine left-arm spinner, like Derek Underwood, quicker and "flatter" than most. He is also a reliable tail-end batsman. Deservedly, he has played in fifteen Tests for England.

1971 was also the year when Joe Lister resigned the secretaryship after fifteen years to return to his native Yorkshire as County Secretary. A gifted administrator, he had a long and successful tenure of office at Worcestershire. He captained the County Second Eleven for fifteen years with success, particularly in 1962 when Worcestershire won the 2nd XI Championship, helping to "bring on" future first team players. Joe, as he was known to everyone at New Road, had a happy knack of looking after members from the Committee downwards, including the "county cousin" writer, who will always be grateful for the Jamaican Tour and the opportunity to play in a few Club and Ground matches. In these games I was fortunate to play under the captaincy of Henry Horton, known as "H", primarily of Worcester but famed as a post-war Hampshire batsman with a Jessop-like crouch. "H" succeeded Charlie Hallows as county coach.

Of the Worcestershire side in the seventies mention must be made of the long and lean Vanburn Holder, the West Indian fast-medium bowler, much in the Reg Perks' tradition; and the trio of professional footballer-cricketers, Ted Hemsley, Phil Neale—both good, reliable middle order batsmen as well as splendid fielders—and Jim Cumbes, ubiquitous goalkeeper cum zestful stock medium-pace bowler. He, over recent years, has served the county well in company with John Inchmore, tall, dark, strong, moustached or bearded—a hardworking fast-medium bowler, who really should be termed an all-rounder after his fine century against Essex in 1974. There were some excellent performances, too, from the Pakistani players Imran Khan and Younis Ahmed, both attractive attacking batsmen, and from New Zealander John Parker.

In 1974 Worcestershire were County Champions again, for the third time in a decade. This time Glen Turner and Ron Headley were the leading batsmen, and Basil D'Oliveira the most effective all-rounder. Vanburn Holder was the top wicket taker, partnered by Brian Brain who had now become a fine opening bowler, while skipper Norman Gifford bowled his left-arm spin as well as ever. By taking seven wickets in the final match against Essex in the rain, it was he who fittingly obtained the vital bowling points to win the Championship. Gifford, by the way, is the only player to have taken part in Worcestershire's three Championship successes, four Cup Finals, and a victory in the John Player League.

Over recent years Worcestershire has been served just as well off the field as on. There is not room here to list everybody who has been connected with the Club, but a few people stand out in my mind: Sir George Dowty, an outstanding President in the sixties, particularly when Worcestershire became County Champions in 1964–5; Gilbert Ashton, referred to earlier as a player, another splendid President; Dick Lygon, a large, expansive, enthusiastic Committee man, a worthy member of an historic Worcester family; the Preb. Chignell, Van Dyck-bearded cleric, the County cricket historian and most recent, respected President; and the "Wing Co" Shakespeare, former President and amateur player in the twenties.

Around the ground there are characters like "Loppylugs", the eccentric sage and wag in his Boer War khaki hat, his braces, sometimes without a shirt, and his infernal hunting horn, at one time banned from New Road as well as Edgbaston! Curly, the scorecard vendor, with his ready quip; the champion groundsman Gordon Prosser and his faithful assistant, Cyril; the Worcestershire Supporters' Club folk selling souvenirs in their little wooden shop near the Severn Bar; and among the regular spectators the debonair Vicar of St John's just up the road, Malcolm Richards—a keen supporter of Worcestershire and, even more perhaps, of his national game at Cardiff Arms Park, as well as being a fellow clerical critic.

Last but not least, there is at the administrative helm Michael Vockins, the able and agreeable Secretary who succeeded Joe Lister ten years ago. He, together with Glen Turner and Alan Ormrod among other experienced players, and Basil D'Oliveira as coach, will see to it that the affairs of the county are well run.

With such promising young players in view as Dipak Patel, who looks a high-class all-rounder in the making, Phil Neale, Paul Pridgeon, David Humphries, D'Oliveira Junior and others, Worcestershire may yet become County Champions again in the eighties.

But, come what may, Worcestershire *is* a Champion County!

Gloucestershire

Alan Gibson: Has broadcast for many years and written on a variety of subjects for a variety of publications, including *The Times* and *Spectator*.

Parker, Goddard, and Some Others
Alan Gibson

Gloucestershire cricket has been known, over a hundred years and more, for W.G. Grace, and several other outstanding batsmen—Jessop, Hammond, Graveney, not counting the more recent overseas imports such as Procter and Zaheer—yet just as much for a remarkable succession of spin bowlers. They were nearly all finger-spinners (C.L Townsend was the principal exception), some bowling with their left hand and some with the right, and they usually hunted in pairs: Dennett and Parker, Parker and Goddard, Goddard and Sinfield, Goddard and Cook.

Later there came Mortimore and Allen. Even today, in an age sceptical of spin, there remain Childs and David Graveney. The last four fall outside the scope of this essay, which is concerned chiefly with the two great ones, Charlie Parker and Tom Goddard, and their contemporaries. No doubt I shall digress from time to time, for Gloucestershire is a likely place for digressions: sometimes too much so, if you take a wrong turning down a Cotswold lane and discover they are in the middle of repainting the signposts.

When Gloucestershire first began playing county cricket, they had a left-arm spinner in the side. R.F. Miles did them sound service for some years. His best performances were against Yorkshire, a good sign, even though Yorkshire were then a collection of talented, erratic individuals, not the powerful machine they became when Lord Hawke took charge. Miles was succeeded in the team by another left-hander, William Woof, Gloucestershire's first professional. In 1884 and 1885 Woof took a hundred wickets in a season. Then he became coach at Cheltenham College, and so was only available for the county in August. Nevertheless, in a spasmodic career which began in 1878 and lasted till 1902, he took more than 600 wickets. In his last match, against the Australians at Cheltenham, he took the wickets of R.A. Duff and Clem Hill.

In 1903, the third left-arm spinner came into the side, Dennett. He was a slow bowler, even as left-arm spinners went. He relied on accuracy and gentle spin, not inclined to take unnecessary risks. By the time he played his last match in 1926, he had taken more than 2,000 wickets. Yet he is not so well remembered in the county as he should be. This may partly be because he did not play for England, nor was seriously considered to be a possibility. It was very difficult for a left-arm spinner to make his way into the England side in those years. Rhodes and Blythe stood before him, then came Woolley, and later Parker and J.C. White. So Dennett just went quietly on with his work for Gloucestershire, collecting his wickets. He had his moments of drama. In 1907, for instance (when he passed 200 wickets), he took eight for 9 against Northamptonshire at Cheltenham. Northamptonshire were all out for 12. When Gloucestershire were batting a telegram was received, on the field, by the Northamptonshire captain, from a disgruntled supporter languishing in Northampton. It read, "Send the boys home, mother". The captain threw it down angrily, but Buswell, the wicket-keeper, picked it up, no doubt for many a laugh in the Northamptonshire professional dressing room. Northamptonshire were not, of course, a power in the land then, though only five years later they managed to come second in the Championship.

Nor, in Dennett's time, were Gloucestershire considered to be among the stronger of the counties. They usually finished in the bottom half of the Championship, twice at the very bottom. Dennett had little bowling support. There was Roberts, a tubby fastish left-hander, a popular character and a hard worker, but never of the first rank. There was Jessop, who had been a truly fast and dangerous bowler, but concentrated increasingly on his batting, though still capable of a sudden bowling intervention. The most famous of these was in 1906, when he put himself on to bowl against Yorkshire, who needed two runs to win with one wicket left, and took the wicket. This was the second-last match of the season, and it was widely said, especially by Yorkshiremen (though not quite precisely), that Yorkshire had lost the Championship by one run. Kent came through to beat them.

Dennett also sometimes had C.L. Townsend at the other end, and this might have been a great spinning partnership if Townsend had been able to play regularly, which he could never do after his early years. Townsend was a back-of-the-hander, right-arm, with a fierce spin. He could also bowl off-breaks. He played 275 innings for Gloucestershire, his first in 1893 and his last in 1922, and had a batting average of over 30. (He batted left-handed.) He took more than 650 wickets, average under 22. He played three years in the Clifton College XI, and his bowling figures were

1892: 59 wickets at 11.67
1893: 55 wickets at 12.80
1894: 85 wickets at 8.49

H.S. Altham thought Townsend "the greatest boy bowler since A.G. Steel". He first appeared for Gloucestershire when he was 16. He played for England twice at home against Australia in 1899, making a fair showing. It was a pity that the googly had not been invented in his formative years, for he had the kind of subtle mind to exploit and develop it. Possibly he would not have had the physique for a full career, even had the law not claimed him. He was tall and slight. Cricket ran in the family. His father, Frank, had played for Gloucestershire in the great days of the Graces. His son, D.C.H. Townsend, won a Blue at Oxford, and though the only county he represented was Durham, was chosen for a strong England side touring the West Indies in 1934–5, playing well enough in three Tests. I knew C.L., a little, towards the end of his long life (he was nearly 82 when he died). He looked very much what he was, an ageing solicitor, and not at all what he also was, an ageing cricketer who could have been one of the great all-rounders of a mighty period. Yet his eyes had a kind of wise twinkle, such as I have seen in the eyes of Mailey and Peebles.

No, Dennett had to labour on without much support. Yet there was potential support, at hand, had anyone in authority recognised it. In 1903, another left-armer, C.W.L. Parker, played his first game for Gloucestershire. His natural talent and inclination were for spinning the ball, but with Dennett in command it was thought that there was no place for a second left-arm spinner. So Parker was encouraged to bowl at fast-medium, something he did not do very well. He was thought of more as a potential successor to Roberts than an aid to Dennett. It was 1908 before he gained a regular place in the side, and not then with much distinction.

After the war, Parker was invited to rejoin Gloucestershire, but refused, unless he was allowed to bowl spinners. The county agreed. Parker was then 35 years old. In 1920, for the first time, he took 100 wickets. He continued to do so for year after year, usually many more, five times over 200. He finished with the astonishing number of 3,278. Only Rhodes and Freeman have taken more. He had an easy, untaxing action, which enabled him to bowl more or less all day, as he often did. He was a quicker bowler than Rhodes (or Dennett) and did not rely on variations of pace and flight. Spin and length were his strengths. His style was nearer to that of Verity, or, to take a modern example, Underwood. Informed judges have suggested that there has never been a better left-arm spinner than Parker. For what my opinion is worth, I would not go so far. I did see Parker bowl, but was of no age to make a technical judgment, and the memories are dim. I would think, on all the evidence, that Rhodes and Blythe were better, Verity and Underwood at least as good, and probably Briggs and Peel, with Lock and Wardle not far behind. But this is mere

169

speculation, and there is no doubt that Parker was a very great bowler indeed.

Why, then, did he only play once for England? This was against Australia in the fourth Test of 1921, the match which H.L. Collins made sure would be drawn (Australia had already won the rubber) by taking five hours to score 40. In the single Australian innings, Parker's figures were 28-16-32-2. This was not thought to merit a place in the next match. He also scored 3, not out, in his only Test innings. This pleased him, that he was never out in a Test match. He rather fancied his batting, and at the beginning of every season would buy two new bats. As he swung them confidently around the dressing room, he would declare that this year nothing would stop him from getting a thousand. He cannot have been too bad, because one year he did reach 500, but his career batting average was only 10.

He was summoned to the third Test at Leeds in 1926, but left out of the final eleven. It was a wet pitch, expected to help the spinners, and A.W. Carr, the English captain, put Australia in. This was a very odd combination of decisions. There was a case, no doubt, for leaving Parker out, and a case for putting Australia in: but not for both. Macartney scored a hundred before lunch. Again, in 1930, Parker was on the brink of the England side. He travelled to the match, after a late summons, by air. But, as he said, "they signalled that the pitch was dry and I flew away again."

Fred Root wrote that Parker "made no secret of his belief that he would never be chosen for England while 'Mr X' was a member of the selection committee." But this cannot be true, whoever Mr X may have been. There were too many different selectors. No member of the 1921 committee served in 1926, and no member of either in 1930. It was, however, the kind of thing Parker was liable to say. Fred Root calls him an "inveterate grouser", and he was a difficult man to captain. B.H. Lyon, when he took over Gloucestershire, managed him with tact and skill. "Who's going to set my bloody field, skip, you or me?", Parker would growl, and Lyon would cheerfully reply, "You are, Charlie. I'm standing here."

Parker was often severe on his own fieldsmen. Robertson-Glasgow tells how when mid-on and mid-off, neither an athlete, both turned to pursue a straight drive, Parker said mordantly, "There go my greyhounds." Cardus tells the same story, only in reverse. A batsman snicked a ball past Dipper, at first slip. He set out to chase it (there was no third man) and Bloodworth, the wicket-keeper, set out too. Neither of these were flyers either. Parker turned to Reeves, the umpire, and said, "Look, Bill, there go my ruddy whippets." I dare say both variants are true. Parker was an artist who did not mind repeating a good remark, or a good ball.

Yet he was a warm-hearted man, and excellent company off the field.
Grahame Parker summed him up, in *100 Years of Gloucestershire Cricket*:

> Geniuses are not easy to live with. Charlie did not appreciate the Establishment . . .
> and to have played in only one Test is proof that they got the message. It was a nightmare
> fielding in the deep to him. You started by taking up one position which experience had
> taught you to mark. Next over you were somewhere else for Charlie was a sequence bowler
> and he reckoned to have a fielder underneath every ball hit into the air. Very soon the
> ground around your station was as thick with crosses as a tray of hot cross buns. If you
> dropped a catch you took the long way round to the dressing room. He bowled all day and
> he talked cricket all night. No one has ever known more about the game. We loved him.

Well, that was the view of a young Cambridge Blue coming into the
Gloucestershire side, of the ageing professional. But that he did not get
on with "the Establishment" is not quite sufficient reason for his omission
from England sides. On tours, perhaps. He did make one tour, an
unofficial one to South Africa organised by S.B. Joel, and was found
reading a book in his room ("a classic", says Fred Root, though heaven
knows what Fred meant by "a classic") when he should have been on
parade at an official do. But many difficult and temperamental men have
played for England, including some of the most successful. So this is not,
in itself, a convincing explanation, any more than that of Mr X.

The feeling was that Parker could not bowl on plumb pitches. There
is little evidence of this, though certainly, especially in the years when he
had no proper support at the other end, the years after Dennett had gone
and before Goddard arrived, he would sometimes wilt under attack from a
great batsman (the same became true of Freeman, though hardly ever, I
think, of Rhodes). But though Parker's chief fame was for being a demon
on a "sticky", he cannot have taken all those wickets on bad pitches.
Cheltenham, it is true, has always had a reputation of being a happy home
for spinners, but Gloucestershire played only three of their matches there.
Bristol has never been thought of as a bowler's pitch, except for a few years
after the second war when it had been neglected. "Too slow for either
batsman or bowler", was the common complaint about Bristol. Tom
Graveney, for instance, found a new spring when he moved to Worcester
in the later years of his career. Gloucestershire pitches were as good as
most, and wet weather occurred there less frequently than it did on the
turners of the north.

This was the thinking behind Parker's omission from England sides,
and I doubt if there was malice behind it; but I believe it was mistaken.

It is tedious to give a list of such a bowler's best performances, but
one of Parker's has to be mentioned. In 1922, in his benefit match, he
took nine for 36 against Yorkshire. In the course of the innings, he hit the
stumps with five consecutive balls. The second, unfortunately (and it was

very unlike him), was a no-ball. Perhaps his other most-remembered performance was against the Australians in 1930, but by then he had been joined by Goddard.

Goddard, like Parker, was a late developer, and began as a not very successful quickish bowler. He played for Gloucestershire first in 1922, when he was 22 years old, and after six seasons of hearty but generally fruitless work left them. He strove to be a fast bowler. His six seasons had brought him 134 wickets at an average of 34. He joined the Lord's ground staff, thankful for the job. He accepted that he was a failure as a county cricketer, but still enjoyed bowling in the nets, now more slowly, even though it was mostly to aged members—"Pick up the ball, Goddard, not so young as I was, ha ha" (this is something Parker would not have stood for long). Nothing might have been heard of Tom Goddard again had he not bowled in a net to Beverley Lyon, who was to become Gloucestershire's captain in 1929. As soon as Tom bowled a few spinners, Lyon spotted the magic. Goddard rejoined Gloucestershire in the same year, took 184 wickets with off-spinners, and went on taking wickets for so long as he could play. Statistically, he did not quite equal Parker, for though he also took 100 wickets in a season sixteen times, he only took 200 in a season four times; also, he only took 2,979 wickets in his career. His average was 19.84, Parker's 19.46. Tom would dearly have liked those last 21 wickets. As it is, only four bowlers have taken more, the three we have mentioned, and, much earlier, J.T. Hearne. Tom's best year was 1937, when he took 248. In 1939 he took 17 wickets in a day, against Kent at Bristol.

Tom was a tall, craggy-looking man. He used to wear a lot of hair-cream, which was not at all in character, but added a touch to his formidable aspect, a little of Al Capone on top of a lot of Tom Cribb. The fierceness of his looks, and his appeals, belied the gentleness of his character, just as the innocent appearance of his off-spinners belied their venom. I count it one of my blessings that I came to know Tom in his later years, and shared conversational pints with him. I recall the pang of grief with which I heard the news of his death. He was 65, no age at all for a man who had seemed so endurable.

He was fortunate in his bowling partners, especially of course Parker. Their most famous joint triumph was that Australian match at Bristol in 1930. The Australians recovered the Ashes—it was Bradman's first and mightiest season—and lost only one match, the first Test. But after the rubber was won, Gloucestershire tied with them at Bristol in a low-scoring match.

Gloucestershire were all out on the first day (when play did not begin until four o'clock) for 72. Australia scored 157 on the Monday. Hammond scored 89 in two hours in Gloucestershire's second innings, but they were all out for 202, so only 118 were needed to win. Lyon, always a man for a gamble, began the bowling with Parker and Goddard, since the pitch was helping the spinners a little, and he wanted to persuade the Australians that it was helping the spinners a lot. But it seemed no more than a gesture when Jackson and McCabe had put on 59 briskly for the first wicket.

Then Parker bowled McCabe, and Goddard had Jackson leg-before. I will not go through the details of the rest of the innings, for there are several good printed accounts of it, but Parker and Goddard bowled them out. The scores were level for twelve minutes, and thirteen balls were bowled without a run being scored. There were about 8,000 present, and scarcely a breath drawn as each ball went up, scarcely more than a gasp as each still failed to produce a result. Several who were there have told me that the uncanny thing about those last few overs was the *silence*. The only loud noises were Tom Goddard's appeals. Twice he called for leg-before against Hornibrook, to be denied, and then he called again, and this time Hornibrook was out, and it was a tie, and all that pent-up Gloucestershire breath was expended in a great explosion. Tom looked back on this match as the most happy experience of his cricketing life, more so even than his hat-trick in a Test in South Africa, a decade later. Charlie no doubt took a quiet satisfaction in it, reflecting that he had been able to get at them at last, without the aid of an aeroplane. Tom took ten for 126 in the match, Charlie seven for 104.

Tom was irritated by few things, not prone to wrath about his fieldsmen, nor with Parker's gift for the sardonic; but he did get a little cross sometimes about his reputation as an "appealer". He felt it cost him wickets, because umpires would tend to say, "Oh, that's only old Tom again", and give the batsman not out. Tom bowled his off-spinners round the wicket, most of the time, but sometimes over the wicket. In either case he would, after delivery, bear off sharply towards cover, and so was not in line to see whether the batsman might be out or not out. If a pad was hit, he appealed on principle. "Them as don't ask, don't get." But I never remember seeing him disputing with an umpire, once the decision was given. The best transcription of that roaring appeal is perhaps OW WAZEE?. The next would contain a cadenza, OW WAZEETHEN?, a bass suddenly ascending to a contralto. He would sometimes vary this, with a contralto descending to a bass. "OO-OWS EE NOW?" When a series of appeals had been turned down, he would simply look at the batsman, and hardly at the umpire, murmuring happily as he turned round, as if to himself, the satisfying words "GOT'N". Out went the batsman, almost shamefaced, while even the most fearless umpire was inclined to pause. I tell you this story not because it is necessarily true, but because I remember Tom telling it in a Cirencester pub.

Dennett had taken two thousand wickets and never been chosen for England. Parker had taken three thousand wickets and was chosen for England once. Goddard took nearly three thousand wickets and was chosen for England eight times, a difference largely accounted for by the proliferation of Test matches (he only played once against Australia). So that these three great Gloucestershire spinners, after taken 8,404 wickets between them, had earned just two Australian caps. It really is no wonder, in the face of such a statistic, that provincial men (I do not count Yorkshire and Lancashire, because they constituted less a province than a rival kingdom) felt in those days that their players were hard done by.

Tom's Australian cap came in 1930, in the fourth Test, when he took two for 49 in 32 overs in Australia's only innings. There is a curious similarity with Parker's Test experience, though Tom's wickets were hardly more than tail-enders, whereas Charlie's had been Macartney and Pellew. He played twice against New Zealand in 1937, and twice against West Indies in 1939. He toured with England to South Africa in 1938–9 and played in three Tests there, achieving the hat-trick which was immortalised because a youthful E.W. Swanton happened to be broadcasting, live, to England at the time. In all Tests, Goddard took 22 wickets at 26.72, which was respectable, but did not bear much relation, compared with the figures of others, to his cricketing merit.

Tom had a theory of his own about why he did not win more caps. "Trouble was they only picked me when they left Hedley out. Hedley used to say to me, should pick us together Tom, then we'd have 'em moving different ways, bowl 'em out in no time." Tom deeply admired Hedley Verity, and there was much force in the argument, as a man who had bowled for years at the opposite end to Parker well knew. But like Mr X, it was an impression rather than a fact: three of Goddard's Tests were played with Verity in the team, and a fourth before Verity had started.

A better reason was that off-spinners were not, in the thirties, thought of as a necessary part of an England side. A leg-spinner and a slow left-armer was the preferred combination. Especially, off-spin was thought to be feeble stuff in Australia. As late as 1946, Ellis Robinson, the most consistently successful bowler of the season, was left out of a weak England bowling side, and James Langridge, a good slow left-hander before the war, was included. He did not play in any Tests. As late as 1950, Berry, a slow left-hander (and I bet you can't tell me which counties he played for, off-hand), was chosen, and Laker left at home. There is no need to go beyond this for reasons why Tom did not tour more often. There is, incidentally, some ground for this thought that off-spinners brought up on English pitches may find themselves in trouble in Australia. Even Jim Laker, when at last chosen in 1958, had no more than an adequate tour there, though he was handicapped by a sore spinning

174

finger. Yet a couple of years before he had destroyed a strong Australian batting side, in England. So if Jim made only one tour to Australia, it is not surprising that Tom made none. Yet how the Australians would have relished his company!

Tom returned to Gloucestershire after the war, embellished with the status of a commissioned officer of the R.A.F. The old Gloucestershire burr was as strong as ever, and he seemed as good a bowler as ever. I saw quite a lot of his bowling around that time, though it was some years before I came to know him. It was thanks to Tom as much as anyone that Gloucestershire had such a good Championship run in 1947. Their challenge to the triumphant Compton/Edrich Middlesex was thrilling to a young man—it was a close win by Middlesex at Cheltenham, a marvellous match, that really settled it. Then in 1948, Tom was given a battering by the Australians at Bristol. Bradman had told Ian Johnson, his own off-spinner, to take special notice of how Goddard, a master of the craft, bowled. Afterwards, Johnson did not feel he had learned much. Tom retired with a bruised hand and bruised feelings. In Gloucestershire it was felt that the old man was at last over the hill. I remember one supporter, of a literary turn of mind, quoting dolefully a line from Byron:

Poor Tom's no more, and so no more of Tom.

But he was wrong. Tom was soon in good spirits again, and taking wickets. It was only in 1951 that he announced his retirement, "because of ill-health" (not a hint that it might be because he was 51 years old). In 1952, with Gloucestershire in some trouble, he came back, with an ostentatious reluctance which deceived nobody, and played in thirteen Championship matches, in which he took 45 wickets. Thereafter he ran a furniture business in Gloucester, pretty well, for he was shrewd despite his innocent rustic air, which he would sometimes deliberately cultivate. For those who knew him, every Gloucestershire spring is a reminder of his absence.

After Parker's retirement, in 1935, Goddard's principal support was Sinfield. He was more of an off-cutter (though we did not know that phrase then) than a spinner, and relied much on inswing. Sinfield had come into the side in 1924 and did not do a lot of bowling for a decade, but this did not worry him unduly, because he was a patient man, and could bat. He was an opening batsman for a long time, later dropping down the order as his bowling responsibilities grew heavier. The pattern of the Gloucestershire bowling in the second half of the thirties was still the same—a few overs from the quicker men, to take the shine off, and Goddard and Sinfield on for the rest of the day. The difference now was that the spin turned the same way from both ends. Hammond and Barnett usually bowled the preliminary overs, and Hammond, certainly, would have taken many more wickets had there not been the overriding need for his runs (in 1928, the season before Goddard rejoined, he took 84, as well as scoring nearly 3,000 runs).

Reg Sinfield came to Gloucestershire via Hertfordshire and the Lord's ground staff, but he looked and behaved very much as you would expect a Gloucestershire man to do. He did not have, in his play or his character, the devil, the sharpness of Parker; nor the commanding, genial public appeal of Goddard. He was a quiet, gentle cricketer, weather-beaten with a ruddy face and grey hair when I knew him. For Gloucestershire he took 1,165 wickets, average 24.37, and scored 15,561 runs, average 25.89. He played once for England. It was the first Test against Australia in 1938, and he had Bradman caught at the wicket. He did not play first-class cricket after the second war, but spent many happy years as coach at Clifton, where he came to be revered.

So who was to bowl at the opposite end to Goddard? There arrived at the Bristol ground, during the pre-season nets in 1946, a young plumber from Tetbury, who said "I'm Cook". His Christian name was Cecil, but for some reason I have never heard explained, he became immediately known as Sam. By lunch-time he had been taken on. By the end of the season, he had taken 100 wickets. In the first Test of 1947, against South Africa, he was chosen for England. Sam bowled slowly, later getting up towards medium, with his left arm. His Test career was unlucky in its timing. He had made some extraordinary performances on the Bristol pitch, which R.J.O. Meyer described in those years as "like the sands at Weston". At Trent Bridge, quite a different problem, he took nought for 127. He never played for England again, though he took 1,768 wickets, average 20.26, before his retirement in 1964. He enjoyed his batting and managed to score more runs than he took wickets. One of the best Gloucestershire cricketers was Sam—still with us, of course, as one of the most popular umpires. But you will notice that Cook, Sinfield, Goddard, Parker and Dennett played in just eleven Tests between them, and only three of them were against Australia.

This was put right, to some extent, when Mortimore and Allen came along. Mortimore played in nine Tests, Allen in no less than thirty-nine, but by their time there seemed to be a Test match every month of the year. Mortimore was the more successful bowler for Gloucestershire, Allen for England. They were both off-spinners, and I must not be tempted (not just now, anyway) into a discussion of their merits. Gloucestershire had a third off-spinner in their side in the fifties, and a good one. This was B.D. Wells, known as "Bomber", and a fair character was he. As George Emmett used to say, when Bomber bowled off his long run (this only happened when Gloucestershire needed to save time) it was like watching the charge of a baby elephant. Wells was a great crossword man. When Gloucestershire had won the toss, and Milton and Young were nicely settled in, he would arrive in the Long Room, or what used to pass as the Long Room at Bristol, take out a pencil, chew it, and ruminate over his crossword. I do not think it was one of the trickier ones, but Bomber took it seriously. He refused all direct help, but was not above asking a bit of advice occasionally. I remember this conversation:

Bomber: Wassorjus then?

Us: Er—how d'you mean, Bomber?

Bomber: ORJUS. How d'you spell'n?

Us: Er—do you mean ORGIES, Bomber?

Bomber (dismissively): No, no, ORJUS, you know, giants.

I bet they never appreciated our Bomber when he went to Nottinghamshire.

A company of great men, have been the Gloucestershire spinners.

Leicestershire

Charles Palmer: Worcestershire, Leicestershire and England. Former Captain and Secretary of Leicestershire, now Chairman of the Club. President of the MCC 1978-9, and current Chairman of the Cricket Council.

My County, Right or Wrong
Charles Palmer

"Secretary and Captain of Leicestershire?"

There was an air of restrained incredulity in the voice of Brigadier Mike Green, the Secretary of Worcestershire, when in early 1950 I told him I was considering an invitation to become Secretary and Captain of Leicestershire. I could see he was weighing his words carefully because he did not want to be unkind nor to deflate me and he knew that I respected his advice. He had been Secretary during the post-war period when I played for Worcestershire and, when I toured with MCC in South Africa in 1948–9, he had been the manager, forming a splendid partnership with George Mann, captain, and Billy Griffith, vice-captain.

Mike Green urged me to study the proposal carefully before I made the move from my relatively comfortable, civilised and ulcer-free job as assistant master at Bromsgrove School. I knew almost nothing about the Leicestershire County Cricket Club; he told me what he knew.

Leicestershire, historically, had not been a fashionable cricket county. There had over the years been a number of fine players such as Armstrong, Astill, Dempster, Geary, King, Knight, Pougher, Smith and others, but rarely had enough played at the same time to make a consistently successful team. Low in the Championship in 1946, '47 and '48, the side had reached the bottom in 1949; the Club had no ground of its own and the accounts were such that it needed some stimulant to face them with equanimity. Poor team performances, no ground, negligible capital, deficits rather than profits . . . I considered all these, but after six years in army service I was feeling a little constrained by the pleasant but what I felt to be introverted atmosphere of a boarding public school and, more particularly, I wanted to play more first-class cricket than school holidays permitted.

So I glossed over what I didn't want to know and with confidence, foolhardiness—call it what you will—but with the full support of my wife, and with a son aged three years and another minus two months,

179

decided to up and away to the hunting county in April 1950. Thus I followed the leads set by Desmond Eagar in Hampshire and Wilf Wooller in Glamorgan.

But there were several things Mike Green did not know.

He did not know the strength of purpose of the Leicestershire Chairman Frank Smith, a very successful self-made businessman who, in the twilight of his active career, having passed most of the daily running of his dairy business to his sons, said that, come what may, he would see that the County Cricket Club would survive successfully into the fifties. Since the war Leicestershire has always had a very small committee, and at the time Frank Smith and I were lucky enough to have the complete support of hard-working and enthusiastic men dedicated to the Club.

There were perhaps times when their dedication and the strength of their loyalty were strained. More than once the Chairman and I, to save time, took action before it had been sanctioned by the committee, and I then had the task of persuading my colleagues to agree to a course of action that had already been taken! This is by no means to say that the committee was there to be a rubber stamp: they were far too individualistic and positive to be cast in such a role. The Chairman sometimes cut corners for expediency but he was trusted by the committee not to betray their faith in him. This was a sensible policy in the days before counties appointed managers or chief executives, and important decisions could often get delayed awaiting committee approval.

I had some wise men of great experience around me at Leicester. The Chairman taught me, in moments of my perhaps unjustified frustration, that it was a common-place of life that the solution of one problem invariably posed another, and I also remember the avuncular words of another committee sage when failure rapidly followed success, "Don't forget, my boy," (I was then 31) "the Lord doesn't give with both hands."

Brigadier Green, my friendly counsellor at Worcester, had not known the calibre of men I was to work with, nor did he know the keenness of the players in 1950 to lift the county off its knees on the field of play. There were no real contenders for places in the England team but there were some fine cricketers and fine men.

Leslie Berry, the most senior, had already served Leicestershire faithfully and well since 1924 in the manner of the highly respected professional of his times. He scored 30,188 runs (30,106 for Leicestershire) including 45 centuries, mostly as opening batsman, and had he played in another era which lacked such established competition as Hobbs, Sutcliffe, Holmes and Sandham, those results would surely have ensured for him a place in the England side. Leslie had only two years with me before he retired and in his last year—his 46th—the spirit was there but the legs sometimes became so weary that he often quoted one of

Leicestershire's greatest cricketers of the twenties and thirties, George Geary. George had had a gruelling day in the field; the captain, at the end of his tether in trying to stem batsmen in full cry, sought George's advice: "George, who shall we put on now?" Looking at the pavilion clock showing 5.45 pm, George, too far gone to waste words, succinctly replied, "The clock!"

Leslie was with us in the side when we played Cambridge University at Fenners, where it was doubtless his intention to call upon his immense experience to take advantage of the normally perfect batting wicket there. As he strode purposefully to the wicket one could sense his unspoken words—he was not the sort of man to say them aloud—"I'll show these damned young amateur undergraduates!" As it happened, the Cambridge side that day included Peter May, Hubert Doggart, David Sheppard, John Warr and John Dewes, all soon to be England players. Leslie has never lived down how he showed them: Berry c Haywood b Warr 0; Berry lbw Warr 0; his first and only pair and at the hands of damned amateur undergraduates! But such was the calibre of the man that we went straight to Lord's where he scored a century. If it is any consolation to Leslie reading this revelation, let me remind him that it was later at Lord's that I scored my only pair: b Moss 0; b Moss 0.

Maurice Tompkin, of blessed memory, died tragically at the age of 37. At the time it seemed one of nature's more unjust acts. Maurice was a generous man; generous with his open friendliness and attractive personality so that people felt the better for having been with him; generous and fair on the field, never countenancing sharp practice. He was, understandably, universally liked and respected by his fellow cricketers. His qualities were widely recognised when, after he died, the County Cricket Club and the *Leicester Mercury* jointly launched an appeal which attracted the sympathy of a wide public and helped to cushion his family from the blow and to secure a good education for his two sons.

As a cricketer, Maurice was a fine upstanding attacking batsman whose straight drives hit the wicket at the bowler's end more than those of any other batsman I have seen. Most of his runs were scored in the arc between mid-wicket and cover, and almost always along the ground. Whenever Maurice was batting therefore the fielders would be packed into that area. Had he been better able to break up the field by hitting the spinners over their heads, he would have scored even more runs; so often he hit the ball really hard, but straight to a fielder.

To my horror, he did once try to hit over mid-on. He and I were on opposite sides in the Gentlemen v. Players match at Lord's in 1955. It was, for Maurice, something of a Test trial and he had batted splendidly, but having reached the late nineties his innings, as happens to so many, had become becalmed and he had become frustrated. At that point I was put on to bowl and I must confess that my wish for him to get his century was uppermost. I never liked giving runs away but I fed Maurice with a ball just short of a half volley which, in his eagerness and frustration, he aimed over mid-on's head. The ball did not rise high enough and went to the fielder's right hand; my heart bled at Maurice's agonised cry but the somewhat leaden-footed mid-on didn't even get a touch. I wonder whether he had been purposely slow; although we fought matches hard, such little "generosities" were by no means uncommon, and I'm sure the game was the better for this.

Vic Jackson and Jack Walsh, so often spoken of as a pair—I suppose because they were both Australians playing first-class cricket in England at a time when there were many fewer overseas players than now—had come to England before the war to play for Sir Julien Cahn's eleven, and then joined Leicestershire in 1946. They were in fact very different types of cricketer.

Jack Walsh was perhaps the most fascinating spin bowler I have ever seen, bowling left-arm Chinamen and googlies. I hope the cognoscenti will forgive me but this breed of bowler has been so rare for so long that some readers may welcome an explanation. The left-arm bowler's Chinaman is, in effect, the off-spinner spinning from the off-side to leg-side of the right-handed batsman, his googly spinning from leg-side to off-side but disguised in delivery to appear to the batsman the same as the Chinaman. Three Australians—Fleetwood-Smith, George Tribe, who played for Northamptonshire, and John McMahon of Surrey—spring to mind as bowlers of this type. One lives and learns: it is only as I write this that I realise that this specialist type of bowler is mainly Australian. There have certainly been other left-arm bowlers who have bowled in this way— Gary Sobers, Denis Compton, Johnny Wardle, Donald Carr, for example, but it was hardly what they were renowned for.

Jack Walsh was an artist of spin bowling, with the occasional touch of artistic temperament bursting through a quiet personality. He spun the ball more than any other bowler I saw, and because of this could at times be somewhat erratic. He was a captain's dream and nightmare; always with a split 5/4 field there were many gaps for the inaccurate ball; a couple of loose deliveries in the early part of an over would be hit for four, then at the end of the over two beautiful balls would so mesmerise the batsman that I felt I had to give him another over to apply the *coup de grâce*. Then the same sequence would follow, and I would find the scoreboard had rattled along alarmingly.

Walsh rarely wanted a leg slip close up for the catch. Vic Jackson, who could "pick" Walsh, always fielded first slip to him and on turning wickets I have seen Vic "see" the ball from Walsh's hand, then, while the ball was in the air, move from first slip to leg slip. He knew, even if the batsman did not, that it was the Chinaman and that there was the possibility of a leg-side catch from the edge of the bat. I never saw him catch a batsman by this ploy but I'm told he once so caught Harry Crabtree of Essex. Certainly I've seen many a single or more saved; and I did once see Vic move to leg-slip, take a gigantic Chinaman and run out a batsman who, having played and missed, had over-balanced out of his crease.

At one time Jackson broke his finger and I replaced him at slip. It took me several matches of constant and intense observation before I felt sure I could detect the googly from the Chinaman. Before I had succeeded, I looked very red-faced one day when I tried to show off by copying Jackson's move from slip to leg-slip, only to find I had guessed wrong and that a fizzing googly had got past the wicket and wicket-keeper and should have been stopped by me in my original position. The difficulty in detecting the Walsh googly from the Chinaman was aggravated by the fact that he would bowl a googly he intended the batsman to detect, and one which he intended he should not. Hence a batsman could be led early into a sense of false security by spotting the former, only to be confounded by the latter. Also at times he spun the ball so much that a long hop would turn and lift more than normally, and so induce a false stroke. It was a true feast for both connoiseur and layman to see, as once I did in 1952, the battle between Walsh in top form on a responsive wicket at Folkestone and Arthur Fagg of Kent, equally in top batting form.

Jack Walsh's batting could perhaps be described as effervescent, unpredictable and unpremeditated. Indeed, in my first year of captaincy there were occasional moments when I wondered if I was in control. A critical moment came in one match at Grace Road just before the tea interval; we still needed many runs and we had lost too many wickets quickly (a not uncommon occurrence) and I was desperate not to lose another before tea. Jack Walsh went in with one over to go and with my instructions not to take any risks. Nervously I watched him play four good length balls defensively as instructed; the fifth good length ball he struck over the sightscreen for six. Over a cup of tea all I got was, "I just didn't stop to think, sorry!", and then with a twinkle and adding yet another wrinkle to his already weather-creased Australian face he said, as though as an afterthought but with pride forcing its way past apology, "Not a bad shot though!"

Vic Jackson's cricket was by no means unpremeditated. He was a calculating player with a fine cricket brain; an excellent all-rounder, off-spinner and No 5 or 6 batsman, who gave splendid service to Leicestershire before he retired to Sydney where so tragically he was soon to be killed in a car crash. He supported me well when I arrived at

Leicester and his advice was always worth listening to.

A number of times, with his blessing, have I dined out on a story against him about the visit to Leicester in 1950 of the splendid West Indian team under John Goddard with the three W's, Worrell, Weekes and Walcott. John Goddard won the toss on a benign Leicester wicket against a benign Leicestershire attack. That great trier Jim Sperry, the spearhead of the seam attack, was ineffectual in such circumstances and I soon brought on the spinners, Jackson and Walsh. Jackson had an early success getting the wicket of Alan Rae for 26. His next great personal "success" came a few overs later when he strained his back and left the field for the day to enforced rest in the pavilion. He was of course genuinely injured but we did not allow him to escape without ribald comment; he certainly knew what the day was likely to offer! The scorecard eventually read:

A.F. Rae b Jackson 26
R.E. Marshall c and b Sperry 188
F.M. Worrell not out 241
E.D. Weekes not out 200
Extras 27
Total (2 wickets) 682

Had either of the two W's failed, Walcott was next in at No 5!

There came a time during the innings when I said to Jim Sperry, "Jim, bowling a line and length at Weekes is getting us nowhere; try seven on the off-side and bowl well outside the off stump." At this stage he was not averse to advice and was happy to hand over all responsibility. "OK, skipper," he replied, "I'll give it a go." The ploy certainly had one effect: it reduced the arc for scoring from 360° to 180°; it did not however reduce the scoring overall as Weekes then ran across to the off-side, sometimes as much as four feet, and crashed the ball to the mid-wicket boundary. The umpires were not given the opportunity to award wides! My next idea, that Sperry should adopt the same tactics but on the leg-side, merely resulted in Weekes running to leg and smashing the ball through the vacant covers.

The score at the end of the first day was 651 for two. At 10.30 the next morning, I summoned up as much optimistic bonhomie as you can imagine the circumstances allowed and went to the West Indian dressing room to say good morning to John Goddard and his team. "We bat on," he said. I must have failed to hide the horror of my thoughts that it was all going to start again. "Don't worry," he said, "it won't be for long, just until Everton gets his fifth double century of the tour." Everton did. His first 102 had taken 65 minutes; the 200 took 171 minutes. At the end of this astonishing partnership we were satiated with brilliant stroke-play; our bowlers were very weary but the fielders less so, as so often they merely waited for one small boy after another to throw the ball back from the boundary. Marshall, Weekes and Worrell between them hit 79 fours and 2 sixes.

As our long-serving regular wicket-keeper Paddy Corrall was injured, we had brought in a good local club cricketer, Jack Smith, making his first-team debut. In the total of 682, he allowed a mere 18 byes. He relates this with amused relish and then his innate modesty (allied to the fact that most of his listeners know anyway!) forces the punchline that throughout the whole innings the batsmen allowed the ball to soil his gloves about a dozen times.

Such astonishing batting reminds me of an even more astonishing performance, that of Denis Compton on the 1948–9 MCC tour to South Africa, when he scored, as *Wisden* records, 300 runs in 181 minutes against N.E. Transvaal at Benoni. It was a privilege to be present to see this phenomenal innings which embraced every stroke that was typically Compton—we fellow tourists naturally failed to rile him when we said it was typical of him in another way, in that, as usual, he was never on schedule for anything on that tour: 300 runs in 3 hours *1 minute*, if you please! It may be a piece of irrelevant trivia but in that match I batted No 3 and Denis No 4, the significant difference between our innings being a matter of 300 runs!

But to return, as I should, to Leicestershire. I have written of only a few of the players who were keen to help me when I arrived at the county in 1950. I would like to write more of them all—Gerry Lester, soon to succeed Berry as senior professional, Paddy Corrall, Jim Sperry—these and others were the players whose personal attributes Mike Green did not know; members of a team which languished at the bottom of the Championship in 1949, was next to bottom in 1950 but which, with newer recruits such as Maurice Hallam, Jack Firth, Gerry Smithson and Terry Spencer, was at the top of the table in August 1953. Even if we did fall to third position at the end of that Championship year, it was a satisfactory transformation.

Before I move on from cricket and cricketers, I hope I may be forgiven if I briefly venture again into autobiographical detail to refer to what in my own career with Leicestershire caused me and many others great amusement—my bowling of "donkey drops". It is not a wholly exceptional irony of life that one may strive for success in one sphere, only to achieve unexpected results in another. Without doubt, I derived my greatest satisfaction and success in cricket from batting, yet although I was only half a bowler, it is for isolated bowling achievements that I am frequently mentioned. Firstly, for a once-in-a-million performance against Surrey in late May 1955—I blush at the sheer, unjust extravagance of the unexpected—when, putting myself on (against medical advice) for my first over of the season merely to change the existing bowlers to opposite ends, I took eight wickets for no runs in twelve overs, and finally eight for 7. Secondly, for my growing propensity for bowling "donkey drops". It may ill-become me even to mention, let alone describe the former, but let me tell how the latter happened.

Bank Holiday fixtures in the fifties, before limited over cricket began, were the main highlights of the county season and were usually games which excited the fiercest local patriotism. Our local rivalry was against Northamptonshire, a strong side which included Jock Livingston, the fine Australian left-hander, who had had great success against Leicestershire. I do not want to depress myself by checking his batting average against us; suffice it to say that it was enormous, and on May 22, 1956, he seemed yet again set fair for a big score.

I was bowling to Livingston—as captain, Heaven knows why—presumably because the other bowlers had cleverly suggested it or by performance proved to me that they had had enough. I ran in to bowl from the pavilion end at Grace Road . . . and to this day I have no idea what motivated me to throw the ball right up into the air. I took a run of only ten short paces and certainly at the beginning of my run-up I had no idea of bowling a "donkey drop".

The success of this type of ball depends on several things: it must be high enough for a steep descent, at least 30 feet, or it will be merely a full toss; it must be straight; it must be of full enough length to land on or very near the wickets if missed; and it must be used sparingly enough to be something of a surprise to the batsman. The one I bowled to Jock Livingston, with beginner's luck, met all four requirements but, since it was my first ever, perhaps the element of surprise was its chief characteristic. It surprised the batsman, it surprised the fielders, it surprised the crowd, and in truth it surprised me. During the eternity it seemed to Jock to be in the air, his eyes appeared to pop out to mid-off and back, then to search upwards like a plane spotter as, mystified, he pivoted and whirled his bat like a Highlander throwing the hammer, finally swatting the ball with a gentle glancing blow off the back of the bat to give Maurice Hallam a simple dolly catch at first slip. The spectators and fielders were in paroxysms of laughter. To his credit, despite his frustrated embarrassment, Jock also saw the amusing side of it, although I suspect the joke had worn very thin by the time he reached the dressing room. I apologise to Jock for making him the butt of this story but there can only be one first time, and if it is any consolation to him, he was the first of a few illustrious victims, including that same Frank

Worrell who with Weekes had mauled us in 1950. Worrell, looking upwards, trod on his wicket awaiting the ball's descent; but I have to record that he had already scored 100.

There is a very readable short story by Sir Arthur Conan Doyle called "Spedegue's Dropper", which tells how a young man in some remote country village strings a rope at the top of two tall trees and bowling over it to a wicket beyond perfects this type of delivery, and then goes on to graduate through all levels of cricket to eventual success in a Test match. Incidentally, a few days after *my* first "donkey drop", I received by post a small parcel containing a cigar which had been rewrapped with a band inscribed: "Guaranteed made of pure donkey droppings."

At the outset I mentioned the accounts. We lost money in my first year at Leicestershire but then, with the apparent profligacy of the suicidal bankrupt, we spent more than half our meagre capital on ground improvements for members in a desperate attempt to prove to our supporters that we would like their presence at the ground even more than their sympathy away from it.

But self-help was at hand. I had left Worcestershire just as they had been the first county club to introduce the heterodox idea of running a football competition to raise money. With well-researched market information on every conceivable money-raising scheme the first elementary requirement of the present county cricket club manager, it seems strange now that a lucrative football competition should not have been welcomed without reservation. Most county clubs had always been hard up but before the Second World War, when the financial devil drove, it had been the local aristocrat, squire or dignitary who had dipped into his private pocket in a rescue act. In 1950 few such individuals could afford this kind of philanthropy, and we were in effect proposing to move the patronage to the man in the street with his "bob-a-week". I followed the lead of Worcestershire and introduced the idea of the football competition, taking the precaution of lobbying each committee member individually to correct any possible misapprehension that anything was being proposed beneath the dignity of a county cricket club.

The committee welcomed the idea and the scheme was launched by the Supporters' Association. The promotion involved much hard work, good organisation and infinite patience but the balance sheet was transformed. Starting from scratch in January 1952, the Supporters' Association presented the Club with its first cheque for £2,000 in June of that year and by the end of 1953 more than £20,000 had been raised, so laying the foundations of a greater financial security.

After the Club had accumulated capital through the football and other competitions, we waited impatiently for an opportunity to get the Grace Road ground for ourselves. Other sites had been investigated but all proved unsuitable. The chance came when the Leicester Education Authority rehoused the Leicester City Boys' School and moved its recreation facilities from Grace Road. We bought the ground in 1966 and the acquisition was the catalyst, if one were needed, to inspire Secretary Mike Turner and the rest of us to improve the facilities.

The team's successes of the seventies, under Ray Illingworth's captaincy and Mike Turner's managership, set local enthusiasm alight. Leicestershire won the Benson and Hedges Trophy twice, the John Player League twice and in 1975, *mirabile dictu*, we won the County Championship. In the wake of this success came more support and more money for the Club. With it we have developed a ground which, while never likely to possess the beauty of a Worcester or a Canterbury, nor the atmosphere and capacity of a Lord's or a Trent Bridge, has at last provided players, members and spectators with reasonable comfort; a ground which is, we believe, suitable to stage at least a minor representative international fixture. Perhaps even more important, it has enabled us to try and create a friendly, *welcoming* atmosphere for members and visitors alike. We want people to feel at home and to come again.

My own playing days with Leicestershire ended in 1958, but, first as a member of the committee and then, since 1964, as Chairman, it has given me enormous pleasure to continue my association with the Club. During these years, two men in particular can be said to have masterminded Leicestershire's progress: William Bentley MBE, President since 1960, and Mike Turner, who was appointed Secretary in 1961 at the remarkably young age of 24.

Over the thirty-odd years Leicestershire has been my county it has certainly been wrong at times and certainly right at times. I hope this does not sound pretentious but, throughout the whole period, we have all been mindful of the splendid heritage of cricket we have been given. We are also mindful of the need to preserve the decencies, dignities and courtesies that have generally characterised the game, its participants and its administrators; characteristics which have bonded me to the sport, whether at county or national level, for the last forty years. Cricket is a game through which many new friends can be made and old friendships consolidated, as my time with the county has happily demonstrated.

I have, in this essay, been unashamedly self-indulgent and somewhat discursive, looking back, as I have, to my early years with the Club. I hope my readers will not think I have need to apologise for this self-indulgence.

Leicestershire Cricket has been kind to me and I have liked it, warts an' all, right or wrong.

Somerset

Tim Heald: Journalist and thriller writer, creator of Board of Trade investigator Simon
Bognor, whose adventures have also been seen on television.

Do Anybody Want a Bannanny before I Do Go Out to Bat?
Tim Heald

I first began to follow Somerset cricket when I was sent to prep school just outside Bishops Lydeard. It was not a good time to form such an allegiance. The summer before I joined the school, in 1952, they came bottom of the Championship for the first time in their history, a feat they repeated in each of the following three years. *Wisden* was withering: "General slackness, particularly in fielding was Somerset's biggest handicap . . . until the whole club develops a more enthusiastic spirit as portrayed by Gimblett they will continue to disappoint their faithful supporters." And, a year later, "Once more Somerset discovered that inexperienced amateurs could not solve their team problems, and it proved no surprise when they finished at the bottom of the Championship table for the second successive season."

They were even beaten by the Royal Air Force—though it should in fairness be pointed out that the Air Force did include a fast bowler named Trueman, F.S.—and the worst moment came at the benefit match of the long serving "Bertie" Buse. Lancashire shot them out for 55 and 79 and beat them in a single day. Their keenest supporter, my great aunt in Creech St Michael, was in despair. "Very poor specimens," she would say, shaking her head in disbelief. She reserved her greatest scorn for the unfortunately named Lobb, who joined the county in 1955 as a fast bowler. She regarded him as the worst specimen of the lot.

And yet there was something about Somerset cricket which transcended such a trifling matter as defeat. As R.C. Robertson-Glasgow, one of the most remarkable in a long line of Somerset characters, once wrote: "In the long view it is not the arithmetical performances of this or that player, not merely the times of success and failure that strike the historian of Somerset cricket. It is rather the spirit—the spirit which win or lose has always been a happy compound of humour and independence."

Besides which, as Robertson-Glasgow also pointed out, "In the matter of cricket, Somerset has ever been a county of surprises." The first time I ever saw them play, in 1957, when they finally began to emerge from that appalling five-year slump (Won 14, Lost 81), they bowled out an extremely strong West Indian touring team for only 78 runs, with Bill Alley taking five for 38 and the much maligned Lobb five for 37. They even achieved a modest first innings lead, though in the second innings the West Indies remembered who they were the Garfield Sobers made a century. The day of our outing there was, as far as I can remember, more rain than play and the most memorable moment was getting the autograph of Gilchrist, the West Indian fast bowler. Gilchrist was not one of the greatest intellects and it was rumoured that he had spent the entire sea voyage to England locked in his cabin trying to perfect his signature, which by the time he reached Taunton was an impressive though not very legible squiggle.

Cricket at the prep school near Bishops Lydeard was a mirror image of Somerset's. It had charm; it had character; it had very little success. The first eleven ground was so pretty it was almost a pastiche of what a cricket ground is supposed to be. To the north the Quantocks, much closer than at Taunton, provided the background to a white wooden pavilion with a thatched roof. On one side a walled vegetable garden, on another a dangerous slope towards a sunken lane.

Our headmaster, Randall Hoyle, was alleged to have played a couple of times for Somerset Second Eleven and there were other masters who could play—notably Paul Cooper who specialised in hitting enormous sixes with a cripplingly abbreviated Gunn and Moore bat—but somehow they never quite passed on their expertise.

Paul Cooper now says that he found looking after small boys' cricket "a fantastic waste of time", to such an extent that he "became a bit bolshie and used to tell Randall that I would soon get rid of an opposing team in a match by giving the opposing batsman 'Guard' well outside the off stump and have him lbw in no time." He never did, but Mr Hoyle was always anxious. From time to time one or two real cricketers were brought in to drill some cricketing disciplines into the boys. One was Jack "Varmer" White who captained England and Somerset and farmed nearby; another was Bill Greswell, who took nine Hampshire wickets for 62 in 1928 and whose son went to the school and was recently Lord Lieutenant of Somerset; when I was there Bill Andrews brought along some of the Somerset team for a work-out in the nets. "All," reflects Paul Cooper, "without exception were disasters. Excellent players in their own right but clueless when teaching small boys who hardly knew 'off' from 'leg' or a long hop from a full toss. It is no exaggeration to say they did far more harm than good and looked at the whole business with a benign superiority."

Certainly none of my generation went on to play for the county. The best batsmen we produced were Paul Cooper's son, Michael, and a boy called Graham whose father played stylishly in father's matches and sported a multi-coloured hooped cap which greatly impressed the spectators. The best of our rivals were St Michael's from over the county border near Barnstaple, and St Dunstan's from Burnham. St Dunstan's were lethal. One day, I played for the Connaught House Under Eleven Team which scored ten all out against St Dunstan's. Wandering over to the first eleven pitch to see how our seniors had fared, we found that they had been dismissed for eleven. It felt a little like playing for Somerset against Yorkshire.

In those days the link between Millfield and Somerset County Cricket Club was not yet apparent, at least not to me. Under the headmastership of successive county players in R.J.O. Meyer and C.R.M. Atkinson the school has now acquired a reputation as a nursery for sportsmen of all kinds, but in the fifties the connection between Somerset and the schools was different. It meant, in essence, that every August the team was augmented by the arrival of one or other of the gifted amateurs who were schoolmasters by profession but cricketers for fun.

The best of these was M.M. Walford who taught at Sherborne, where his legendary abilities as an all-round games player (he captained the British hockey team in the 1948 Olympics and played rugger for Oxford and the Harlequins) were somewhat belied by his unprepossessing appearance and manner. His much imitated catchphrase was "Oh Lor", accompanied by an expression of defeat and perplexity. Walford's county batting average, however, was higher than W.G. Grace's and he hit seven hundreds for the county, including 264 against Hampshire at Weston and a not out century against the Indian touring team.

Sherborne, being in Dorset, had no first-class county allegiance so that Somerset would be the natural first choice for any suitably inclined and talented players among staff or boys, but oddly enough the only other master I know of who played for the county was the dapper M.R.G. Earls-Davis, the ex-Irish Guards officer who was in charge of the C.C.F. His record was less impressive than Walford's, for he played only once, in 1950, scored four runs and took nought for 18. Although it was no more of a cricket school than Connaught House, Sherborne had the peculiar distinction of providing two England captains of cricket. A.W. Carr, who led England against Australia in 1926, had been expelled from Eton before arriving at Sherborne where he was the model for the Corinthian Lovelace in Alec Waugh's novel, *The Loom of Youth*. Neither he nor Sherborne's other England captain, David Sheppard, now Bishop of Liverpool, ever played for Somerset.

Another distinguished Somerset schoolmaster was D.R.W. Silk who averaged over 33 between 1955 and 1960 in summer holidays from teaching at Marlborough, and is now the Warden of Radley. Silk was born in the United States and the year he topped the Somerset averages the birthplaces of the five leading players were: California, Sydney, Georgetown Guyana, Stockport and Sydney. Colin McCool, the Australian Test player who was one of the two Sydney-born Somerset men, once commented harshly that part of Somerset's trouble was that the county "suffers from the theory that the Somerset team ought to come from Somerset." If this really was the theory in McCool's day it was seldom put into practice, then or later. In recent years, as always, Somerset has been a broadly based team of disparate geographical antecedents. Of the present side Victor Marks, for example, was born in Middle Chinnock, Phil Slocombe at Weston-super-Mare, and Peter Denning in Chewton Mendip. Ian Botham may have been born elsewhere and even choose to live in a planner's aberration called "Humberside", but he was at least at school in Yeovil. On the other hand the county's recent prosperity has depended greatly on Yorkshire's cast-off Brian Close, as well as such gifted expatriates as Viv Richards, Sunil Gavaskar, Greg Chappell, Kerry O'Keefe, and Joel Garner.

It was ever thus. Or sort of. In the very beginning when the Somerset Club was formed in 1891 (in the Devon town of Sidmouth, which is a typically Somerset way of going about things), the team's star player was the irrepressible Sammy Woods. Woods was one of that rare breed of binational sportsmen who played for two countries, in his case Australia and England.

That was at cricket. He played rugby for England too. Between 1891 and 1910 Woods scored more than twelve thousand runs and took more than five hundred wickets for his adopted county, as well as captaining them from 1894 to 1906—longer than any other player in their history. He was, alas, before my time and as a player even before the time of my correspondent, R.G. Besley of Bishops Lydeard, who never saw him play but got to know him a bit in the early twenties when he, Besley, was a boy at Taunton School. It was clearly Woods who set the tone of Somerset cricket: aggressive, hard hitting, devil-may-care. Besley remembers him addressing a meeting of rugger players where he was being consulted about tactics, when someone enquired meekly, "Please, sir, what about the dummy?" "Then," writes Besley, "Sammy (the heroes of whose stories were always Sammy) told of the England v Wales match when he kicked off for England, a high one into the arms of Billy Bancroft, the Welsh full back. Sammy following up very fast arrived just after the ball which Billy poked towards him to put him off balance. 'Thanks, Billy' said Sammy, and taking the ball, scored a try. 'Is that what you call a dummy?' asked

194

Sammy."

On another occasion, Woods was asked to speak at the annual dinner of the Taunton Light Car Club. He accepted and made a speech in which he denied all knowledge of light cars but spoke instead on his favourite sport: "Ratting. The pursuit and destruction of rats." On Sundays in the middle of county matches he would invite the visiting team for a ramble in the Quantocks. At about midday, he would complain of a thirst and bemoan the fact that the nearest pub was miles away. A little later he would start sniffing the air and swear he could smell beer, and sure enough a crate of the stuff would materialise, hidden down a rabbit hole by an accomplice earlier in the day.

Like his fellow Australian Bill Alley, Woods achieved a sort of honorary Somerset native status, though there was never any pretence that he came from anywhere but Sydney. But by the early twenties McCool's law was coming into practice. People talked of "Somerset qualifications", and there was a pretence that Somerset players should be Somerset men. It was never more than a charade. The best known example was Tom Lowry, who attracted Somerset attention while an undergraduate at Cambridge. There was great excitement when it was discovered that Lowry was born in Wellington, and he was enlisted at once. Only later did it transpire that the Wellington in question was the New Zealand and not the Somerset one. Lowry played four years for Somerset and captained the first New Zealand team to play England (as well as in Woodsian fashion, touring New Zealand with the MCC).

The case of Robertson-Glasgow's qualifications was even more absurd. "Crusoe" was born in Edinburgh but the Somerset captain, John Daniell (who also captained England at rugby), argued that there was a Robertson-Glasgow family connection with Hinton Charterhouse and that his cousin Charles Foxcroft was MP for Bath (which was then still in Somerset administratively as well as in fact). He was also a great nephew, though only by marriage, of Prebendary Wickham, the vicar of Martock.

Wickham, of all of them, is the Somerset cricketer I should most like to have met. Apart from cricket his other great passion was butterflies. He had previously played for Norfolk and although he had 136 innings for Somerset, he averaged a mere 9.44. This scarcely mattered. He was an immensely accomplished and colourful wicket-keeper.

My mother's family lived in Martock for years and my grandfather was the scorer for the village team. If there is Somerset cricket in my blood it comes from here. The female members of the family, in particular my aunt who used to collect their autographs, were much taken with the glamour of the county cricketers and the legendary deeds of their vicar. (The village team had its characters, too, notably Mr Alexander the greengrocer who always brought along his wares for the benefit of his colleagues, shutting them away as his own innings approached with the words, "Now do anybody want a bannanny before I do go out to bat?"; a question which survives in our family as a recurrent and, to outsiders, quite unfathomable joke.) Apart from finding her old autograph album (she had Daniell, Considine, Ingle, Lowry and many others), my aunt was also able to produce a yellowing newspaper clipping which told of the moment the vicar of Martock came to Lord's. The picture it conjures up, as well as the effect it had on the presumably metropolitan writer, is typical of Somerset at its best.

"A peculiar picture presented itself at Lord's in the person of the Rev. A.P. Wickham, the Somerset wicket-keeper standing with legs so far apart that his head just appeared above the wicket. He looked a queer figure even without his eccentric attire. He wore white leg guards with black knee pieces. Above these were grey trousers and a black band or sash. A white shirt and a brilliant parti-coloured harlequin cap completed his curious 'get-up'. Apart from the excellent batting of Woods and Poynton the only redeeming feature of the second innings of Somerset was the stand made by Nichols and Wickham for the last wicket. When the reverend gentleman went in last man it looked as if the innings would not realise 150 but thanks to their plucky batting the score mounted and mounted, each fresh hit being punctuated by rounds of cheering till the total reached 157. Certainly Somerset did not fail for the lack of enthusiastic supporters."

It must have been depressing at times. Wickham was behind the stumps in 1895 when Archie Maclaren came to Taunton and scored 424, and another day he kept wicket when W.G. made 288. He used to claim that only four balls passed the doctor's stumps in the entire innings. Another reverend Somerset wicket-keeper was F.E. Spurway, who played between 1920 and 1929. Reg Besley remembers playing against an MCC team for Taunton School with Jack White bowling. "Jack tossed up a harmless half-volley at which I swiped and missed, and a deep parsonic voice behind me said, 'Young man, if you do that again I shall stump you'." Two balls later he did.

There are no clergy in the Somerset team these days and although Taylor, rubicund, burly and perfectly satisfactory behind the stumps, is in a stout Somerset tradition, it would be fun to have a reverend wicket-keeper again. Unfortunately cricketing clergy are thin on the ground nowadays. On Ascension Day, 1976, I was at Taunton to see Somerset play the West Indies in the company of Christopher Hollis, a Somerset supporter of more than forty years' standing and the son of a former Bishop of Taunton. When I remarked on the sad shortage of clerical collars, even in deck-chairs, he replied laconically, "Fewer vicars". The dearth is not just confined to the playing fields of Somerset. It is a national shortage.

That was an auspicious day because it was the first time I saw Botham bat. Somerset have always had fine hitters: G.F. Earle; Arthur Wellard; Harold Gimblett himself, whose maiden century in his first match at Frome took all of sixty-three minutes; Viv Richards; but for sheer power and arrogance Botham takes some beating.

At first it looked like a typical Taunton day. Daniel and Roberts, bowling decidedly fast, took the first five home wickets for only seventy. At one end old Close, bald and belligerent, exuded solitary defiance but it seemed pathetically obvious that Somerset would be all out for under a hundred. We knew very little about Botham then. He was said to be promising. That year's *Wisden* had spoken of his "useful" seam bowling, his "brilliant" fielding, and his batting "laden with potential". But it was 70 for five, Daniel and Roberts were very quick and he was only a young lad. It is the only time I have seen a six over long stop. He went for the hook. It took a thickish top edge and sailed over the boundary behind him. When he left a few minutes later he had made 56, including two sixes and nine fours. Forty-eight in boundaries. Eight other runs. Boys' Own Botham. Three years later I went to interview Botham for the *Telegraph Sunday Magazine* and he said, "My attitude to cricket is that when I'm bowling there's no one in the world good enough to bat against me and when I'm batting there's no one good enough to bowl at me." I can imagine Sammy Woods saying something like that and laughing with it, just like Botham.

"Good as the cricket could be, it is the companionship and fun that I chiefly remember," said Robertson-Glasgow. Nowadays Somerset have gone back to the winning ways of the 1890s, but the sense of fun remains. Perhaps it is nostalgia or sentiment but there is no team I would rather watch even in defeat. Perhaps especially in defeat, or at least winning against all the odds. I like to think of them as perpetual underdogs capable of overturning the odds, but not too worried if they don't. Perhaps they were *too* amateur in the old days when it was alleged that Daniell would go down to the barrier at Bath station and invite anybody who got off the train and could play cricket to come and make up their numbers.

Rather that, though, than the aberration of 1980, when in a Benson and Hedges match at Worcester, Brian Rose declared at one for nought in order to throw the game yet make the semi-final on a technicality. That was very un-Somerset and, one gathers, much regretted. Even if the Walfords and Wickhams, the Palairets and the Rippons (father and brother of former cabinet minister Geoffrey) are figures of the past one wants their spirit to live on. Hard graft and canny tricks are all very well for north of the Avon, but they don't belong in Somerset.

McCool, a hard man, would not have agreed. He thought Somerset club cricket "with its soft, social atmosphere just about the worst possible breeding ground" for county cricketers. I, on the other hand, like village cricket and what I like about Somerset cricket is that it was, and in the person especially of Botham himself still is, village cricket elevated to an art form. Which takes me back to where I started, on that exquisite ground outside Bishop's Lydeard where, for me, it all began. The prep school is gone now and the field is played on by the village team. Years ago Sir Dennis Boles, who owned it, held jolly country house cricket weeks. At one such, after a particularly alcoholic lunch, Robertson-Glasgow came on to bowl concealing an enormous croquet ball behind his back. The batsman, inebriated, failed to recognise the truth but thought simply that he really had his eye in and was seeing the ball extraordinarily well. He swung, connected and the bat shattered in his hand. "Well, sir," recalled the Boles' butler, one Burgers, who was umpiring that day, "It wasn't cricket, was it, but there were some merry gentlemen who much appreciated the hospitality."

That was Somerset cricket. Not quite cricket anywhere else and none the worse for that. Long may the gentlemen of Somerset be merry and the spirit of Sammy Woods remembered and, in the matter of cricket, let it always be a county of surprises.